BEHIND THE BIG TOP

BEHIND THE BIG TOP

David Lewis Hammarstrom

SOUTH BRUNSWICK AND NEW YORK: A. S. BARNES AND COMPANY
LONDON: THOMAS YOSELOFF LTD

A. S. Barnes and Co., Inc.
Cranbury, New Jersey 08512

Thomas Yoseloff Ltd
Magdalen House
136-148 Tooley Street
London SE1 2TT, England

Library of Congress Cataloging in Publication Data

Hammarstrom, David Lewis
  Behind the big top.

  Includes index.
  1. Circus. I. Title.
GV1815.H34   791.3   78-69647
ISBN 0-498-02205-6

PRINTED IN THE UNITED STATES OF AMERICA

for

ROBERT L. MITCHELL

Contents

	Key for Illustration Credits	9
	Foreword, by F. Beverly Kelley	11
	Acknowledgments	13
	Introduction	15
1	To Hell with Roman Chariots	19
2	Barbette Originals	30
3	Sex and Other Fringe Discomforts	39
4	And the Word Was Wallenda	48
5	The Red Wagon Laid Bare	58
6	A Trip to the Clouds	66
7	Your Money's Wirth	75
8	Life, Liberty, and the Right To Be Hoodwinked	85
9	The Garden or Your Circus	96
10	The Curse of Blacaman	106
11	Le Sacre Du North	114
12	Gargantua, It's Your Honeymoon!	127
13	King behind the Throne	138
14	The Last Great Big Top	151
15	Jackpot Season	165
16	Mysterious Great Traditions	177
17	The Feld Bandwagon	189
18	Move Over, Mother Circus	203
19	Cry, Clown, Cry	215
20	Ten More Bars!	227
	Index	239

Key for Illustration Credits

The following abbreviations are used in the captions for illustrations:

CC   Capital Centre, Landover, Md., courtesy Bob Zurfluh and photographer Jerry Wachter.
CF   Circus City Festival, Peru, Ind.
CK   Circus Kirk, East Berlin, Pa.
CV   Douglas Lyon, Circus Vargas, Burlingame, Calif.
CW   Circus World Museum, Baraboo, Wis., Robert L. Parkinson, Chief Librarian.
HC   Glenn Parkins, Hanneford Family Circus, Sarasota, Fla.
HT   Mack Goeth, Photographer, the *Sarasota Herald-Tribune* Venice Bureau.
JS   John Strong, Thousand Oaks, Calif.
KD   Ken Dodd, Sarasota, Fla.
KW   Karl Wallenda, Sarasota, Fla.

LJ   Mrs. Larry Jensen, Manitowoc, Wis.
LP   Paul Lubera and Bill Poehner.
ME   Merle Evans, Sarasota, Fla.
MO   Melvin J. Olsen Collection, courtesy Mrs. Melvin J. Olsen, Indianapolis, Ind.
PF   Terry Lorant, Photographer, Pickle Family Circus, San Francisco, Calif.
RG   Robert D. Good Collection.
SF   *San Francisco Chronicle*, courtesy Dianne Levy. Photo by Vincent Maggiora.
RL   Ronnie Lewis, Houston, Texas.
RM   Ringling Museum of the Circus, John Hurdle, Curator, Sarasota, Fla.
WT   Walter B. Hohenadel, Editor, the *White Tops*, Rochelle, Ill.

Photographs not credited are the property of the author.

Foreword

Authors of circus books who have lived in the red-and-gold world of the big tops are prone to take a jaundiced view of outsiders who, although lacking in circus experience, nevertheless embrace the subject in literary adventures. Too often the scribe is inclined to feel that because the circus is a colorful and exciting place a book about it can just about write itself. But, to borrow a title from a song in the theater classic *Porgy and Bess*, "It Ain't Necessarily So." Nothing ever writes itself, with the possible exception of the moving finger of a reasonably well-known author named Omar Khayyam.

I feel that none of the old pros among writers of circus stories will deny to David Hammarstrom a membership in their ranks. This young man has put together a circus history book through the use of interviews with highly placed circus men and women who were there when it happened or who had access to authentic information. The research for this book is most impressive, and Hammarstrom has been tireless in tracking down his people—from whom he was determined to hear firsthand the things he wanted to know. Because these circus personalities are the sources for the stories in the book, any inaccuracies occurring should be charged to their occasional imperfect recollections. Hammarstrom has brought off a very good job indeed. He's a good reporter, and one who adds his own special literary sheen to his task. He walked with his source people down a street called memory lane, and they loom large as life—especially to readers who know them. And for the first time, I think, not only the stars of the rings, the air, and the hippodrome track, but management luminaries as well receive center-ring position in a circus book. So for his initial circus literary adventure, congratulations, David, and welcome to the club!

Bev Kelley

Acknowledgments

The preparation of this book has afforded me the once-in-a-lifetime luxury of meeting and interviewing many outstanding producing and performing personalities. To say that I consider myself lucky would be an understatement, for they comprise a veritable galaxy of all-time big top greats. Their combined work spans the entire century, and their insights and observations about circus life, past and present, are the exclusive property of seasoned troupers. For the interviews they each granted me, greatest thanks on earth are due: Merle Evans, Maestro of the circus world; Arthur M. Concello, managerial genius and honored veteran of the flying trapeze; the late Floyd King, press agent, advance man, and show owner; the late high-wire patriarch Karl Wallenda; the late equestrienne marvel May Wirth; center-ring stars Tommy and Struppi Hanneford; Ringling Bros. Circus ringmaster Harold Ronk; producing clown Ken Dodd; Douglas Lyon, Vice President and National Marketing Director, Clyde Beatty-Cole Bros. Circus; famed costume designer Miles White; single trapeze flyer Cookie Arturo; comic wild animal trainer Tarzan Zerbini; and Jane Johnson and Nena Evans, former executive secretaries to John and Henry Ringling North.

This undertaking has benefited greatly by the generous concern of F. Beverly Kelley, spangleland's noted author, press agent, and poet laureate. For the foreword he penned, and for the constructive interest he took in the completed manuscript with comments and factual corrections, I am especially grateful. His endorsement is highly valued.

During the planning stages of this book, Malcolm White of San Francisco offered important advice. At that time, the late Mel Olsen, editor of the *White Tops*, was a positive influence. Cecil Byrne, Cochairman of the Imperial Shrine Circus Committee, answered in candid detail my questions concerning Shrine circuses. Dyer Reynolds, of Los Angeles, granted me access to his rare tape recordings of actual Ringling circus performances during the last years under canvas. I conversed on the telephone with Ronnie Lewis, who now resides in Houston, Texas, about his famous mentor, the late, great Barbette. Mrs. Hedy Trostl helped me reach her son, Cookie, for an interview and favored me with her humorous recollections of things past.

I was made extremely welcome by the Showfolks Club of Sarasota, Florida, where I gained further information from Ricki Wallenda, Ernie Burch, Danny and Sarah Chapman, Alfredo Landon, Bill Smith, and many more wonderful people. Added insights along the way have been given to me freely by John Strong, "Doc" Boas, Jimmy Ille, Charles Carter, "Baldie," and Bill Keller. Valuable, too, has been the assistance of *Washington Star-News* reporter Louise Lague.

Throughout this project, my good friend Robert L. Mitchell, of Sells & Gary Circus, has readily clarified many queries and has helped sustain me with his unfailing encouragement. Equally supportive have been others close to me, including my sister Kathy, Michael Kohl, John Cowan, and Dora Williams. On our way to a performance of the

Ringling Circus, Ken and Flo Reeves and I put our heads together and came up with the book's title. Terry McHale and Liz Johnson lended strong moral support.

To be sure, my own travels on the sawdust trail have contributed to the text, as well, as have my many blurry-eyed wanderings through numerous back issues of *Variety*, the *Billboard*, and the *White Tops*. Although a bibliography is not in order, I should call attention to Earl Chapin May's monumental gem, *The Circus from Rome to Ringling*, upon which I have relied heavily for historical perspective. Another fine source was John and Alice Durant's *Pictorial History of the American Circus*.

For the superb illustrations herein contained, I wish to acknowledge the spirited cooperation of many individuals. Primarily, I am indebted to John Hurdle, the affable curator of the Ringling Museum of the Circus in Sarasota. Mr. Hurdle graciously allowed me total and free access to the museum's photo vault and the subsequent loan of every picture I chose to use. Robert L. Parkinson, Chief Librarian and Historian at the Circus World Museum, Baraboo, Wisconsin, and his assistant Bill Metzger extended similar courtesies and were very helpful in filling the "gaps" with photographs not obtainable elsewhere. They have also made available the excellent sampling of old circus lithographs to be enjoyed in these pages.

Other prime providers were Bob Zurfluh, Director of Public Relations for Capital Centre at Landover, Maryland, who secured the fine color transparencies of Circus America taken by their photographer Jerry Wachter; Mack Goeth, photographer, and Shirley Bennett, the *Sarasota Herald-Tribune*, Venice Bureau; Mrs. Melvin J. Olsen, Indianapolis; and *White Tops* Editor Walter B. Hohenadel, Rochelle, Illinois, whose father Walter H. Hohenadel had the blessed courage to publish the work of a fourteen year old in the form of my first circus review. The *White Tops*, by the way, is the official publication of the Circus Fans Association of America.

For additional illustrations, I am equally indebted to Ronnie Lewis; his mother Mrs. Larry Jensen of Manitowoc, Wisconsin; the Circus City Festival, Peru, Indiana and Ken Hasselkus; Glenn Parkins, Executive Director, Hanneford Family Circus; Circus Kirk, East Berlin, Pennsylvania; Terry Lorant, photographer, Pickle Family Circus, San Francisco; the *San Francisco Chronicle*, courtesy of Dianne Levy and photographer Vincent Maggiora. Also, to Douglas Lyon and Circus Vargas, John Strong, Ken Dodd, Merle Evans, and the late Karl Wallenda.

And finally, my very special thanks to the editors at A. S. Barnes, especially Ronald B. Roth, for their careful, understanding assistance.

The invaluable contributions of all these people have helped make the project a joyful experience, although it has not been without its darker moments. Sadly, I report a telephone call I received in May, 1977, from Fran Olsen, informing me of the sudden death of her husband, Mel, only weeks earlier. Mel had been editing the *White Tops* for several years and, at the time, was helping me secure illustrations for the book from his vast collection of photographs. Some of them are featured in these pages. Although I had never met Mel personally, through our telephone conversations I came to regard him as a very good friend. He was an unusually affirmative man, quite amazing considering the ailments that had befallen him in recent years arising from an automobile accident. The continued encouragement he offered me was perhaps the strongest I have received from any single individual. Mel is now up on "the big lot" as troupers say, there enjoying, I am sure, his favorite circus stars in some wonderful grand entrees. Along with Mel, now, are three legendary circus figures, all integral to this book, who have, since their participation in it, passed on: Karl Wallenda, Floyd King, and May Wirth. They were true wizards of circus magic. For them, and for their enchanted followers (of which Mel was one), this book was written.

Introduction

Children of all ages! Welcome to the circus, the once thriving monarch of American amusements that is today threatened with mediocrity, and tomorrow may be pitching pressurized tents and parading pachyderms in space suits on the moon!

A book of this nature should begin on a note of enthusiasm, I *agree,* although I will argue at intervals along the way for a sense of sobriety. My aim is to "tell it like it is." Not a likely undertaking, I concede, in view of the traditional treatment of circus in this country as something akin to God, Motherhood, and Walter Cronkite.

The simple fact is—the circus is not what it used to be. *Why?* What once made it the entertainment colossus of America, and what has happened to it since the advent of movies, television, and rock? Those are the questions that underlie my narrative, and they cannot be answered by reeling off a series of cliches. To answer them I have gone behind the big top—behind the glossy bannerlines and the glittering press agentry—where the basic facts of how circuses have survived are to be found and studied. There, we will examine a world of strange contrasting moods and goals, of breathtaking artists reaching for celestial shores, and of grim-faced promoters haggling over the bleak realities of profit and loss; a world at times gay and gallant, other times foreboding and riddled with harsh reversals. It's driving axiom is "the next town," and, within the changing pattern of its methods of operation over the

years are to be found the reasons not only for its genius to adapt, but why its existence today is in peril.

Indeed, it is, as museum curator John Hurdle characterizes it, "a very special world." A world of dedicated individuals, restless and forever on the move, whose passions and foibles, whose colorful struggles and incredible achievements, are no different today than they were 100 years ago. No, they have not changed. But audiences have. So has the march of time. And who is not perplexed by the age-old penchant for comparing past with present? How else, though, can we correctly estimate where we are today? I was not around during the "golden age" of circuses—an age that is considered to have matured during the twenties—yet an understanding of that period is essential in establishing a standard of showmanship by which the circus today can better be appraised.

Is the circus dying? Sophisticated doubters have entertained the notion since the great depression years, when our major tenting enterprises began surrendering to their own inevitable obsolescence. Following the last under-canvas engagement of Ringling Bros. and Barnum & Bailey, in Pittsburg, Pennsylvania, 16 July 1956, the evidence of further decline in solidly organized, regularly touring tanbark companies is difficult to offset. You can argue futilely with sheer optimism, with contrived lists of dozens, even hundreds, of so-called titles of shows on the road during the seventies. You will only fool yourself. The plain truth is, red wagon caravans of a rich bygone era in American history have rolled permanently into museum vaults, there to be revered as glorious artifacts of an unretrievable past. Moreover, our most daring creators of circus art in modern times have vanished from the scene. The striking artistic influence once exerted over circusdom by John Ringling North, now retired, is sorely missed. So, too, are the captivating directorial splashes of a Barbette and the innovative producing achievements of an Al Dobritch, both now deceased. Producers and directors of that ilk seem to be in scarce supply these days.

Perhaps a better question would be, is *showmanship* dying? No, not completely. Not *yet*. The "ever-changing, never-changing circus," as Earl Chapin May so wisely called it, may be far less in size and grandeur than it once was; it is not, however, anywhere near the end of the road. Circus entertainment in the United States has effectively endured every change in our nation's diverse history. It withstood the early onslaught of motion-picture shows and weathered the initial novelty of radio. Television has taken by far the greatest toll on big tops, although it's possible that more people see circuses today than ever before. The country has grown by leaps and bounds, and red wagon troupes have adapted, if not brilliantly, from the position of dominance they once held in outdoor show business to the optional status they now enjoy among a growing number of diversions competing for the public's amusement dollar.

Showmanship is a human dynamic, and there are on Yankee soil today a handful of true super stars (and super impressarios), some yet to be fully acclaimed, providing thrills and chills annually to millions of big top enthusiasts. Don't forget that Gunther Gebel Williams is currently performing on *our* side of the Atlantic. And who can guess when, out of the ever shifting alliances between operators and newcomers to the executive ranks, a new partnership comparable to that of Barnum & Bailey, or North and Concello, will emerge? Along to take the place of a retiring entrepreneur comes a Cliff Vargas, with seemingly unlimited potential and the sort of determination that precedes the birth of a rainbow. Along, too, comes a building contractor by the name of Abe Pollin, to assemble virtually overnight a five-ring extravaganza of unforgettable magnitude, called Circus America. Realize, if you wish, its implications for the future: Simply stated, when gifted artists are presented in an exciting manner and ballyhooed with grit, anxious crowds will form at the ticket windows.

Therefore, it is the purpose of this book to celebrate great showmanship in whatever form it may be found—be it the incredible stamina of May Wirth atop a circling horse in the twenties, or the unprecedented aspirations in the seventies of flying trapeze star Tito Gaona going for the quadruple somersault; the bizarre creation by George Balanchine of a ballet for elephants nearly forty years ago, or the sloshy trek, Circus Vargas style in 1974, of a single pachyderm through a Hollywood car wash! Admittedly, I am partial to great moments in circus history and to the men and women responsible. Hopefully, therefore, my preoccupation with the meritorious will do justice to today's as well as yesterday's heroes and serve to enhance the reader's interest in the unique and wonderful people of the big top—those honored immortals of the center ring.

Changes in the circus world are happening so fast, especially in these precarious times, that I hasten to warn the reader of possible discrepancies that may crop up in the text by publication time. For example, will Cliff Vargas by then have produced a really outstanding three-ring performance—something all of us who believe in him so much have a right to expect? Likewise, other matters about which my opinions are herein expressed, such as current glaring deficiencies in the Ringling organization, may have changed, resulting in my comments having less relevance. Such is the risk I take in declaring myself on a number of controversial issues. Hopefully, changes in every respect will nullify my criticisms!

Finally, I have a theory that the circus is also necessary to the survival of the human spirit. Should its demise actually come about, surely somebody with the true spark of genius will invent it all over again. Man cannot live without his symbols of magic, and the circus is perhaps the most potent symbol of them all.

The show is now on, and there's still *plenty* to see!

D.L.H.

San Francisco

BEHIND THE BIG TOP

1
To Hell With Roman Chariots

TO say that the circus as we know it sprang from a Roman festival of horrors called Circus Maximus is to do great injustice to a world of entertainment that has inspired man with its spirited symbols of magic. To the perpetrators of such nonsense, I will argue that the American circus laughs at reason and flies over mortality with incredible vigor; that its reach is upward and its effect infinitely beneficial to us all.

As John Steinbeck noted, ". . . the circus is change of pace—beauty against our daily ugliness,

The Cristianis, 1941. RM.

Circus magic! Children at a performance of Big John A. Strong's Circus, 1976. JS.

excitement against our boredom. Every man and woman and child comes from the circus refreshed and renewed and ready to survive. What doctor can do as much?"

Yet tradition has it, through a number of scholars who have taken a crack at circus history, that tanbark amusements evolved from the ashes of that desecrated Roman midway; that the Leitzels and the Codonas, the Wallendas and the Hannefords represent the artistic descendants of gushing gladiators and demented chariot drivers.

Roots. We all must have them. Pity the circus for

Los Tonitos, 1966. RM.

such ill-deserved origins. Among its pagan progenitors in action, there is the graphic example of Pompey returning from fresh triumphs and dictating a free spectacle of virility for 150,000 freeloading supporters. Deranged lions cavorted sadistically with helpless pachyderms. Lunging tigers charged head on into a rabble of condemned criminals. The systematic slaughter of "500—FIERCE NUMIDIAN LIONS—500!" was perversely advertised and executed. A "Camelopard" giraffe was attacked by imported tigers and allowed to bleed freely, to fulfill the promises made by Pompey's press agents.

"The Circus of the Century" they billed it. Pompey reveled in the publicity that Circus Maximus afforded him. The crowds howled with insipid delight while boxers and wrestlers dismembered their weaker opponents. Chariots crashed sideways into their rivals, raising the dust of bloody aggression in this carnage-crazed arena.

So popular were these sadistic tournaments that Circus Maximus expanded its seating capacity to 250,000. Man's inhumanity to man (and to the animal kingdom as well) approached eerie proportions. A flamboyant, if somewhat jaded emperor with money to burn presented the piece de resis-

tance: 1,000 Christians were delivered into the jaws of a sea of starving lions and tigers. Gulp. Forgive us this day, and lead us out of Rome . . .

Relevant to *what* are these scenes of brazen viciousness? A modern day destruction derby, perhaps, when all ambulances are engaged, sirens blaring, or an evening at Roller Games. The spirit of Circus Maximus lives on through a Hell's Angels reign of terror, when the Ku Klux Klan convenes, and on television screens across America crowded with the repellent images of violence. It is not manifested in any center ring where gifted artists gather to enchant and delight children of all ages. The road from Circus Maximus to Barnum & Bailey is strewn with historical hokum.

The late Karl Wallenda, a man of legendary stamina, assured me that the goals at the Roman Coliseum exhibitions were actually commendable: "They had acrobats. They had jugglers. That was circus."

I queried him about the brawls. "No," he said, "that was just once in a while when they had the blood bath . . . fed Christians to lions in front of the public. It was really a circus, too."

Other voices disagree, some with distinct disdain for the big top's alleged "past."

Curator John Hurdle, of the Ringling Museum of the Circus in Sarasota, Florida, concedes that Pompey's gutsy showmanship is a dubious forerunner to the great Yankee circuses that specialize in breathtaking feats of human skill. "The world *circus*," says Hurdle, "is the only thing that ties it in." Having dispatched a scholar's pronouncement, let us progress upward to the wisdom of the press agent.

The Ward-Bell Flyers, in the 1950s. CW.

20

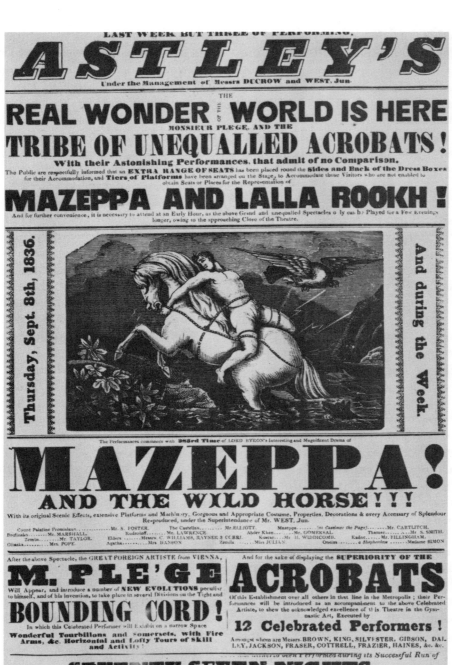

Real roots of American circuses: Astley's equestrians, acrobats, and thematic spectacles. RM.

I give you the words of none other than the late Roland Butler, the guiding spirit of Ringling tout-masters, who in the 1951 circus program magazine had this to say: ". . . for it is a historical fact that the character of a nation may largely be determined by the character of its amusements. The gory thumbs-down amusements of the ancient Romans in the coliseum presaged the decline of the Roman empire and reflected the character of their patrons."

Slobs.

Amazing, is it not, how much a circus press agent really knows? Listen further. Mr. Butler, then in assessing the comparative virtues of his own employers—Ringling Bros. and Barnum & Bailey—defers to the good man from Yale, William Lyon Phelps. The noted professor tutored John and Henry Ringling North. In 1943, he was moved to write about their circus: "I would advise everybody to spend an afternoon or an evening in wonderland and I wish to congratulate the famous managers of this show for giving so much happiness to so many people at a time when happiness was never more needed."

Neither the cry of extinguished convicts nor the agony of consumed Christians were anywhere to be found when Professor Phelps attended a perform-ance of the "Greatest Show on Earth." Nor were such dastardly deeds evident 100 years earlier when Dan Rice, America's favorite one-horse show buf-foon paraded his trained pig, Lord Byron, around the ring and sang "Hard Times." A century before that, star equestrian John Bill Ricketts leaped over elephants and danced a hornpipe on a galloping horse, bringing fresh excitement to his good friend, George Washington. Our first President loved the circus. Good reason had he.

From the circular foresight of the eighteenth century English horseman, Sergent-Major Philip Astley, we emerged—tumblers, jugglers, acrobats, and aerialists. Our roots are deep in the images of Astley's first magical ring!

No circus act has done more to keep alive the last vestiges of macho Rome than wild-animal displays, that did not emerge before American audiences until late in the nineteenth century. Featured in the center of a cage full of "ferocious, man-eating lions and tigers" are the daring men in white, those death defying, fearless and fading wild animal trainers. Usually, their actions are underscored by a ringing crash of symbols and by an ear-splitting blast of brass power and pounding drum rolls. The ringmaster's

vital announcements are essential to heighten the urgency; nor will the trainer be convincing unless he can, almost single-handedly, project great danger on his face and in all his moves. Usually, the fear factor is mere showmanship. Not always have these noisy confrontations between man and beast thrilled the public.

In 1925, our genteel British neighbors began passing laws against the exhibition of wild animals. At the same enlightened hour Charles Ringling, the most humane of the original five brothers, declared that the restless cats and the attendant harassments of their trainers offended the public. Mr. Ringling decided there would be no more cage acts in his circus and sold his beasts to the rival American Circus Corporation. Soon thereafter, Mr. Ringling proceeded to bad mouth his competitors for present-ing the brutes under their Sells-Floto big top!

Was danger and fear not what the public wanted?

Sells-Floto Circus opened in Chicago on 14 April 1925, and the former Ringling terribles were a sensation on new sawdust. Enthusiastic audiences proved Mr. Ringling wrong. Noted one reviewer, "It is a circus pure and simple, wild animals and everything . . . anyone who thinks that they are not as popular as ever is sadly mistaken . . . and if there was any fear on the part of any of the audience when they were presented, it was not noticeable to the average observer."

What was there to be frightened of? While three soloists delivered an original operatic score, the fragile Miss Della Reed portrayed a virgin about to be sacrificed to a den full of beasts, in a pageant titled "The Bride and The Beasts (a Lyrical Spectacle)." Needless to say, since the beasts scheduled to devour the leading lady were traditional circus "wild animals" (probably the clunkers Charles Ringling disposed of), nothing eventful happened. Big cage stars are rarely dangerous. More often these routines are futile exercises in sound and fury. When a tiger does escape, it's cause for a true victory. Something big has finally happened; the act has delivered!

Today's Wolfgang Holzmair, a recent Ringling center ringer, huffs and puffs in his red vinyl Roman charioteer's costume—thrusting his barrel chest defiantly forward like an old steam engine sputtering through an abandoned switchyard without a real train to pull. Not too long ago, Trevor Bale, known mostly for his equestrian acts, cluttered up the center ring with his cumbersome props and lethar-

Wolfgang Holzmair, keeping alive old macho myths. WT.

gic beasts. The sluggish charges stayed clear of the trainer while he spent most of his time rearranging the props. "The furniture mover," he was facetiously dubbed. He was forever engaged in the process of setting the stage for the next item of business—reerecting or redismantling a ton of heavy iron pedastals, ramps, hoops, bolts, and nuts. For what, nobody could ever quite figure out, not even the lions and tigers. Alternately, Bales' subjects posed half-heartedly on the endless array of *rearrangements*. Was Bale awaiting a photographer? A "Bekins" man on overtime would have brought more excitement to that act. I often wondered if Bale had another calling in mind. The animals were thoroughly ignored.

Back to the benign Charles Ringling. He may have been bored by wild animals, too. Without them, his circus coasted splendidly for several years. Seals and trained pigeons sufficed. How could audiences miss what essentially was a dull duel between whip crackers and snarling cats?

King of grizzly hoopla, Clyde Beatty. CW.

Dynamo for the distaff side, Mabel Stark, taught a school for lady animal trainers. CW.

Clyde Beatty changed all that when he stormed onto the scene. Hagenbeck-Wallace patrons were thrilled by Beatty's new brand of bravura, here was something you could get worked up about. By 1931, Ringling Bros. and Barnum & Bailey (without Charles Ringling, now deceased) again put up the steel arenas and scared 'em to death—not with wild animals. No, with *Clyde Beatty*. The grand exponent of the chair and the whip, *he* was something to be feared. Animals took note and their performances improved markedly. In Beatty's shadow followed a steady stream of brave, quasi maniacs, like the "thrill-a-minute" John Helliott, or the strange Hindu animal hypnotist, Blacaman (about whom, tales of terror come later).

Attractive Mabel Stark wrestled with her beloved Rajah, risking eyesight and facial tissue two times daily. She inspired women with her peculiar sense of independence; they flocked in droves to see her perform on the Al G. Barnes Circus. Show officials, wondering how long Stark's reign could last, scored a lucky publicity coup by launching the Mabel Stark Lion and Tiger Training School for Women. The press boys were astonished when thousands of inquiries poured in from all over the country. If Rajah decided to have his mistress for lunch, there were scores of willing gals waiting in the wings for a crack at Rajah's tender embrace. The show was forced by the tremendous response to establish the school at its Baldwin Park, California, winter quarters. Professor Stark gave classes in the etiquette and/or combat techniques of the big cage. The Stark truth is, there weren't many true Starks to be found. Lunacy is not something you can teach. Some people are blessed with it; others are less fortunate.

The ghost of Clyde Beatty refuses to die. That thundering whip still cracks in the ears of a host of hopeful heir apparents (one is yet to be spotted). The competing successors to the throne all dash dramatically into and out of their steel enclosures, all dressed in white, all banking on the odds that someday in the big cage something somewhere will wake up and attack them and nearly destroy them. It's the only way to get a rise from fickle audiences and suspicious media representatives.

None exemplifies better the strained drama of a lost cause than Beatty-Cole's Captain Dave Hoover, the "favored protégé" of all the protégés of the late Clyde Beatty. How frustrating it must be that he is only Captain Dave Hoover. He must feel on occa-sion like the former Clyde Beatty cage boy who, following a stand-in appearance once for the master, lamented the feeble results: "I do everything Beatty does. I shoot the gun at the same time. The lions snarl at the same time. I get out by the skin of my teeth. The lions charge at me up against the door. I do precisely the same thing and I just don't get the applause."

Although Captain Hoover is fighting a losing battle, I suspect he is having a dandy time fooling what few souls there are left to fool. Hoover comes off like an unconscious comedian miscast in a lion's den. His efficient exasperations give him away. Closeup, he's a delight. The lines of caution on his face have a whimsical edge. Is he overacting, or maybe having a good laugh on us all? Whichever, the effect gives his arduous task a sly comic quality.

Jungle myths are gradually collapsing. During his first season in 1940 with Ringling-Barnum, Alfred Court, the great French trainer, called everybody's bluff by politely hosting in one ring black jaguars, a Siberian snow leopard, black panthers, a mountain lion, pumas, African spotted leopards, and Indian spotted panthers. In another ring he presented Bengal tigers, Abyssinian lions, polar bears, Himalayan bears, and giant ocelots. And, in a third, there were Berber lions, polar bears, black bears, black jaguars, and Great Dane dogs!

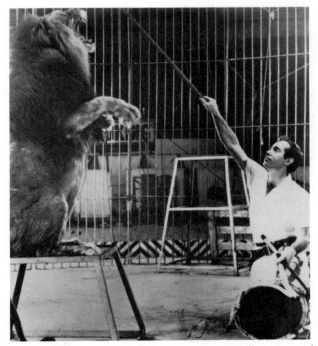

Dave Hoover, one of many "heir-apparents" to Beatty's throne. KD.

Alfred Court stressed rapport with the animals, a startling contrast to Clyde Beatty's "shoot 'em up" bravado. RM.

It was, according to program notes, "An extraordinary display in which natural jungle enemies perform together in the most hazardous and exciting exhibitions, without gun fire, crow bars, electric persuaders, or dramatic pretense."

Court was a sensation. Calling him "the man of infinite patience," circus-story man Frank Braden wrote: "We, of the Big Show, honestly believe him to be the finest trainer of wild animals that ever lived. We know he is the kindest, the most understanding. . . . We watched him with bated breath the first day he entered the arena. His animals had just arrived from England, Norway, and Sweden after a most dangerous threading of mine fields. The war and the journey had forced a four-month layoff, and we expected a terrific struggle for mastery. But we knew not Alfred Court.

"Court stood quietly in its center speaking in soft, gentle tones, as the animals circled excitedly. The low voice seemed almost a whisper, but it rallied and directed the milling jungle beasts like a far off cavalry trumpet. Almost instantly the confusion resolved into order, and the animals, so bewildered by strange surroundings, were on their pedestals. Their eyes were on Court, who had not moved . . ."

A delighted John Ringling North—the man who had wooed Court to American shores—boasted to a corps of adoring photo hounds, "To see another trainer like my friend Alfred Court, you'll have to wait a century."

The ghosts of Circus Maximus were squelched. Suddenly the most unlikely types were showing up behind bars. Six stately showgirls strutted sexily among a circle of infatuated Bengal tigers. One of the lookers casually draped a cat around her shoulders, and the live fur piece, whatever its gender, breathed heavily, obviously satisfied. You've come a long way, baby.

The shattering of old illusions has given rise to a new order of animal experts, inspired mainly by Court and his gentler directives. Currently, the gracious Charlie Bauman and the dazzling Gunther Gebel Williams are fine examples of civilized behavior between man and beast. They display respect for their performing partners, at least in the ring.

While our congressional legislators decide if growling men and grizzly pets have a legal right to continue perpetuating the myth of a circus born out of Roman brawn, I shall enjoy the antics of a few trainers who offer decidedly successful parodies of what tradition would have them be. A rollicking

Court's ultimate put-down of big-cage theatrics was
achieved in 1945 with six unafraid showgirls. RM.

Charlie Bauman, opting for gracious coexistence. WT.

Courage and charisma: Gunther Gebel Williams. WT.

Facetious Tarzan Zerbini. "I'd rather deal with animals. They're smarter than people." RM.

Since hanging up her trapeze, Tajana (Struppi Hanneford) has found life in the big cage no more hazardous than it was in the air. HC.

Spaniard, Pablo Noel, tickled his way through one tour with Ringling-Barnum then returned to his homeland. We are the losers. Noel's wry, self-satiric bravado in the face of his deadly enemies is the work of a gifted jester. Noel satirizes in a devastating way the shoot-'em-up gusto of the antiquated animal routine. After rushing the big kittens back into their individual cages, Noel literally chases the last guy in, following so closely on his tail that seconds later the master finds himself inadvertently locked into the last tiny compartment! With all the anger that no lion would ever have the talent to feign, Noel shakes his furious fists against the bars, howling for immediate release.

We have come to the end of the macho line. No practicing whip master knows this better than Tarzan Zerbini. In a recent engagement with Circus America, Zerbini swung in on a rope, Jungle Jim style, only to stub his toe on the ring curb.

Zerbini told me, "I'd rather deal with animals. They're smarter than people."

Could you explain, I asked.

"They have more sense than human beings running loose in the wild country of United States. . . . How many lions and tigers get killed every day in the United States?"

I wasn't sure.

"How many people get shot."

I think I see what you mean, Tarzan.

Zerbini's act is a doozy. He's got everything. Beautiful animals, neat feats, well-rounded programming. Most of all, a zesty spirit of renunciation. Hold on, you Circus Maximus freaks, you haven't seen the light, yet . . .

Tarzan grabbed hold of a big cat's jaws, pried open the awesome dentures and examined with revulsion the cavity of danger into which he would lodge his trusting noggin.

Too sharp? Too deep? Too hungry?

No, complained T.Z. to the audience.

"Bad breath."

2
Barbette Originals

ENCHANTMENT, maintained Barbette, should be the prime element of any circus. Certainly it was the prime element of any circus *Barbette* got involved with. Strange enchantment, indeed.

Who is Barbette? I must try to explain, and it may not be simple. A child prodigy by choice, Barbette became the sensational "siren" of Parisian aerialists (as a female impersonator). Finally, he became the "World's foremost creator of circus spectacles" (some say by default). It was in the capacity of the

Barbette, the "Entrepreneur of Enchantment," reviews costume sketches for Cole Bros. Circus, 1949. RM.

latter that Barbette came to my hometown of Santa Rosa, California. The fading trapeze star was now supervising a chorus of showgirls in the aerial numbers presented by Polack Bros. Circus.

Also billed as "The Entrepreneur of Enchantment," Barbette led into the Sonoma County Fairgrounds Pavilion (just a few blocks from my home) a fascinating procession of theatrical trunks, odd mechanical contraptions, rough-looking roustabouts to put them together—and me. Small enough to snoop without looking suspicious, I was about to get an eyeful of circus life behind the scenes. I could never have guessed what lay ahead.

The strange images of make believe, like scattered parts of a great puzzle, came rolling out of the trunks and crates: Huge butterfly wings, enormous deflated clown heads, piles of twisted cable and pulleys, silver bars and hinged platforms, light fixtures the likes of which I had never seen. The entrepreneur's artifacts swelled in complexity like a box of toys mushrooming . . . into a surrealistic fantasy.

Through this maze of confusion forming behind the rusty grandstand seats, somewhere always loomed Barbette. Prop hands carelessly assembling the mammoth bird cages were chastised. Local boys, recruited to pump tons of air into the huge clown heads, required close supervision, perhaps an occasional pat on the back. There were broken bulbs to discover, dead batteries to recharge, loose screws and nuts to inspect. Barbette hovered over the details like a possessed puppeteer in control of every string.

Then, out came the costumes—sequined, exotic fabrics arranged in the most unpredictable designs. Outrageously shaped plumes and feathers, audacious hats, chiffon hoop skirts that spiralled to the outer limits. The weird color combinations posed a veritable challenge to ordinary esthetics. So did the gaggle of young ladies who began arriving and would that evening be wearing them. They were "Barbette's Aerialovelies," the dozen darlings who executed aloft the creator's fantastic ideas. Say what you will, no chorus line extant ever matched the sheer nerve of these twelve sturdy lookers.

Whatever their collective attributes, program notes deified the girls beyond recognition: "An astral assemblage performing in graceful unison under the deft direction of the celebrated Barbette . . . swallowlike patterns of flight and fantasy in seraphic synchronization by an olympian corps de ballet . . . sweeping arcs with reckless dives and plunges . . . darting, diving deeds aloft by beguiling damsels . . . roseate hues of springtime . . . matchless in magnitude and munificince . . . an airborne bevy of beauties whose massed maneuvers reflect Barbette's directorial genius."

Under various aliases they flew: The Bird Cage Girls, The Swing High Girls, The Whirlgirls, and The Cloud Swing Girls. The year before, with Clyde Beatty Circus, they were the "Beattyettes." (Before that, with Biller Bros., I assume they were the "Billerettes.") To me, there were only two types—

The "Bird Cage Girls," Polack Bros. Circus, 1956, directed by Barbette. RL.

31

Barbette's "Aerialovelies"—a sigh of poetry between catapulting acrobats and flyers. RL.

the attractive ones and those who chewed gum. The latter were usually of the roseate-hue type and they took longer to get "airborne." Nevertheless, I thought that any girl who would subject her life to Barbette's "swallowlike patterns of flight and fantasy" was amazing, if not insane.

Can you imagine hanging by your teeth in midair, being whirled at speeds unsafe for the human anatomy with ten-foot-long silk wings pulling against your arms, all the while projecting, with or without chewing gum, the untarnished grace of a "human butterfly"?

As the girls wandered into the Pavilion, trying to avoid Barbette (an impossible feat), tempers flared. I struggled for bits and pieces of the delicious dialogue.

"You missed practice in Denver!" snapped Barbette to one of his human butterflies. "Where were you?"

"With my boyfriend!" she growled back, feeding possible scars of jealousy in her aging boss.

"Stretch your wings wider, or you come down!"

A sunburned Whirlgirl bounded by. The mentor was enraged.

"Don't you know when to come out of the sun?"

"I fell asleep."

"When you are peeling, you'll look like Bozo the Clown up there in the lights."

The sun beauty blushed and vanished from sight.

"And take that gum out of your mouth!"

Given Barbette's high artistic vision, very few of the Aerialovelies ever tasted the thrill of victory.

Barbette cuts up with his showgirls. The director reveled in circus spotlights, outlandish egotism, and good restaurants. RL.

From their perfectionist director came constant bitchiness. The seraphic synchronization was too "reckless." The reckless dives were too "seraphic." Still, no cooperative young flyer was beyond eventual grace, nor beyond Barbette's ultimate compassion. The director could offer deep consolation when really needed, and I suspect the girls looked to their taskmaster in times of personal grief as a father figure. Barbette was feared and respected.

Ronnie Lewis, a principal assistant to Barbette, remembers the famed aerial choreographer standing behind his girls. "He did the best he could for them," says Lewis. "He would try to up their salaries; he gave them money out of his own pockets, paid for their abortions, and rarely got his money back."

Lewis met Barbette in 1952, when both were working on the Clyde Beatty Circus in California. A promising acrobat from Manitowoc, Wisconsin, Lewis had landed a spot in a trampoline act; shortly into the season, Barbette offered him the job pedalling an aerial bicycle that powered four "winged" Aerialovelies. Lewis jumped at the opportunity and eventually played a key role in other Barbette creations. Later, he went on to his own independent bookings with a three-person swaying ladder routine, the Ronnie Lewis Trio.

The eccentricities of Barbette amused Lewis. "He was artistic and fussy. He could be hard to get along with, and he liked to argue. He had high opinions of himself and he let people know it. He told me what a star he had been till the day he died."

Lewis admired Barbette's genius "to create nice numbers that would tie a show together." As well, he was intrigued by the brash sense of humor of one fun-loving taskmaster: "He was full of jokes and lots of fun to be around. He made cracks right in front of anybody, said anything that came into his mind. He enjoyed hotel dining rooms. He *excelled* in restaurants."

Recently, the magnificent trapeze ballerina, Struppi Hanneford told me how scared she was of the great circus director. As Princess Tajana, Polack Bros. decided to garnish Stuppi's wonderful talents with a Barbette-conceived production, "Spangleland Powwow." Struppi was nervous at the outset, continually dreading humiliation, ever aware of Barbette's reputation for ostentatious displeasure with feminine figures. Finally, when the director spoke, Struppi was startled.

"Tajana," sighed Barbette, "I just must tell you that you are the most beautiful thing I have ever seen. You're just so artistic when you go up there."

Struppi knew she had arrived in the eyes of the highest judge. "If Barbette threw a compliment at you, you must have been something good."

The olympian corps de ballet more often experienced the agony of defeat. If the imperfect beauteous belles were a threat to the retired Parisian star who cajoled them on, who in Santa Rosa would ever know, let alone care? The Shriners may have winced over this peculiar character responsible for staging the great Polack Bros. Circus. I was then a mere

Little Chris Munoz, primed for flight by Barbette, backstage at Ringling Bros. Circus, 1954. Flanking the wee flyer are showgirls, from left to right, *Anna Del Monti, Eileen Slater, and Mary Lou LaSalle.* RM.

twelve year old discovering Barbette, awed by the stunning originality of "The Bird Cage Girls" and "Beauty on The Wing."

Those Barbette originals fired my imagination to the possibilities of circus art. None were more arresting than "Carnival in Spangleland," a little ballet most circuses would have shunned, that centered around a lovely ballerina and two rival jesters fighting for her love. From the band came a melody of dissonant longing, Morton Gould's touching "Pavan." The three central figures sprang to life off a portable stage that had been wheeled into the center ring. A parade of clowns with enormous heads sauntered gaily on, and a magician followed, bringing forth a garden of blossoms and yards of festive garlands. The tense yearning of the music increased. The lovers seemed lost in a maze of hopeless make believe.

In the shadows I discovered Barbette, alive with rapt attention. I wondered if this was the world as Barbette saw it, a world where magicians and fools cavort in endless illusion, where two clowns struggle for the control of a mere dream? Was the creator living out a lost love through the beautiful ballerina? Why did she give her affections to the grotesque clowns?

The bigger-than-life harlequins danced off; the figures of fantasy slowed to stillness on their tiny stage. The curtain was drawn. Above, the Nine Ward-Bell Flyers were now soaring through the upper reaches of the pavilion. The crowds were cheering another act; I remained entranced by the haunting rhythms of "Carnival in Spangleland." I knew I had seen the work of a great artist.

Who was Barbette?

He was a native of Rock Round, Texas, believe it or not! Born with the name Vander Clyde Broadway, he seemed destined for the international fame he would achieve. At age fourteen, his mother permitted him to travel eighty miles from his home to San Antonio, where he joined an act known as the Alferetta Sisters. Barbette became a partner to "America's Little Aerial Queen." A year and a half later, he switched to Erford's Whirling Sensations, a teeth-suspension act, that gave him his first real taste of big-time vaudeville. In a couple of seasons, the ambitious Texan, now billed simply as Barbette, soloed across the continent on the Orpheum circuit. In January, 1923, at the age of twenty-one, he landed solidly on the stage of Broadway's Palace.

Paris followed. To the French shores sailed Bar-

Barbette as himself. RL.

In his youth Barbette gained international fame on the single trapeze as a female impersonator deluxe. RL.

34

bette with twenty-five trunks of costumes, scenery, and cosmetics for a dazzling female impersonation on the single trapeze that culminated in Barbette exposing his masquerade by removing his wig. Unsuspecting men who cheered Barbette's tantalizing "figure" were shocked, amused, and even disappointed. For nearly two decades, the acclaimed aerialist (all traces of Rock Round removed) flew triumphantly over Australia, South America, the Middle East, and the Orient, always returning to the city of love.

In between there were film appearances—in Scallera's *La Tosca* and in Jean Cocteau's *Blood of a Poet*. Grounded permanently by a serious fall at the outbreak of World War II, Barbette's return to America was rewarded by a contract from John Ringling North to stage his sixty-girl aerial spectaculars. Other producers beckoned as well. Rock Round's eccentric wonder worked with Billy Rose on his *Seven Lively Arts* and contributed enchantingly to Orson Welles' stage epic, *Around the World*. More film contracts followed, for the supervision of circus sequences in *Till the Clouds Roll By*, *Jumbo* and others.

Barbette coached Kathryn Crosby (pictured here in the arms of Ronnie Lewis) for Irwin Allen's movie The Big Circus. LJ.

Widely acclaimed, Barbette's stunning "Monte Carlo Aerial Ballet" for Ringling Bros. and Barnum & Bailey in 1948 featured a multiplicity of routines such as those seen here. CW.

Ten years later, Santa Rosa got its first live look at the former rage of French aerialists. Sad. Barbette's presence evoked a wistful eulogy to the terse brevity of youth.

A strange atmosphere surrounded the declining star.

From the beginning, when I should have been too young to sense it, there seemed a mysterious quality about Barbette that I could not put my finger on. Mind you, there was I, a fully mature twelve year old and a budding circus fancier. Unknowingly intrigued, unconsciously driven to understand whatever it was that fascinated me.

My initial inquiries—an autograph request the first year; some silly questions about John Ringling North the next; and at age fourteen an attempt to evaluate the greatness of the Bird Cage Girls—were all civilly reciprocated. The ears of the entrepreneur gracefully turned in my direction whenever I bounded forward with another proclamation.

"Those girls in the bird cages, boy they were something!"

Barbette smiled. "Two of them belong on a crash diet."

Aerial rehearsals for the movie Jumbo. LJ.

It was obvious most of the Aerialovelies had fallen from grace in the eyes of their creator. Soon, I learned to enjoy Barbette's rare humor by baiting it with leading questions.

"You'd think that girl would have enough sense to remove the gum from her mouth?"

"She might remove her teeth, also."

I laughed on cue. The producer glided away to adjust a lamp and remove some dirt from a ring mat.

I was too young, however, to be properly amused when one evening, as Santa Rosa citizens poured into the Fairgrounds Pavilion, I shot off about how exciting it must be to travel with Ringling Bros. Circus.

"Oh," replied Barbette, "it's like a sex holiday."

I grinned with uncertainty. Was Barbette complaining about the morality of the "Greatest Show on Earth"? Suggesting that Santa Rosa was a bore? I was full of indestructible virtues then. . . . I preferred the brilliant fantasies out front, where pastel spots shone on the swallowlike patterns of the Swing High Girls and the Ballancerinas, and where crowds sighed with childlike delight. The producer of such magic had chilled my fantasies with his odd remark.

I remained an admirer from afar. A decade passed. I chanced again upon Barbette, reinstated with Polack Bros. Circus. Clearly, the great days were behind. Gone were the lavish production contracts that allowed Barbette free reign. No room now to transport the Whirl Girl apparatus or the slide-on stages. Virtually an independent producer, Barbette came to Oakland with the circus on a shoestring budget and hurting.

A tiny motor (of washing-machine size) purport-

Actor Stephen Boyd in the air, Ronnie Lewis below, at work on Jumbo. LJ.

edly lifted the "Human Butterflies" into orbit. Due to a faulty mechanism, the olympian corps de ballet had been of late floating through space like a dump truck on unleaded fuel. Barbette was in search of replacement parts. The prestigious San Francisco stand followed. With some trepidation, the butterflies encountered no turbulence in Oakland. Would they fly as smoothly over the city by the golden gate?

Sensing the urgency of the situation, I offered my battered Chevy for the taskmaster's use. Gracious acceptance was immediate. We journeyed to a nearby hardware store. I escorted my rare guest down the aisles of pragmatic technology on what I considered an errand for some simple mechanical fixture. It lapsed into a stroll through a section of cut-rate fabrics, accompanied by my guest's attendant tacky remarks about today's shoddy materials and the wretched prices. I came to realize a sale was not humanly possible. I doubt anybody understood what we were in search of. Certainly not Barbette.

The temperamental little motor was moved intact with the show—what there was of it—to San Francisco. An opening-night audience, myself being the starring member, viewed with quiet apprehension the Aerialovelies in the throes of some eerie ethereal executions. Barely more than a few inches off the floor had the motor lifted them when its overtaxed guts emitted a foreboding slur of sparks and sputters. For several crackling seconds, it was anybody's guess whether the "seraphic" butterflies were about to be hung in effigy or propelled promptly through the Civic Auditorium ceiling.

The world's foremost creator of circus spectacles was stymied. By the fickle whims of an imperfect machine? Or was it sabotage at the edge of paradise? Rumors had it that a certain resident of a small town in the Lone Star state skipped out leaving a whopping electricity bill, and that a Texas power company official flew to California to cut off the offender's juice, on the spot. Was this not taking things a little far?

Barbette examined closely the overloaded economy power winch. You can push your dreams to infinity, but the instruments of mortal men have breaking points. The lovely ladies on high, stranded in a holding pattern, did not convey cheesecake confidence. Nor did the ringmaster who squelched any further take-off plans for the evening with a brazen apology.

"Technical difficulties!" And the olympian *corpse de ballet* came down as ordered. Barbette's Aerialovelies were grounded.

The road to the end encompassed at least one brighter chapter. For three years, beginning in 1969, Barbette toured with *Disney on Parade* through Australia, overseeing the operation of an electrical carousel of six butterfly girls. He had

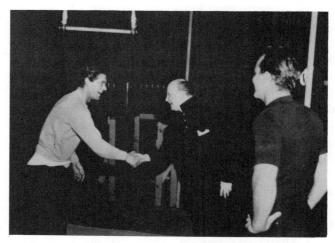

Barbette extends warm praise to Boyd, far left, *for a job well done.* RL.

With Disney On Parade, in Australia, 1972, Barbette,
second from left, *drew great satisfaction.* RL.

fought long and hard to win the assignment, and his moments with Disney were among his happiest.

Then came more unemployment, along with the increasing agonies and frustrations of old age. Unable to cope with these discomforts, Barbette opted for what old timers fondly call "The Big Lot." This he did by indulging in an overdose of sleeping pills.

In the foyer of the Cirque Medrano in Paris, the entrepreneur of enchantment, now a deceased dynamo, is permanently enshrined as one of the "TOP TEN ALL TIME CIRCUS GREATS." The French know a true artist.

To my knowledge, there are no monuments in Rock Round, Texas.

Whatever Barbette did, there was magic. And in adversity, marvelous humor. That night in San Francisco I closed my eyes in retrospect and remembered the haunting "Carnival in Spangleland," remembered the exciting "darting, diving deeds" of the Whirl Girls and the Swing High Girls. Remembered how in the fairgrounds pavilion of my youth my eyes were opened to the strange magic of the circus and to the special people who create it. Finally, I admired in retrospect the director's long-suffering patience in teaching so many average girls to do such extraordinary things. Was that in itself not the essence of greatness?

What a genius. What an *incredible* person. I tell you, this Barbette was some man.

3
Sex and Other Fringe Discomforts

THIS next exhibit, ladies and gentlemen, is not recommended for the children. For you adults, as well, who are offended by alternate, unusual lifestyles, it is suggested you move along to the Wallenda display, where we will join you momentarily.

No, if you prefer your fantasies untarnished, *don't* go behind the big top. From a distance it may be the "ageless delight" that Ernest Hemingway once described. Up close, it's not something you'd want to take home with you. Having served my apprenticeship as a "first-of-may," I am still recovering from the culture shock of a lifetime—lingering bed bugs, a permanent distaste for anything cooked in flour by a fire eater, and a firm suspicion that Freud was a repressed circus clown out to get me.

What my mother didn't know.

The romance and glamour of running away with the circus. Ah, the open road at moonlight, that special person by your side in the shadows between shows! Proclaimed John Ringling North, "People love this colossal thing that roars out of nowhere, set up its rigging, offers a fleeting vision of breathtaking enchantment, and on the morrow vanishes mysteriously into the night."

More than a few dazed dreamers have vanished mysteriously with it, many of them in broad daylight. Since I number myself among the fallen, I will assure you that not all of us escaped from a nut house. Actually, I believe I escaped *into* one when I attended, one bleak day in Cleveland, a performance of Wallace Bros. Circus and failed to leave promptly thereafter. Instead, I decided this was the ageless delight I could not live without. Somebody mistook me for a nut and gave me an usher's job. I started out on a "room and board" basis—a bunk in the musician's sleeper and a note of introduction, by the great Papa Cristiani, to the "gut foundry" (slang for cook house).

Wallace Bros. Circus sideshow grind commences. MO.

39

Wallace Bros. Circus provided employment for a sagging branch of that once-celebrated family of Italian bareback riders, The Cristianis. Those of us who did not ride horses were considered accessories after the fact. Our tour guide was the irascible Pete Cristiani, a Robert Mitchum type who seemed bored with circus life and bent on shepherding his flock over the worst roads and onto the testiest lots. The Cristianis were too absorbed in their reputations to concern themselves with homicidal feuds among canvasmen or the indiscretions of wayward clowns.

It was either hire or fire. Shortly after I joined, Pete gave walking papers to Jimmy, a young jester whose unauthorized escapades with female members of the audience along the route were beginning to bring heat upon the show. Who did they ask to fill Jimmy's forbidden shoes?

Yep. I became the new in-house child molester. A total flop.

Clown alley contained a number of bigger-than-life characters. Their raucous spirit belied a deeper sense of frustration and heartache that shadowed most of their personal lives. Changing the names, of course, there was Steven, an imitation Emmett Kelley who pouted over the audience's failure to recognize that Wallace Bros. was presenting the world's most famous tramp. Bobby Flake, an aging diabetic, had once (in his opinion) been the greatest cloud swing (aerial breakaway) artist ever. His brother Harry, an aging alcoholic, had once been a youthful alcoholic. Getting Harry to make a complete circle of the track during a comedy routine was a notable feat. Paulo was a European midget who felt intimidated working with such a tawdry group of American "fun makers."

To complete the tawdriness there was Horace, beneath whose superfluous baby fat and malcontent spirit there throbbed a dedicated, aspiring ballet dancer. What was he doing with Wallace Bros.? Waiting, he claimed, for a certain aunt in Alabama to kick the bucket, since she had willed him a large sum of money that would pay for ballet lessons. In the meantime, Horace was perversely satisfied to pass his time in a lesser form of art (usually in the capacity of its principal critic). Besides, Horace loved appearing in drag, and considering his bulky anatomy the only place he could bring it off without immediate threat to his person was in the twilight zone of circus comedy. Seldom, though, were his labored female impersonations met with much laughter or even serious attention. They were neither funny nor convincing, and Horace was pathetically unaware of the lost and lonely image he portrayed. Barbette he was not. I wondered how many circuses would have tolerated his odious aura.

Horace spent most of his off moments bitching. Wallace Bros. was "a rag." The hair spray one of the Cristiani women used smelled like a streetcar named desire "at the end of the line." In our dressing tent, his continual sarcastic remarks about the sexual orientation of everyone connected with this free-wheeling enterprise earned either quick approval from a fellow joey or a decisive "shut your damn mouth" from one of the "ballet broads" making up on the other side of a thin canvas partition supposedly separating the boys from the girls. Animosities bounded between the two sectors. Neither half depicted femininity in its ideal state, though both tried.

Kinky company, oh yes. What ordinary folk would have tolerated this seedy expedition? Pete's brother Lucio once said, "I like to go into strange places." Evidently, Pete found unknown territory just as exciting. The tourmaster whistled our sleazy room-and-board caravan over forgotten cemeteries, fields of trash, and cultivated weed patches. We slosh-buckled our way from one condemned lot to the next, even giving circus day on hillsides. Truly, this was showmanship.

Add to these flights into the wilds of rural areas the assaults of the elements. Pete pursued rain and mud with perverse passion, laughed when cloud forma-

Grim beginnings to another day of magic. Crews unload the canvas. MO.

40

"Towners" watch our strange, transitory world rebuild itself. MO.

tions appeared, brought winter to Georgia in August. In one unified sense, it was a perfect tour—all downhill.

In a small Tennessee town during a sudden rainstorm, while the show was in progress, the clowns scampered through mud puddles in ruffles and greasepaint "guying" out the dressing top (tightening the ropes). Water pounded against my funny face, dismissing my colors to a blurred rainbow. Dodging the downpour in an outrageous nurse's costume, Bobby complained about what a "woman" has to go through, bitched about Harry being too drunk to help and Paulo too short to count. We tugged away at the ropes like giggling children at play. Horace did not laugh. The ballet student seemed possessed of his own problematical existence. Waiting, I guessed, for this wretched day to end so he could get on with another night of intrigue and denial sulking over his unrequited loves.

Behind the big top, there are no apparent restraints on a person's proclivities. The souls who inhabit this transitory world are governed by the amoral attitudes which they bring with them. Essentially, they are nonconformists. They live and let live and they go after and get each what they want. They tend to form relationships without pretense, and prostitution flourishes. If the circus is, as Barbette told me, a "sex holiday," it is certainly not a free one. The atmosphere is harsh.

In a formal sense, sleeping arrangements reflected a tradition in the circus of strict separation of the sexes on the train and on the lot. Our sleeper was divided into two impenetrable halves. The single musicians and clowns crashed in the rear; the ballet broads bedded down up front, under possible duress, at the edge of a locked private compartment—the imperial traveling boudoir of the closest thing on this show (excluding the durable Cristiani unions) to a man, wife, and child combination. The cheerful family unit consisted of: Bud, an ex-con (every other night, when he was not at the wheel); his feminine associate Ruth (unless Bud threw her out that day), and, during daylight hours, their prized darling, Mimi—a goat, the most faithful member of this menage a menagerie. The secret transpirings of that threesome were the talk of the show.

Performers with some seniority might acquire possession of one of the small sleeping compartments built into the various utility trucks. Harry and Bobby Flake had survived a lifelong brutal friendship and were thereby pronounced "brothers." They commanded a private suite at the rear of a wild-animal truck. The Flakes slumbered in close proximity to a spotted leopard and some African lions. Each night (whether the moon was or was not in Scorpio), the brothers, with bitter subdued high hopes, ascended to their throne of honor adjoining the lion's den. Their crib was a nightmare of useless paraphrenalia, and when Bobby crawled in, there was little hope left at this inn. No wonder Harry had a professional drinking problem.

There we slept—the musicians and clowns in the rear compartment; the "ballet broads" up front. MO.

41

Breakfast at the "gut foundry" (slang for cookhouse), site of the famous fried-flour controversy. MO.

Gossipers had lost interest in the repetitious brawls between the haggard brothers. Occasionally someone might question which occupants were likely to go mad first, the lions or the Flakes. The natural jungle killers were actually good neighbors, quite tame compared to the ballet girls who represented the "girls next door" in my new-found world. I envied the Flakes for their peaceful home in the wilds.

A few notches below these private quarters were the trucks that hauled "Big Top Jim," the boss canvasman, and his crew of abiding wood alcoholics. The gruff roustabouts sprawled over the bunks and aisles with zombie-like abandon; the sleeper transported with unfailing precision every one of their comic books, poker chips, and bad odors.

Far above anything I have so far detailed, there was a social order of sweeping distinction—the sleek contingent of Airstream house trailers, monuments to the elete class of performers and show officials. These prestigious quarters were coveted by those who did not occupy them, and occasionally a single performer or working person might maneuver his or her way into one of them by fostering a liason with its owner. Most everyone was apt to swing with whatever winds might carry them to such a favored station.

Fred, a husky candy butcher (concessionaire), was one of the privileged, having recently set up quarters with Alfredo, the sword swallower and proprietor of an Airstream. Heavily tattooed and muscled,

Fred moved with easy confidence. On some nights, he could be seen departing the lot with an attractive female escort, and rumors had it that somewhere down the road a girlfriend of long standing was waiting on him. In the meantime—on dateless nights, at least—he availed himself of the good life, circus style. The living arrangement that Fred had established with Alfredo proved compatible. The roommates were visibly nondestructive.

Quickly, a group of envious malcontents led by a vexed Horace called it the case of a candy butcher finding a sugar daddy. Over lunch one day in the gut foundry, Horace lashed out at Fred's credibility, claiming behind his back and right there in front of everybody that he and the candy butcher had made similar plans at the end of the previous season.

I was struck by the ludicrous implausibility of such a live-in. The two may have once been tentatively close, as Horace lamented in the wake of his loss. Practical limitations surely ruled out their moving in together. Neither had Airstream accommodations. Horace's assets were virtually nil, save for his one enormous green trunk crammed with a clash of toiletries, Betty Grable gowns, and gauche wigs (no doubt, Alabama originals). Worse yet, Horace wielded the sharpest tongue on the lot; who possibly could have survived his lethal association?

The deal was never consummated; instead, Fred joined domestic forces with the sword swallower, a man of some maturity. The blow to Horace's ego was deafening, and it added another lyrical sour note to

Norma and Pete Cristiani. MO.

42

Aristocrats at the front door: Papa Cristiani keeps an eye on the money; Cosetta, next to him, watches a sponsor take tickets. MO.

his repertoire of misery. Of course, he exploited this like a masochist in his glory. Through Horace's pathos, I could hear an unreachable lost soul crying in an endless night of rejection. What an alien, restless world this was, filled with unappeased, disfigured spirits and nomadic scavangers—looking, looking, looking, for what? For the hoopla of continual motion, for the quasi security of an escape, but never an out . . . when you have reached the abyss, where *then* are the exits?

Alone in splendid isolation I slept, without the means of a rich man nor the marketing whims of a candy butcher. I accepted a movie invitation now and then, always conveniently slipping away before the live after-encounter was to have commenced. In the prenatal position my mattress was bearable enough. I wondered if the day would ever dawn for me to begin clawing my way up the ladder of opportunity . . .

Across from me slept the bandmaster, Enrico, an old world figure who looked terribly out of place in this company. Enrico had spent his whole life with circuses; his current nadir of despair did not speak well for a career under the big top. Enrico had already been fired once during this season, only to be rehired when Pete discovered Enrico had taken the music and that the windjammers were improvising their way to the lost chord. Enrico returned and

was treated like a hero for a few contrived performances. Then his grumblings began anew: The Cristianis were ill-mannered, his musicians disrespectful, the wages an affront to his integrity, and the food a threat to his health.

That day in the gut foundry, "Miss" Alberta, the show's fire eater (and the latest in a succession of lambasted, short-lived cooks) had served a chicken dinner. Enrico's tuba player, Leo called it "fried flour." Everybody roared, except the bandleader. Enrico could barely stomach Miss Alberta's raunchy recipes. How would he ever bring his wife to this dive when she visited him enroute? She would probably commiserate with her husband at a nearby Holiday Inn, avoiding the circus like a plague.

On his bed now, the music maker clutched his stomach. Was it the food that bothered his intestines, or something else? No, it was the bed.

"What's wrong with a my mattress?" he mumbled to himself. "It's likea sleeping on fried flour!"

Enrico told me the show didn't have half the class of other circuses he had toured with. "It's nota the same," he said, smoothing the blankets, "Nothing around here isa any damn a good!"

Enrico tossed and turned on the uneven surface, talked about quitting, said he'd "show them." The truck suddenly lunged forward, then screeched to a halt. Bud was at the wheel, and I could hear him cursing hysterically.

"Damn fucking arrows!"

One of the musicians jumped out apprehensively.

Norma Cristiani and some friends wait for their entrance cue. MO.

There was an angry exchange over directions between Bud and somebody else. We jerked back and forth in short, jagged motions. Bud had taken the wrong turnoff and charged up a hill into a near impossible bend. For several spine-tingling minutes, I felt like we were being exorcised through the eye of a needle. I braced the edge of my bed should we finally careen down the mountain onto Pete's next trashy lot.

Enrico ranted and raved quietly to himself. The truck started moving normally again. We were back on the road. Thank God, I sighed. Turn over and go to sleep!

. . . You may be reaching for the stars when you join a circus, reaching out for the fantasies of youth. Gradually, you'll settle for a gas station across the street with hot running water and a lock on the door so you can keep your associates out while you enjoy the luxury of a private shave. Your quest for romance and glamour will fade into a struggle for the basics. The simple day-to-day functions take on great significance. Who has time for the higher pleasures?

Looking back, was Wallace Bros. atypical? "I'll be truthful with you," says Kenneth Dodd, the gifted young producing clown for Clyde Beatty-Cole Bros. Circus, "the conditions that we live in are not the greatest. Moving every day, and in bad weather and the cold springs, the lack of privacy. Above everything else you've got to have a love and a want."

Struppi Hanneford recounted for me her dreadful first year with Mills Bros. Coming from Europe, where living conditions for artists are decent, the contrast startled Struppi. "It was rather threatful. We were just shocked. A small room with four girls, the rain came through. It was plain miserable," says Struppi. "You just have to fight your way through."

No, Wallace Bros. was not atypical for a tent show, and I write with respect for the remarkable Cristianis, appreciating their tolerance in allowing me to recount these recollections.

A "love and a want" it takes, indeed, to compensate for the lack of good days down the road. A beautiful lot was like playing in heaven. One Sunday morning, I stepped out of the sleeper to find us parked on a green meadow surrounded by billowing trees. It was the kind of a setting Grandma Moses would immortalize. What were we doing *here*?

Our spirits brightened. Bobby had a smile on his face, and Harry swore off any more beer. Horace danced a little ballet. Mimi the goat nibbled at the grass approvingly. Big Top Jim had a song on his lips

while he and I (his guest for the day) pushed the marking pins into the earth to indicate the placement of stakes and poles for the main tent. Soon, the rich blue canvas would be waving over green turf.

"This is *not* the place!" yelled some idiot.

The idiot was right. No, one of the drivers—was it Bud?—had misread the arrows posted down the road by our twenty-four-hour man, and diverted to heaven, with everyone behind following him to the wrong lot.

Up came the pins that I placed, back to the trucks we scrambled, blushing like itinerants in somebody else's garden. To another one of those sorry Pete Cristiani circus sites we drove, and was *this* one a doozy. . . .

We were directed to the edge of a deserted airstrip. Without identifying the state, I will say it was near a town called Newport News. A flat, rotting piece of land it was, stretched out like Frankenstein's face. There were tree stumps and unearthly protrusions resembling dinosaur bones. A greyish, powder-like haze enveloped us; it was like being on the beach at the end of the world (without the water), like having set foot on the ruins of a nuclear holocaust between consenting adults. Ooooooo.

Clouds of dust hovered like aimless tumbleweed.

The band emitted lively dissonance and occasional harmony. MO.

44

On with the show! Holly the Hippo sloshed forward, oblivious to the changing elements that plagued our circus lots. MO.

The Arturo Twins included Cookie, left, later to become the accomplished Great Arturo. MO.

The sum emitted a muted, hazzy glare. Horace and Bobby skipped off to a naval base in the vicinity to make a personal inspection of the troops. Harry was completely gone, and Paulo may not yet have arrived. That left only Steven, the tramp clown, and myself to assemble the dressing top. Groping with the canvas, straining to unfold it, I felt listlessly suspended in a vacuum, and my movements seemed to be in slow motion. My sledgehammer fell lightly, the stakes under its indifferent weight sinking into the earth like wood pegs in hard clay. There was silence everywhere. I stopped to observe the big top going up. I could hear the tiniest squeaks and scrappings of the cables being pulled up around the four great king poles and the swish of taught canvas following. The huge performance top rose with ghostly disapproval over this baren wasteland.

This *was* the place.

Who in their right mind would come out to see us perform *here?* Human beings? The next day, two jam-packed houses filled the tent. The canvas rafters rang with the happy sighs of thrilled customers. Cosetta Cristiani breezed her way around the ring—a sight I will always remember—dancing stylishly on the back of her horse; Enrico's band swayed, too, snapping out sultry rhythms to match Cosetta's high-kicking savvy. The crowds responded with feverish delight. We all performed at our peak. Harry Flake did not that day have to be badgered

Cosetta's inspired turn. Performing was a luxury for the Cristianis. MO.

into the tent by his nagging brother. Bobby spoke of returning to the cloud swing. The swell of heat and pulsating action was hypnotic. There was magic in this tent, and in the eyes of the lowest paid prop hand, true pride. Above the scorched patch of earth, the world to our music soared. . . .

But when the crowds went home, the tawdry seldom-inspiring drama behind the scenes resumed . . .

45

Horace caught Fred and Alfredo in an argument over gasoline expenses.

"What did I tell you?"

That put the first smile I had ever seen on Horace's face.

Harry was back on booze.

Paulo was mad at everybody.

Enrico said this was the most disgusting lot he ever played on, and the Cristianis should be ashamed. Enrico cursed the white powder, said it made his trumpet sound like a french horn, and the band like Spike Jones at a funeral. He said if he could get his hands on the tape a circus fan made of the performance, he'd destroy it (and the fan, too).

"This fucking show makes me sick to my stomach!"

The next morning, a couple of hundred miles beyond the end of the world, the flag was up at the "ptomaine joint" (more slang for cook house) and breakfast was being served in a dried-out gully. (The big top was rising over a felled power plant.) In progress when Enrico entered for his first meal of the day was a heated discussion over Miss Alberta's eggs:

Horace argued they tasted like "fried marshmallows."

"No!" interjected Bud, "They're cotton dipped in food coloring!"

"Maybe Miss Alberta's burnt out her taste buds," said Nancy, rising to her feet, "but I can tell the difference between dog food and horse shit." She shimmied out in a huff.

Leo sampled Miss Alberta's version of sunny-side up, Wallace Bros. style. His face turned purple. He rose from the table, pushing away the specimens in disgust.

"Fried flour."

The tuba player roared off.

Now it was Enrico's turn. The bandmaster again made a valiant attempt at pretending. *This* was a cookhouse, and *those* were eggs, and *that* was food, and there was life during life and death after death, and the Cristianis would not be admitted beyond the Pearly Gate but ordered to the worst circus lot in hell. That's what he was pretending.

Enrico didn't have to pretend at being surprised or attacked by sheer bad taste when he bit into one of his "scrambled" eggs. With a scornful finger he mocked the plate of plenty before him.

"What a crock of shit! What a damn rotten dump!" Enrico ditched the cookhouse (alias for gut foundry)

and headed straight for his berth.

Why did his back ache? Was he sleeping on fried flour? Fried eggs? Cotton dipped in food coloring? Rocks dipped in cotton?

"Room anda board—what a joke!"

The music man assailed Pete Cristiani's production down to the smallest bed bug. He shot up the stairs to the sleeper with finality.

"The toilet paper's probably contaminated. My shit isa probably contaminated! What a damn dump this place is!"

I was removing myself from the prenatal position. Leo was auditioning an orange he had purchased himself. The other musicians were joking about fried flour and the few lousy bucks dolled out to them begrudgingly on Fridays. Enrico, ready to take the music and run, stormed through his belongings. A suitcase already packed many towns behind came crashing down to the floor. The bandmaster snickered over his despicable lodgings.

"I'm not gonna die here!"

His shoulders jetted upwards in violent rejection of everything around him. He pushed the blankets aside, flung the skimpy mattress off the bed, and howled over the revelation:

"Look ata that! Look!"

We all gazed in shock at the bed. One of the planks was missing.

"Somebody stole mya board!"

No wonder Enrico's back felt like an accordion. He observed the remains of a bad season with unconscious good humor. . .

"Whata job. I gota the room and a board. But look at this, I gota the room, but *where's the board?*"

Down goes the big top! MO.

46

Riotous laughter ensued during the next meal at the gut foundry and a lively conversation about Enrico's room without board took marked precedence over Horace's tired commentary on Fred and Alfredo's first argument.

Sex in the circus isn't much without an Airstream.

4
And the Word Was Wallenda

GREAT circus artists have a passion for their work that transcends muddy lots and "fried flour"—all the petty irritations that perplex would-be clowns. Their tempers are pointed to strange, far-off regions. They fling themselves with reckless grace to the edges of infinity, frolicking like astral vagabonds along wires, cavorting over the backs of horses, tilting upwards with dizzy abandon off teeterboards. Are they dissatisfied with earth? Bored? Afraid?

"I feel like I belong to the sky," said the French daredevil Phillipe Petit.

Ethereal wizards before Petit have expressed similar affinity for the cosmos and beyond. In 1905, Octavie La Tour, the driver of Barnum & Bailey's thrilling somersaulting automobile, wrote for the *New York World*, "Human daring has but one limit: human imagination. Human courage dares all, and there is no task, no feat, no exploit of bravado you can suggest to it that it will not venture . . . Demand what feat you will that requires physical skill and physical courage, and we in the circus will attempt it. Nay, we will perform it successfully . . . get your mind fermenting; give your imagination free play; and invent the real limit of human daring. Show us how to fly to the moon; direct the way to Mars; point the signboards down the roads of human daring. And I for one will go."

The volatile Alfredo Codona flew like a restless bird, possessed by the uncertainty of open endless sky. Lillian Leitzel, his wife, spun like a carefree butterfly at the top of the tent. Over and over went the dazzling Leitzel, a symbol of man's eternal longing for flight. Both Codona and Leitzel were doomed to the physical world—she, by the snap of a crystalized iron ring in Copenhagen, releasing her suddenly to a fatal death below; he, by his own madness which drove him hastily into a disturbing second marriage, and finally into a frenzy: Codona shot both himself and his new bride. Some say the great flyer was tormented by his declining powers.

When Leitzel and Codona thrilled circus-hungry crowds, nineteen-year-old Karl Wallenda was the most famous wire walker in the world. Fifty years later, up until the day he died, in 1978, he was still the most famous wire walker in the world.

Some people thought the great Wallenda was crazy; I think he was incredible. Having seen the Wallendas astound audiences on countless occasions, it was a unique experience to observe them on the ground and at home during the off-season in Sarasota. Aloft they are proclaimed heroes; below, not so different from average declared mortals.

The young man with long hair and a friendly mustache, ambling his way around the pool table at the Showfolks Club in Sarasota, was twenty-one-year-old Ricki Wallenda. He walks the wire and he is an easygoing fellow with deep religious convictions.

". . . I did a wire act myself in a Christian night-club in St. Pete and I just did the work for Jesus. I

71-year-old Karl Wallenda in London, 1976. ". . . I have always an idea. I want to do something that nobody else did before." KW.

*Volatile Alfredo Codona turned triple somersaults with
flawless ease, later shot himself.* RM.

Leitzel in the air. Gushing like a butterfly. CW.

Lillian Leitzel, ready to go on. RM.

was all by myself and I was doing tricks that I'd never done before at any height except for three feet, and I just gave the glory to God for that."

Ricki took a sharp wack at a striped ball. It missed the hole. He relaxed while his girlfriend—who claimed no aspirations to the high-wire realms—took her turn.

Karl Wallenda's grandson could not recall when he learned how to walk the steel cable. "I've always known how as far back as I can remember." Nor did he show the traces of inherited temperament. "I have confidence in myself because I've put a lot of hours training into it, and confidence in God that he's going to see me through it."

Rick's turn again. This time he was more careful, directing a striped ball into the pocket.

"I'm in prayer when I'm on the wire and I feel like I'm just entertaining somebody and that I'm doing something that not everybody else can do."

His next shot failed.

"I really don't think it displays a whole lot of courage because I'm not really brave. I *run* at the sound of danger . . ."

I gazed at the photographs of famous circus personalities which lined the walls of the room— dramatic views of Leitzel and Codona, Con Colleano, the Hannefords, La Norma . . . did they run at the sound of danger?

"There's a lot of things I wouldn't do on the wire," said Ricki.

While he dispatched the remaining balls, the young Christian talked about going whenever the Lord leads him, about what his life-long circus friends mean to him. He told me about the Monday-night bible-study class he conducts for show folk.

"Circus people need Jesus a lot."

They probably do, I thought to myself.

Returning to the main topic—Karl Wallenda— Ricki reflected, "He's immortal in his own time. He inspired me. He didn't make me do it. It was my own choice. I started when I was thirteen, the first time I worked professionally. Then I left for a while, then came back in the act because he needed me and I was starving. He pays me good and I feel tradition. You know, I feel like I want to carry on."

The game was over. I'm not sure who won. It must have been a Wallenda. Seldom is their will overridden.

A few days later I walked up the steps of a stately old wooden house. A big porch shaded by oak trees suggested an "Our Town" hospitality. Inside, the

La Norma blended beauty and grace with death-defying mid-air maneuvers. cw.

living room was cozily enhanced with cultivated European images—a deep carpet of rich design, clocks and nicknacks, paintings, trophies. Beyond an arched doorway, three women chated lightly, one of them sewing sequins to a costume for a three-year-old performer about to make her debut in a famous high-wire team.

An American soap opera flickered aimlessly across a television screen in one corner of the living room. Nobody cared or listened. Occasionally the telephone rang—callers at the other end seeking vital information, percentages offered a Detroit sponsor; how many shows on Saturday in Toledo; the name of a trampoline act booked for Buffalo. Politely these and other interruptions, including the intermittent barks of a hound dog in search of a thief, were deferred to his wife and other relations for their handling by my host—the great Karl Wallenda.

We sat around a circular marble coffee table, where Mr. Wallenda answered my questions with unflinching candor. One might expect of a wire walker—especially an "immortal" one—a decisive approach to verbal communication. That I got.

"A man can walk the high wire just as quick as a child can go with a bicycle. I practice with anybody.

51

I say, 'Look, remember, on that wire is your life, below is your death.' That's how I practice, even when I practice about two feet high. I holler like crazy, I say, to bawl them out, 'How *dare* you jump off! You know you could have been killed already!' I keep them up there, keep them on that wire."

What drove Mr. Wallenda on?

"I don't show off, but I pray to God in my own way. I say, 'God, help me, give me the strength that I can do it.' It is exciting. Most people in life, they want to go up there, they want to do better than they did before. I have always an idea. I want to do something else that nobody else did before. Like, I'm going now to Six Flags, got a phone call this morning, in Texas. A tower 300 feet up and big parachute jump tower 250 feet. I'm gonna work from that tower to this parachute—that's a thousand, five hundred feet apart. And to my knowledge, it's never been done before."

Karl Wallenda was then in his seventies when I spoke with him.

"There's a lot of people sitting, they fall to pieces already. They say, 'Oh, I'm old now, I'm gonna die pretty soon.' That's all that's ever in their mind. Then they see a man up there, seventy-one. He goes over that wire and he's still in shape. That gives them more ambition. They say, 'Look what a man can do!'"

What nineteen-year-old Karl, his brother, and two partners did at Madison Square Garden in 1928 with the "Greatest Show on Earth" electrified opening-night audiences, as it did John Ringling who discovered the young German troupe during a Havana engagement. The Wallendas were executing stunts that Karl had been innovating since his seventeenth birthday when he climbed on the shoulders of his headmaster and completed a headstand. Simple? Prior to that historic display of originality, wire walkers strictly walked the wire. Wallenda's acrobatic feats presented new artistic possibilities. "The performers all were speechless; they couldn't believe it. They said they never saw something like this."

New Yorkers rose to their feet in a standing ovation unprecedented in circus history. The honored aerialists misread the cheering signals and feared they represented scathing disapproval.

"The people started screaming and stampeding," recalls Karl. "Such noise, I had to hold my ears. I said to my brother, Herman, 'Let's get out of here. We're gonna get tomatoes on our heads!'"

The riotously successful Germans vanished in shame to the dressing rooms, convinced they had flopped. They were followed by Fred Bradna, ordinarily the self-contained equestrian director. Bradna shouted at them in amazement.

"Wallendas! Wallendas! What's the matter with you? You crazy? You have to go out there!"

"No, no," pleaded Karl. "I don't want to have rotten eggs!"

"You crazy!" repeated Bradna. "People want to admire you so much! We never had that before!"

A horse act in progress was halted so the Wallendas could return without interference and take the victorious bows the audience demanded. They basked in cheering acclaim for five solid minutes, the crowds had been on their feet for fifteen. Karl walked around the ring in his white sailor costume and "made like a fighter."

They were a featured act with Ringling Bros. and Barnum & Bailey for seventeen consecutive years. According to their master, the most difficult feat they presented was a four-person pyramid involving two bicycles. Supporting his wife Carla in a standing position on his shoulders, Karl balanced on a chair that rested over a bar bridging the shoulders of two men on separate bicycles. "Harder than the seven-high," stated Karl. But not so deadly. . . .

The famous seven-high pyramid took the Wallendas to the summit of greatness. There has never been anything in circus annals to approach the complexity or magnitude of this mind boggling achievement; it's a shocker, a fantastic, almost transcendental display of human trust and perseverance, and it lives up to every accolade ever invented. It was mastered by the Wallendas, ironically, after the troupe left the Ringling show, and it has never been performed at Madison Square Garden. I saw it one afternoon in the Fairgrounds Pavilion in my hometown of Santa Rose. I was only eleven. You don't have to go to the Garden in New York to see the greatest circus artists. The Shriners, God bless them, brought this spine-tingling troupe—and others—to Santa Rosa.

Who could have visualized what was about to take place? The Wallendas moved over the wire with clairvoyant ease, their balancing poles wavering slightly like the oars on a ship at rest. Then came Wallendas on higher plateaus, their pyramid growing. Finally, a Wallenda on a third level sitting atop a chair like a Greek Goddess at a ship's mast. All of them were now on the wire, moving slowly through

"Harder than the seven-high," said Karl Wallenda of this routine performed at Madison Square Garden to standing ovations. RM.

The famous seven-high pyramid, a Clyde Beatty-Cole Bros. Circus highlight during the 1960s. CW.

an icy, mystifying silence . . . step by step in flawless precision, inching their way to the other side. . . .

Could hypnosis take me back to that day, would I feel more vividly than I do, as I write these words, the chill, dazed rapture of disbelief and total awe? If anything converted me to the circus and its powerful symbols, it was that one matchless moment.

"On that wire is your life; below is your death."

Forty feet above a tanbark-covered cement floor in Detroit's State Fair Coliseum ten years later, the seven-high formation is moving slowly across the wire. Tensely, the Wallendas are traversing the dark chasm of danger they have traveled so many times before but have never completely conquered. Each successive journey is a new test. Tonight, the lead man, twenty-three-year old Dieter Schepp, is making his first performance with the group. He and his sister, seventeen-year-old Jana who stands on the

chair at the pyramid's peak, are East German refugees, the nephew and niece of Karl Wallenda's first wife. Up in the spotlights now, they may hear Karl's promise of a year ago echoing in their minds: "Come to America. It's a good life there. You can be free. And I will teach you."

The taskmaster found Schepp in training "hard as nails." Tonight in Detroit, only ten feet from his destination, Schepp begins quavering. His hands become sweaty. His forty-foot balancing pole pulls against him and he feels weak.

The pyramid is in trouble.

"I feel something is wrong" thinks Karl to himself, standing proudly at the front of the second plateau on a brace over the shoulders of Schepp and Richard Faughnan.

Schepp should be holding his pole in the palms of his hands. Instead, it has slid to the tips of his

54

fingers. He tosses it up slightly to get a better grip.

> Seven souls symmetrically spaced,
> Faithfully, no time for haste.
> Hushed, intrepid footsteps err,
> All is lost up there . . .

"I can't hold any longer!" cries Schepp.

Karl can not believe what is happening. Schepp falls from the wire, his pole crashing after him. Faughnan, Jenny Wallenda's husband, topples over. Then comes Mario Wallenda, Karl's adopted son. Karl falls against the wire, wrapping his legs around it. Miraculously, Jana Schepp plummets against Karl, grabbing him like a tiger for her life. Karl's brother Herman clings to the cable by his legs, dangling in tortured pain. Gunther, Herman's son, is the only member to remain erect; he moves quickly to Karl and Jana, taking Jana's hand and helping Karl hold her while prop hands below race to assemble a make-shift net.

Into the blanket spread beneath them, Karl and Gunther release Jana, screaming. Then the three who are still aloft—Karl, Gunther and Herman, clutching the wire with torn ligaments and bones—maneuver their way stoically to safety.

The act is over.

Dieter Schepp and Richard Faughnan are dead. Mario Wallenda suffers skull injuries and will be confined to a wheelchair for the rest of his life. Jana Schepp and Karl are hospitalized. The next day, Jana is allowed to fly home to be with her mother. That evening, twenty-four hours following the tragedy, Herman, with a patch over his eye, and Gunther return to the high wire before a cheering sell-out crowd. After the show is over, Herman says, "We all have to go on. This is our life. There is nothing else to do."

Gunther adds, "Yes, the show must go on. But every once in a while you get to thinking—*why?*"

In the hospital with a pelvic fracture, Karl was not asking "why?" to the ways of showbusiness. Simply he wanted to know when he could get out.

Madness was setting in.

The death-defying invalid refused to lie down and be still. He had seen Gunther and Herman on television and he knew he must join them. Was he driven to prove a point, that there still was life up there for him? Driven by the primitive forces that had fueled him through countless adversities? He had walked the wire over gorges, to the edge of earthquakes, under the flaming canvas of the tragic

Family solidarity. Gunther, Karl, and Herman, far right, examine the bicycle they will ride aloft. RM.

Hartford fire in 1944. What on earth was he doing in a hospital?

The patient put on a deceptive smile, concealed a badly bruised leg from the doctor and agreed not to work right away. The doc acquiesced before the patient escaped.

The next night, missing only one performance, Karl rejoined his brother and nephew, along with Gene Mendez who flew in to buttress their depleted forces. Herman removed the bandage from his eye. Karl disguised his painful inability to raise his feet barely more than six inches. He stood on the chair at the top of a three-high pyramid, more triumphal than ever. A crashing ovation greeted the greatest Wallenda. He was back up there, up where there is life . . .

Another ten years passed, another seven-high pyramid was being drilled and molded to reality by the relentless taskmaster. And the word was Wallenda.

"It makes you happy when you open up the paper and you see you're always on the front page. That's what they called me, 'Front Page Smasher.' So that makes me happy. I *am* somebody."

The mid-air monarch had a will as strong as the

55

steel strands he walked. Not all of the others, actual family members, adopted or aspiring ones, were as lucky. On one of the rare occasions when Karl consented to the use of a net, his brother Herman fell into it and bounced onto the concrete floor. He was killed instantly.

On another occasion, without the use of a net, Karl's brother-in-law Philip lost his balance, slipped and fell, breaking his arms and legs. True to tradition, in short time he was back on his feet and well enough to rejoin his redoubtable relatives on high. But for Philip, however, adversity struck again. There are no assurances that your courage alone will carry you through life, nor that skill is an infallible saving grace. You live with other mortals and you are subject to their quirky whims. The daring men and women who walk the wire are not exempt from mortality's cruel reversals.

Philip encountered his final blow. His nerves were put to rest, his fears silenced forever. The crowds had gone; maybe the fanfares of a better day

The Wallendas practice a feat they never presented in performance, an eight-high! RM.

Karl Wallenda crosses San Francisco's Candlestick Park, May 1977. "On that wire is your life; below is your death." SF.

56

continued ringing through his departing spirit. On his way to a Philadelphia date with the great Wallendas, he had stopped to fix a flat tire on his house trailer. Now he lay dead. A speeding automobile had run over him.

And finally, luck ran out for the lead man himself. On Wednesday, 22 March 1978 in San Juan, Puerto Rico, Karl surrendered to the winds of adversity when he fell ten stories to his death from a wire extended between two beach-front hotels. A strong, sudden gust refused him another triumph. The following Sunday, in Sarasota, thousands viewed his body as he lay in state. Included among the pallbearers were Emmett Kelly and Merle Evans.

They called him "The King" and his body was buried about five miles northwest of Sarasota in Manasota Memorial Park, between the graves of his nephew, Dieter Schepp, and Richard Faughnan, and near his sister-in-law, Rietta Wallenda. The tombstone bears the inscription—"The Wallendas—Aerialists Supreme."

There will never be another Karl Wallenda. Irascible, dauntless, unwilling ever to "retire," he was a powerful symbol of the will of man to endure through every age of his life. Karl died the way he preferred, doing that which he loved best.

"On that wire is your life, below is your death."

5
The Red Wagon Laid Bare

LEGION are the crimes, petty and otherwise, that have been committed in and around the crucial zone (usually referred to as the red wagon) where tickets are sold, wages dispensed on some solvent Fridays, and show officials hobnob with shady characters who smoke cigars incessantly and look like business consultants on loan from Chicago.

Operating it in the black is a bloody business, ladies and gentlemen, a sport of arbitrary rules not fit for genteel administrators. By hook or by crook the shrewdest showmen keep their banners in the air and themselves out of jail. No simple feat, even on the run. Big-time hoopla costs a fortune. The government does not subsidize elephants and clowns—nor do complimentary press passes that are distributed by the thousands to local police chiefs, fire marshals, beauty queens, and their offspring (sometimes the whole town). When the ticket lines are not long enough to satisfy your daily nut, you have a problem.

Enter the bad guys: fixers and phonemen, short-change artists and pickpockets; card sharks and shell workers, alias precocious little devils in their youth. Scoundrels of all persuasions who come alive wherever crowds form and there are ample distractions to keep their defenses down.

Bluntly stated, con artists prey on circuses and vice versa. Survival down the road has rarely meant a square deal for the customer. On the midways of yesteryear—and even on some today—gimmicked

On the midways of yesteryear lurked all sorts of grift, from pickpockets to three-card-monte sharks. CW.

sales pitches, unadvertised additional fees, wheels, and other rackets ran rampant. Early American circus lords engaged slippery charlatans to relieve patrons of their spending money.

Through the 1870s, Pogey O'Brien managed ruthlessly well a syndicate of shows. At one time O'Brien's domain included control of the Barnum show through its northern states and Canadian stands. Pogey was a pedantic teetotaler who suffered from asthma and the ever-nagging fear of fore-closure. To offset the latter, O'Brien specialized in

"ripin 'n tearin"—his own language for short changing and crooked gambling. Sound business principles in a free-wheeling market, Pogey believed with
all his (congested) heart. Maybe so, but not as
ordinarily practiced by Pogey's grifters. When a
dispute erupted over a towner's complaint of fowl
play, Pogey's fiesty Irish canvasmen defended with
brutal finesse the lucky boys from their enraged
victims. The ripin 'n tearin manager burned up town
after town. In time he exhausted the territory he
could return to without facing local lynching mobs.

Adam Forepaugh conducted graft on a higher
level. By 1888 the big-top tycoon, who began as a
humble meat butcher, was gifting (and grifting) his
customers with a formidable three-ringer and a
traveling menagerie bigger than most city zoos—all
for the single price of one ticket purchased, plus any
unreturned change. Forepaugh relied heavily on

*Ticket sellers working from high counters diverted the
patron's attention to his change.* CW.

the light-fingered boys as well as on a host of other
assorted parasites. From these accomplished rascals
old Adam exacted vital show-sustaining "privileges"
(payoff money for the right to engage in their sundry
skills on his midway). For $20.00 each week, the
pragmatic manager commissioned a sightless
woman to sell her alms near his front door. Together
they stole the public blind.

Only the most puritanical executive would turn
down a qualified shyster applying for a position on
his premises. Slick operators competed for assignments on the biggest shows, and they were hard put
to explain why the five Ringling brothers from
Baraboo, Wisconsin, would not welcome their tune.
A steady succession of flimflam artists tried to
convince the unmovable Otto Ringling that ripin 'n
tearin was a necessary evil subscribed to by the
nicest chaps.

One of the dapper callers offered Otto $2,000 a
month for the joy of extracting loose change from his
patrons. Otto's face swelled up in reddish hues.

"Try it and you'll be thrown off the lot," roared the
affronted showman.

Sensing a hard sell on his hands, the pesty visitor
upped his projected payment plan to the sum of
$2,500 every month, in advance. That drew an
immediate advance from Otto, who beckoned a
husky roustabout to remove from his sight the
unwanted hack.

The bad guys could not tolerate being snubbed by
a bunch of pretentious upstarts. "Sunday School
Showmen" they called the Ringlings. Worse than
that, what if the pristine policies of these moralistic

*Adam Forepaugh commissioned a blind woman to sell
alms at his front door for a cut of the action.* CW.

brothers were to contaminate other shows?

The spurned villains followed on the trail of the Ringlings like a horde of gnats, preying on crowds as near to the show grounds as they dared go. The Ringlings retaliated by sending a man ahead to warn local sheriffs and town mayors of the riffraff element infesting their immaculate enterprise. They stationed a clean-cut fellow by the ticket wagon to warn patrons:

"Count your change! Beware of pickpockets! Count your change!"

Insulted and humiliated, the antagonists shot back with a mud slinging manifesto charging gross hypocrisy:

> When thieves fall out honest men get their dues.
> WARNING!
> Neighbors unchain your dogs.
> Get out your shotguns.
> Keep your children at home.
> THE MARAUDERS ARE COMING!
> Beware of them.
> They go by the name of the Ringling brothers.
> You will know them by their appearance.
> They look like a gypsy camp.
> They are thieves, liars and scoundrels.
> They have no show worthy of the name.
> They sneak from town to town under cover of darkness.
> They plunder and steal even the washings hanging in backyards.

The authors of this civic-minded rat bill touted their own integrity by making a rare confession: "We who give this warning are also thieves, but have fallen out with the greasy pack and now tell the truth."

The Ringlings hired Pinkerton detectives and exploited their grift-free showmanship. CW.

Entertainment seekers of the day were baffled and amused. The Sunday School boys established a reputation based upon honest business principles. A battle for righteousness ensued, with every major show now ballyhooing cleanliness, virtue, and half the bible. The so-called morality showdown between the Ringlings and their ignoble competitors "reformed" the circus world—according to a tale told by historians. It's a lovely story.

In public, big tops shunned the lucky boys. In private, behind every reformed impresario there lurked a new game plan. Detectives appeared on midways, demonstrating management's concern for the rights of the customer. Publicity releases laden with the rhetoric of rectitude rolled forth from sanctified press kits. Lavish circus pageants portrayed religious themes. Before a man's resources might be tapped, you must now first gain his respect.

Long-fingered opportunists followed circus crowds far into the twentieth century. In 1921, a sheriff in Watertown, New York, slapped a pair of handcuffs on John Robinson's head ticket man, Arthur Bigson, and hauled him down to the police station. There, Bigson was looked at by a couple from a town the show had played in the week before. The man and his wife claimed to have received two dollars in change for a twenty dollar bill they tendered for a pair of tickets. No, decided the couple upon close examination, this was not the person who took their order. Off came the handcuffs and the charges were dropped. Where was the culprit? Conveniently incognito.

Fifty years after the Ringling-inspired reformation of circus ethics, John Robinson and other shows were doing business as usual. That day in Watertown on the Robinson lot, a towner made a heated beef about being shorted seventy-five cents by a rough guy at the ticket wagon. This time the victim was a patrolman, not the kind to be suckered easily. He aired his ire to a detective traveling with the show. Promptly the ticket shark made good, offering profuse apologies for a "mistake."

In 1929, Christy Bros. reportedly "notified" all racket men that their contracts would not be renewed for the coming season. According to *Variety*, ". . . with Christy dropping the gyp, this leaves all major circuses free of chiseling." In retrospect, the conclusion was naive. The bible of show business had failed to see the light.

During those years, the seven-show American Circus Corporation, one of the largest syndicates of all time, was presided over with uncanny fortitude

Ringling customers enjoyed lower ticket counters and were exhorted to "Count your change!" RM.

by Jerry Muggivan, a devout Catholic who may have led two lives. Floyd King once asked Muggivan, "Would you have those games with the circus?" Replied Muggivan, a revered magnet, "A thousand times *no*. I'd have no part of the grift whatsoever. I'd have a legitimate circus all the way through." Muggivan knew how to answer a leading question.

Recently at the Ringling Museum of the Circus, one of Muggivan's old ticket wagons was stripped down for restoration work. It was a revelation to behold what was inside. As the warped, soiled boards were removed, greenbacks fell freely from within the frames. The evidence was damning, though experienced old-timers were not surprised. The scattered bills had been routed through a "lip" in the counter of the ticket wagon. Hurriedly the foxy cashier would lay out the "sucker's" change in a stack of bills then proceed to push the pile forward so that much of it was directed beneath the surface through a slit in the counter to a jackpot area below. The price of admission has dropped considerably since those hurly-burly days.

The red wagon laid bare revealed the undeniable truth. In the words of Arthur M. Concello, "Grift moved the show."

Did the extraordinary funds gathered by Jerry Muggivan's ticket sellers go to the parishes he patronized along the route? Muggivan could well afford to be a practicing Christian and an untarnished showman as well. He had two capable partners, Bert Bowers and Edward Ballard, who

Ben Davenport, in the 1940s, whose Dailey Bros. Circus fleeced the public royally. CW.

61

could enter behind his well-turned back into lucrative arrangements with the lucky boys.

Daily Bros. Circus flourished during World War II in "ripin 'n tearin" good order. Starting out, if his press agents are to be believed, with "but two lions, three monkeys, a hyena, and five ponies," Ben Davenport engineered to frightening proportions one of the most wretched enterprises that ever grizzled down the tracks. To this day troupers flinch whenever Davenport's name is mentioned. The despicable headman, a disciple of the old school, pirated his sleazy pack of con artists through California and other unfortunate West Coast communities.

"We'll pay our salaries every night and we'll not buy anything until we have the money to pay for it," Davenport told his wife when they made up their minds to hit the rails.

What did the surly operator have on his mind? ". . . through all the dark days, a bright idea was burning." Davenport stalked his midway with a hip pocket filled with pennies. Each time he noticed a good "take" at one of the shell games or card tables, the chief crook tossed a penny into a shirt pocket. Thus, he could keep tabs on the stolen funds being suckered to "pay our salaries every night." When he settled each day with the fast boys, Davenport knew from the weight of his shirt pocket roughly how much to expect.

"Even on the Ringling show," speculates one well informed fan, "I dare say they couldn't stop it completely. There was bound to have been some shady characters around."

The Ringlings, nonetheless, engaged Pinkerton detectives to keep an eye out for suspicious intruders. And when, in 1929, they bought out the American Circus Corporation shows, the family's reluctance to continue running them on grift is cited by old hands as the primary reason for their demise.

The Ringlings well-known impatience with riffraff did not extend, however, to the ranks. Through the 1950s, gambling among personnel of the show was treated as part of the modus operandi, sanctioned and supervised for set charges by top management. Other strange happenings were enshrouded in mystery. A labyrinth of intrigue unfolds as layer by layer the allusions to high moral standards are delicately peeled away. In the closets of the past are locked skeletons that may never be exposed. Some are beginning to emerge. . .

Very frequently the red wagon was instructed not to sell tickets for a particular seat wagon. "Strike number 210. It's down at the runs with a broken axle." Official records reflected numerous problems with "inoperable" seat wagons. Once inside the big top, however, general admission ticket holders desirious of better seating locations were directed by helpful head ushers to the "inoperable" seat wagon, where each and every cushioned chair could be secured for the proper price. Cash flowed freely from hand to hand.

No circus has ever relished the thought of squaring off with the IRS. In 1937, John Kelley, chief attorney for Ringling Bros. and Barnum & Bailey Combined Shows, Inc., the amusement institution that "reformed" the circus world, was sent to prison facing a two-year judgement for conspiring with the late Charles Ringling over fabricated tax reports. Government auditors estimated the show may have reneged on amounts up to several million dollars, going back many years.

Keeping a grift-free show on the road is not very feasible. Somebody, somewhere has to pay the price.

Meanwhile, as the old order of midway sharks died off, a modern breed of bad guy entered, the man accepting donations for the "underprivileged children." Expedient souls adapt well to the times. When the Knights of Columbus sponsored the Hagenbeck-Wallace show in 1922, circus officials were unconsciously dabbling in an area of promotion that would someday spell their salvation: the charity tie-in. That same year, the Shriners ordered every seat in the tent at a matinee performance of the Ringling circus in Buffalo, New York. The noblemen marched through town with the circus parade and dined in the cookhouse. Little did they suspect they would someday rival the Ringling name itself.

By 1929, the idea of circuses "under auspices" was on the move. Fraternal societies of all ilks derived an easy cut of red-wagon revenue by lending their good names as sponsors. Many of the early ventures fizzled. The Old Ladies Home of Lexington, Kentucky, failed to put a kick into the ticket campaign of Hubert Shieve's 1932 trick. About the only thrill the ladies got was watching Shieve hit the skids and end up in jail. Shieve's performers took legal action against him for his refusal to pay them for three days work. The unlucky producer confessed to this and sustained attachments to his auto to satisfy claims totaling $500.00. Working in collusion with local sponsors was a brand-new ball game, yet to be mastered by skilled professionals and Old Ladies Homes.

Rogers & Harris Circus during a sea-saw 1925 tour

encountered extreme difficulties in South Bend, Indiana. The local sponsor proved to be, ironically, a decided embarrassment. Both local dailies refused, as a result, to acknowledge the show's presence in town or to accept advertisements. For a charitable cause? Yes, billboard space was denied the billposters. Norman Bece, representing the controversial fraternal order bringing the show to town, offered to let the circus advertise without making reference to his group. Still, the newspapers refused to cooperate. Rogers & Harris were coming to South Bend under the auspices of the Ku Klux Klan!

Pitching charity became a hukster's paradise in the hands of telephone solicitors. "When grift went out," continued Art Concello on the subject of how circuses kept going, "the phones came in."

"Hello, Charlie? Charlie Gimble of Gimbles Paint Store? . . ." begins a typical pitch. "Charlie, this is Sergeant. . ." (Here the caller clears his throat so as to conceal his true identity while he garbles out a fictitious name.) "I'm calling for our great Policemen's annual Athletic League Circus . . . yeah, Charlie, wasn't it great last year! You know the tremendous things we do for all those underprivileged kids out there. . . . Listen, pal, *you* make it possible. Yes, we are having another one, on the seventeenth of June! That's great. Say, Charlie, how about going for *two* books this time around?" (A pause.) "GREAT! Listen, pal, I'll have one of our girls drop them off, is tomorrow around eleven okay? Fine. . . . Fifty, right, leave it at the desk, Charlie! Okay, thanks!"

And that's how the tickets are sold. Sponsors are courted with flattery. "YOUR MAJOR ANNUAL FUND RAISING PROJECT," heralds a gaudy fold-out brochure detailing to prospective fraternal groups the road to a fortune.

Here's the Deal. Your Sponsoring Organization Assumes No Financial Risk WHATSOEVER!

Twenty-five sample auspices, from catholic parishes to policemen's benevolent funds, are listed. States the add, "The above list is not in order of importance. All our sponsors are important!"

In the boiler rooms (phone rooms) of today are to be found an army of sophisticated technicians—friendly persuaders adept in the arts of deception and intimidation. Rarely do they see the circuses they sell, and they couldn't care less. It's not uncommon for the promoter to skip town with a satchel of checks and tabs (the cards containing vital information about merchants for marketing purposes). When they are operating in normal behavior, these fly-by-nighters unload far more tickets than the show could possibly accommodate. Most of the books of children's coupons pawned off on intimidated merchants are tossed in corners and circular files. Fifteen or twenty percent of the "free" tickets may be distributed and used. The majority do not find their way to "needy" hands.

Working as general press representative for James Bros. Circus in 1969, I was ordered to refrain from seeking publicity in St. Louis. Token news adds of the smallest size were to be placed for the first day of the show's run. The reason: local sponsors feared an overflow of crowds should a fraction of the advance tickets sold be utilized. The preshow sale had been a bonanza for the promoters, although the circus did not turn away a single soul. The businessmen who purchased the tickets, weary of these transparent charity grinds, did not break their backs to pass them out.

Selling charity rather than the circus has taken a tremendous toll on showmanship. It has put many circuses in the hands of men so far removed from big top entertainment that their contributions at best are mediocre. Although it may be academic, I think some of today's unethical promoters are far more destructive than yesterday's Adam Forepaughs. The latter breed at least delivered a viable product, whereas the modern-day boiler-room showman will often take advantage of the sponsor's name to compensate for his own shoddy goods. Showmanship or phonemanship? I prefer the former.

Take James Hargrove—the quiet, conservative promoter who developed a reputation for a unique style of selling. Invitations began pouring in—usually in the form of summons—to appear in various courts throughout the country to explain himself.

I recall the suave phoneman as he stood before the Charity Solicitation Commission in Oakland, California. Local board members were bothered by repeated complaints from citizens of harassment by Hargrove's telephone solicitors. The man in charge shook his head in disbelief. At a loss for words, Hargrove could not understand how such tactics were being perpetrated by his staff and promised to remedy the situation with his assistant in the area. The chairman of the commission noted this was a position Mr. Hargrove had taken at a previous visit for similar complaints. Would things really be any different this time?

"Yes," assured Hargrove. "They will."

John Strong, left, *with the late Arizona telephone promoter, James Hargrove.* JS.

Months later, Hargrove was again summoned to appear in Oakland. Nothing had changed. Hargrove's license to solicit in the area was revoked.

Elsewhere, Hargrove was not up for any man-of-the-year awards. In Seattle, Washington, where a new charity solicitation ordinance would have severely curtailed his thunder, Hargrove advised the Jaycees to conduct their annual circus promotion on a "noncharitable" basis. Thereby, they could justify exemption from the constricting new ordinance. However, angry residents throughout King County testified to having received through the mails tickets in envelopes imprinted, "If you find you cannot attend the circus yourself, the Jaycees have requests for tickets to our show from many residents and less fortunate children's institutions through the King County area."

County officials accused James Hargrove Productions of "outright deception" and ordered the promoters to produce a list of all ticket purchases so that refunds could be facilitated. The odds were starting

to turn against the clever Arizona telephone magnet, as they were now also turning against his associates. Seattle had been blitzed by the boiler-room rip-offs of several high-powered California based operations. Miller-Johnson Circus callers, over a three-year period, talked $588,000 out of the city. The show moved away with seventy-five percent of the proceeds. The Police, who sponsored the sham, retained twenty percent for themselves and passed along to the charity that was pitched a whopping four pennies on the dollar. Greed in reverse also characterizes the fast transactions between circus promoters and local fraternal honchos. Invariably, the art in the center ring suffers because it is not what is being sold.

Hargrove was a crack modern-day pusher who exploited the crippled kids and burned up a score of angry towns. In the process he had, in polite terms, demeaned John Strong's delightful vintage one-ring 1869 Circus, while begetting for himself the means to sustain the life style of a multimillionaire. In Arizona he luxuriated while the summonses mounted. The heat eventually became more than he could handle. Hargrove's options were running out. In 1974 he committed suicide. His passing was not mourned by the circus world.

The sordid, dishonest operations of the Hargroves are being muzzled by laws enacted in many states that regulate the conduct of charitable campaigns. In California, a phoneman must now identify himself and give the actual percentage of the funds earmarked for the good cause, while a recent Michigan law makes it mandatory that at least seventy percent of the proceeds raised go directly to the charity. Boiler rooms may vanish completely from Michigan.

Perplexed by the enactment of such legislation in other states as well, phonemen have grouped into a national organization of dubious goals—the International Telephone Solicitors Association. Strongest among their ranks are the circus producers who argue the advance telephone campaign is imperative to their survival. *"Wrong,"* says Douglas Lyon, an advocate of the "cold date" operation (playing without sponsors, thus without the phones), who has proved his point with Circus Vargas and was recently hired by Clyde Beatty-Cole Bros. Circus for similar reasons.

Contends Lyon, "How do the ice shows survive? How do rodeos survive? How does Ringling survive? Phone rooms are on the way out. That's the writing on the wall. They should really be talking daily and saying, 'How do we lick this? How do you and I sit down and change the law to make it fair for all of us?' But they're afraid of losing their dates, of losing the policemen's association or the firemen's association . . . because a phone room *needs* a sponsor."

Frustrated producers advance such arguments as the following: "The telephone solicitation is the backbone of our business and employs hundreds of performers, students, and older people. It provides for underprivileged children seeing a circus as well as countless thousands of dollars reaching the coffers of charitable institutions." Who knows, some of today's college students employed in these boiler-room operations may become the circus kings of tomorrow, devising for future generations new ways of keeping the show (or the charity) on the road.

I have faith the "ever-changing, never-changing" circus will find a way. Ultimately, circuses may be forced to drop the needy children and change their pitch to something signifying their own fate: "Hello, Charlie? Charlie Gimble of Gimbles Paint Store? Yeah, I'm this here ringmaster calling on behalf of a couple of starving elephants, three needy clowns, a part-time wire walker and this dynamite goat act. Things haven't been going too good; in fact, I'm calling you from this here pay phone, in case we get cut off. Hey, pal, yeah, it would help our circus greatly if you could purchase a book of tickets! There's a truck with all our props, about 100 miles down the road. Replacing a broken clutch is our first priority. And we need $500 for a deposit on the rodeo grounds. If everything goes all right, we might be able to open this Thursday! Who will the benefits go to? I don't quite understand. Charlie? Charlie, are you there? Operator. OPERATOR!"

If it's the product that's crippled, why not pitch *that?*

6
A Trip to the Clouds

THERE are two traditions you observe strictly in the circus if you expect to get very far. One is that you make yourself "generally useful." The other, that your usefulness continue even when the show cannot afford to pay you.

The exploitation of these sacred customs by successful owners made possible the evolution of the American circus from a one-ring infant to a spectacle of runaway proportions. Showmen judged a performer's value by how many tricks he might turn during a single performance. And if he could double between shows to help out the canvas gangs, he might be considered a worthwhile asset.

Typical of contracts entered into before the rise of labor unions is the following ditty, authored by P. T. Barnum for Bob Sherwood. The wide-ranging stipulations might conceal the fact that Mr. Sherwood regarded himself, at least in a general sense, as a clown. ". . . Bob Sherwood (Petey) hereby agrees to give his services as clown, pantomimist, tightrope and wirewalker, trapeze, tumbler and horizontal-bar performer, principal and scenic rider, object holder and to make himself generally useful."

The same applied in reverse for the workingman. If a ropedancer could be expected to pitch stakes in wind and rain, the roustabout was not below filling artistic needs. In fact, in the early days canvasmen commonly assumed costumed positions in the opening specs. The results sometimes riled the reviewing fraternity, as exemplified by *Variety's* strained look

at the Sells-Floto opener in 1921: "The circus started with what was supposed to be a spectacle called 'The

Ethel Jennier in the afterglow of a great performance. The love of circus inspires a performer to endure many hardships. CW.

66

Birth of the Rainbow,' and consisted of all the performers, stake drivers, roustabouts and hostlers dressed up in medieval costumes. They were of an ancient vintage and showed the wear and tear of many parades."

Rare is the performer who makes one appearance and is wisked away amid a crush of autograph seekers to a luxurious hotel room. So you can grace a flyer's tights like nobody's business; you're a crack juggler, a promising equestrian, and a handy fill-in clown. How are you with a sledgehammer in a blizzard? Would you mind terribly being the second vertebra in the dinosaur during the Creation spec? Have you any objections to connecting random black cords to circuit boxes on muddy lots without an electrician's license? Can you drive a semi with a broken clutch? Are you a suicidally inclined schizophrenic?

Individuals who aren't afraid to diversify and don't mind working overtime without being paid overtime have a habit of staying around. Charles Siegrist in the early part of this century acquired the graces of a fine horseman, added to that talent the skills of a juggler, acrobat, leaper, aerialist, and (of course) funny man (and who knows what else). The five-foot Oregonian possessed the striking demeanor of an Austrian prince and the versatility of a Yankee jack-of-all-trades. He never wanted for a good job under the big top. With the Ringling Bros. and the Barnum & Bailey concerns for twenty years, Siegrist appeared in each performance upwards of four times, usually winding up his chores as the principle flyer in a top-flight trapeze act. When the seats were vacant, the agile Oregonian of many facets practiced boxing and wrestling. To his death in 1953, Mr. Siegrist, then seventy-two years old, reaffirmed on a regular basis his ability to accomplish a two-and-one-half somersault through the air. The vigorous veteran may still have heard the inspiring roar of the crowds applauding his stamina. Whether he savored the memory of his paychecks is another matter.

Siegrist was the sort of talent that circus men keep on the roster. It's easy to imagine the little dynamo being available at all times, so expansive were his energies. Possibly he filled every role on the books at one time or another, although it's doubtful he ever went so far as to coerce gifted acrobats and ropewalkers into contracts requiring them to "double" and "triple" for piddling sums of money. Siegrist fell short of the heights of a show manager. He was a dedicated artist.

Two recent headliners with Ringling Bros. and Barnum & Bailey were too good to be useful. Pablo Noel, the zany animal trainer lasted but a season. The captivating juggler Picasso, not much longer. Why? The answers may vary, yet neither gent, for all he could offer in his respective area, seemed ready to spread himself in subsidiary directions. Both preferred remaining incognito once having presented their superb specialties. They were short-lived wonders with the most solvent of circuses.

Of a briefer duration, yet, was the highly popular French wire walker, Philippe Petit, who did not last a full season with the Ringling organization. It may be ego crushing for acclaimed European stars to observe their cohorts commanding the spotlight three and four times at each show.

On the other side of the coin, still gainfully employed after ten continuous years of service are Elvin Bale on the "Blue" unit and Gunther Gebel Williams on the "Red" unit. Bale swings with clean competence on the single trapeze and has fortified his job security by augmenting his credentials with additional insane undertakings: he poses as a reckless maniac on the Strato Cycle (a glorified motorbike) and walks with spine-tingling nonchalance over the fast-revolving Gyro Wheel as the "Phantom of Balance." He is also now being shot from the head of a cannon. Bale has earned a high place for himself in circus history.

Gunther Gebel Williams will train and show off almost any animal who is amenable to being drenched in sequins and taking quick orders in German. The so-called "super star" status of Williams is based as much on his radiant good looks and self-assured charms as it is on his remarkable

Diversified aerialist Elvin Bale. HT.

Multitalented animal trainer Gunther Gebel Williams. HT.

the founding spirit, took a crack at every known routine. He presented a few homemade tricks of his own, including balancing a fifty pound plow on his chin! As prosperity set in, Al gave his plow back to the farmers and focused his attention on directing other performers. Diplomatically he coaxed from each, sufficient additional routines to keep three rings occupied continually with warm bodies. Al was a grand illusionist at creating so much action from so few heads. He earned the coveted reputation of being able to get more out of an artist than any other ringmaster.

The early day non-Ringling employees had to face at the red wagon, where contracts were signed and weekly stipends dispensed, the tyrannical Otto Ringling, of whom it has been said with brevity, "He was too tight to drop his drawers" (for reasons self-explanatory). The "King" as he was called guarded the treasury like a squirrel hording over the

Big tops survived on cheap labor, employed local boys in each town for free tickets. RM.

compatibility with animals. Is he indispensable? A contingent of devoted admirers think so. Their adoration may elude reason. Nonetheless, it testifies to the impact a single man can make in the generally useful world of the circus.

Who knows what other undeclared talents or mad vocational hazards these two Ringling headliners may be harboring in the privacy of their dressing rooms? Bale's father, Trevor, a distinguished equestrian by preference, free-lanced in a cage full of wild beasts whenever the front office put out the call. Has Elvin a similar disposition? As for Mr. Williams, how would he fare in white tights as a flyer on high? Beneath the blond-haired aura of the graceful German may lurk a true aerial crazy.

The employment practices of our nation's leading circus did not develop overnight. When the five Ringling brothers embarked on the windy road to fame and fortune in 1884, whatever they could not afford to have somebody else do they did themselves. Al Ringling, the oldest of the brothers and last uncracked nut in captivity. Getting Otto to let go of a mere penny required the majority vote in its favor by the five brothers; then, Otto executed each expenditure, no matter how minuscule, as if he were being held up in disguise. King Otto's frugality was considered by showmen to be one of the Ringling's greatest assets.

"They'd whittle a man down as cheap as they could get him," Floyd King told me. "Maybe a clown could get $30.00 from the Hagenbeck-Wallace show; The Ringlings would hire him for $25.00."

A sideshow manager from Cole Bros. Circus journeyed with high expectations to Baraboo one winter for a job interview with Albert Ringling. With Cole Bros., he had enjoyed fifteen percent of the gross; naturally, he suspected he could improve his lot on the bigger circus. Al offered him a "counter" proposal amounting to ten percent. The applicant was insulted.

"I've been getting *fifteen percent*, Al!"

"You're now with *Ringling Brothers*," emphasized his prospective employer. "When you go back to Columbus, Ohio, you'll walk down the street in the fall of the year and they'll say, 'Where have you been all year?' 'I've been over at Ringling Brothers.' That'll give you a lot of prestige and honor."

Protested the disillusioned job seeker, "It might give me pride and honor, but when I go into the grocery store, I'll have no money to buy no groceries." So eat your pride.

The wayward Cole Bros. sideshow boss returned to the fold. Ringling Brothers continued interviewing for a ten percent man in search of pride and

The Nelson family between shows. "Generally useful" circus people seldom rest. RM.

Lillian Leitzel, one of the select few who commanded private quarters. RM.

honor, and they continued turning a big profit. On to the next penny pincher.

When John Ringling scouted European acts for his brothers, he tempted foreign stars with glowing visions of the land of opportunity. Perched atop a bale of hay, Ringling watched the Wallendas perform in Havana, then after the show went to work on young Karl. Ringling promised the wire walker a rich man's future. Karl's indifference surely relieved the tight circus proprietor.

"I don't want to be a rich man; I just want to come over and see the cowboys and Indians."

Mr. Ringling jumped up.

"We have lots of cowboys and Indians!"

"That's good," said Karl, turning to his partners. "We make one season then go back to Germany."

Clown alley in the old days, Joeys bathed from buckets of cold water, dressed in mud and rain. CW.

69

Salary was never a very perplexing issue, for the Wallendas lasted out seventeen years under the Ringling Banner.

"But I didn't see cowboys and Indians," Karl hastened to add. "I saw cowboys and Indians only in the circus—they made the finale of the wild west show."

Not so fortunate was John Ringling in dealing with other performers. Con Colleano loomed high on a select list of artists deserving special treatment (no doubt a painful practice for the Ringlings). Colleano demonstrated a flair on the low wire that has not since been matched. Dressed as a Spanish toreador, he danced to Ravel's pulsating "Bolero." Then suddenly he threw a backward somersault—removing his trousers in midair—and landed dramatically in tights. It was a supreme achievement that only he could bring off with regularity. He and his fans knew this.

Colleano grew tense and irritable whenever John Ringling approached with a new contract. At $450.00 a week, Colleano was deemed a detriment to the payroll, and his bosses were famous for effecting wage cuts if possible. One season they tried it on the wire wiz. John Ringling ignited fire in the Australian's eyes by asking him to accept a slightly lesser fee.

"No!" stammered the fiery Colleano. "My salary is $450.00. If I don't get that, I won't work. I'll go with a smaller show, pay what they can afford. But this big Ringling show—I'm entitled to what I'm getting!"

That did not make Mr. John very happy.

At Greensboro, North Carolina, a few weeks later, the last day of the season, the star had not budged, and Ringling realized he would make no concessions. Hearing the crowds cheer the toreador along the wire, Ringling could not fathom his circus being deprived of Colleano's unique thunder. The frustrated executive ordered his secretary to type out a contract, same as the existing one. He affixed his signature to the document and returned it to the typist.

"Take it back to that guy and get him to sign it, too."

The wiredancer was standing near the performer's entrance to the big top when he noticed Ringling's secretary approach with paper in hand. Colleano sense victory in the air. He examined the typed figures, saw the big man's autograph in fresh ink. $450.00 warranted tacit acknowledgement. Colleano shoved the contract up against a splintery quarter pole and signed it right there the night the show closed in Greensboro. Neither man's john henry

Leitzel and one of her doting attendants. RM.

Poodles Hanneford, miffed by a proposed Ringling pay cut, moved on to more lucrative bookings. RM.

exemplified his best penmanship. The transaction was a strained one.

The Ringlings, because of these backward salary reviews, lost to other circuses the funniest man who ever stepped off a horse. That man was Poodles Hanneford, whose troupe consisting of four riders and four horses collected $250.00 weekly. Tommy Hanneford, a nephew of Poodles, recalls how his popular uncle "stopped the show and was back in the dressing room, and people still wanted him to come out. Encore after encore."

How did management remunerate such showmanship? "Due to the tradition of Ringling Brothers," explains Tommy, "and they still do it, they wanted to get him cheaper, so they cut his salary to $200.00 a week."

Poodles did not consider the adjustment a laughing matter. Patiently he concealed his contempt until the Hanneford family rode in with the circus to New York, where they accepted, with no guilt feelings whatsoever, a three-year offer to appear at the New York Hippodrome for $1,250.00 a week. The producer's name was Dillingham, not Ringling, and Poodles on Dillingham's stage became a great star, later doubling for Fatty Arbuckle during the comic's Hollywood scandal.

Henry (Buddy) Ringling North compensated for low wages with countless loans to workingmen, seldom repaid. RM.

Eventually, the Hannefords were wooed back to the big top by the shrewd American Circus Corporation. In the center rings of Sells-Floto, Hagenbeck-Wallace, and Al G. Barnes, Poodles proved to be one of the greatest box-office draws of all time and strong competition to his former employer.

All of which should not be construed as a diatribe against the durable Ringling balance sheets. Rare is the producer from whom half-way acceptable wages do not have to be extracted like wisdom teeth from the jaws of a lion. Big top impresarios—the ones who survive—are a uniformly miserly bunch. None are below the self-demeaning ritual of confessing casually on a dark Friday that they lack the funds to effect payday. When the red wagon is empty, what do you do? If you're truly "with it" you remain calm, project the image of compassion for the show's bad luck and continue being as useful as ever. Having no assurances that next Friday will be any different, you go about your chores filled with a deeper inner peace: you have a bunk that will shelter you partially from wind and rain; access to three meals a day in the cookhouse (at your own risk); and guaranteed employment for as long as the show can survive on a volunteer staff. Heady satisfaction, that.

Well, give the Ringlings credit for a near-perfect record as paymasters. One clown, who prefers anonymity, puts it like this: "Every Friday there's a paycheck waiting for you on the Ringling show. Granted, it may not be the biggest paycheck, but there are no ifs, ands, or buts. You go up there and you get paid. Many times in the circus throughout my life, I've gone up on a Friday and there was no paycheck there. The big answer I always got was, 'Just think of all the hundreds of kids you've made happy.'" Producers love instilling in their ranks a sense of guiltless involvement.

Henry Ringling North understood well the realities of circus management. That did not diminish his generosity among show hands in need. Known affectionately to them as "Buddy," Mr. North made himself eminently available and over the years "loaned" thousands of dollars in ten and twenty bills to countless hired help—mostly canvasmen and roustabouts who would squander their stipends away on booze and poker. Henry's friendly loans were seldom repaid, nor were the debtors denied subsequent assistance up the road. Comradship goes a long way on the sawdust trail.

In the "good old days" it was a risky business to

protest not being paid. A motley of canvasmen with Robins Bros. Circus in 1931 rose up one evening in assignation against their bosses for back wages owed them. One by one, the "ungratefuls" were discharged—from a fast-moving train in the night. One victim died, twenty-four others walked—bleeding and ruptured—eleven miles to Mobile, Alabama. Indictments were issued by a grand jury in Mobile against Ralph Nobles and Earl Sinott for manslaughter. Circuses have endured some sordid struggles to keep their tents in the air.

Fewer men today are viciously disposed of when their skills are not required or they begin quibbling over obscure pay scale arrangements. Etiquette has improved for the better. Still, it takes a tight wad with irresistible charms or an i.o.u. artist on the run to manufacture a big splash in three rings and stay out of the bad graces of the Internal Revenue Service or any number of child labor commissions. Today's crushing economics have reduced most shows to one-ring affairs.

Not so for Dory Miller, who operates yet like an old pro with a tent full of action. Under the canvas of his marvelous five-ring confection, Carson & Barnes, Miller has been treating Bicentennial audiences in small towns to a wonderful sampling of the robust big-top magic of yesteryear. How does the show owner of forty years do it? Not with the looks of a man on his way to a jackpot in the sky. Miller is down-to-earth, a humble chap who rumbles around his assets on circus lots across the country behind the wheel of a tractor. Miller's secret code is no secret at all: get a full season and keep a lot of people anxiously engaged at rock bottom prices and don't let them out of your sight.

Most of Dory Miller's artists are of Mexican descent. Allegedly they jump and twirl to the cheapest of rates. They are energetically free souls and they have made Carson & Barnes a feasible joy to behold. Not being signed, sealed, or delivered, however, to lucrative contracts, they are also more likely to fly away without notice. Sunday was no day of rest in Del Rio, Texas, a couple of seasons back, where Miller and his general manager Ted Bowman found themselves in troublesome proximity to the Mexican border, only a brief tantrum away. Wondering why they booked the company so close, they feared the possibility of losing half their performers back to the country from which they came. Midway in the tour would the Morales family of teeterboard exponents get itchy feet and withdraw?

Arguments were carefully avoided; it was a day of extreme tact. Bowman wasted no time in dispensing with two early shows, ordering the tent struck el prompto and dispatching the company up the road as far north as possible without skipping the next scheduled stand. Holding a big splash of aerialists and tumblers together on a depression budget is the mark of an accomplished showman. Commented the man who conducts his business from the edge of a tractor, "We don't make much money, but we enjoy trying to satisfy the public."

Who *does* make money, anyway? As Ricki Wallenda pointed out, "Any show's good enough as long as I'm working, getting paid. That's the main thing."

Many producers are today bemoaning their decreasing returns. Some flaunt their tepid profits as if there was a contest on to see which one can show the greatest loss. Hubert Castle made some stark confessions to a Canadian reporter. Stated Castle (or was he boasting?), "I used to make more money as an act than I do as a circus."

Hubert Castle, with Cole Bros. Circus, 1947. "I used to make more money as an act than I do now as a circus." CW.

Castle went from a star performer on the low wire to a prime producer of Shrine circuses. During his 1973 tour, Castle claims, a top act cost him $80,000.00, while he recouped for himself just $20,000.00 profit on a half million dollar investment. Castle might consider returning to the status of a generally useful performer.

Since 1942 Louis Stern had been at the helm of Polack Bros. Circus. Until he sold the show in 1977, he attended every performance. "What else would I do?" he asked. Stern, in his eighties, had been with it too long to let go with ease. Expenses in the meantime had soared, and his dates had dwindled in number. Therefore, Stern was forced to pay premium rates to his performers in compensation for numerous idle days between stands. Reportedly the producer was sinking sixty to seventy thousand dollars annually of his life's earnings into the show, and he then had no plans of retiring from his costly pastime. How could he be "with it" if he did? Nobody paid the price of admission that Louis Stern did—to see his own circus.

The tanbark trail is strewn with the ghosts of men and women who have given far more to the world of big tops than they ever received in return.

In his book *Circus Kings*, Henry North reflected on this subject with graphic firsthand knowledge: "The circus is a jealous wench. Indeed, that is an understatement. She is a ravening hag who sucks your vitality as a vampire drinks blood—who kills the brightest stars in her crown and who will allow no private life to those who serve her; wrecking their homes, ruining their bodies, and destroying the happiness of their loved ones by her insatiable demands. She is all of these things, and yet, I love her as I love nothing else on earth."

Fussbudgets unwilling to bear the grueling sacrifices fade quickly away to less chancy walks of life. Edward Greer regarded himself as the crowning thrill act with Barnum & Bailey. The aerialist opened the New York season of 1914 performing the loop-the-loop in a routine billed "A Trip To The Clouds." Greer gained increasing momentum on a swinging bar until he spun over and over in rapid-fire revolutions. The shrieks he heard from the crowd below were all for him, he thought; actually, other acts in his display were contributing to the commotion.

Greer developed a star complex. He began quibbling over the extra duties required of him. He objected to appearing in the opening spec—a labori-

ous half hour pageant, "Wizard, Prince of Arabia" that dragged endlessly on beneath the sweaty oppression of ostrich plumes, a turgid original score, and the heavy sighs of participating canvasmen. Greer did not fancy the notion of marching in the daily street

Whirlwind of versatility, John Strong, Jr. has perfected a host of circus skills. JS.

73

parades once the show commenced touring under canvas. He made it known he would not be available.

Show officials went into a huddle. They had a nonproductive man on the payroll. A hasty decision was reached: examine Greer's rigging, take notes, and have it duplicated. At the same time scan the roster for a replacement to begin rehearsals immediately.

The gates of opportunity opened for nineteen-year-old Ella Hackett. The daughter of a New York physician, Ella and her sister Sarah had come to Barnum & Bailey following tours with the John Robinson and the Hagenbeck-Wallace shows. The girls were show-business crazy. They rode in the hippodrome races and marched in the opening spec. Ella was vulnerable to any and all suggestions issued to her by management. Useful she was.

Greer's services were terminated at the end of his first week. Miss Hackett was assigned to "copy" his act, while property crews assembled similar rigging. Greer later maintained it was an "economical move" and "an impossible trick for a girl." In trade journal adds he flaunted the harrowing outcome. . . .

At 5:30 P.M. on a Wednesday in Madison Square Garden, Ella Hackett climbed excitedly to the top of the arena for her first run through. Elated with the anticipation of stardom—perhaps someday rivaling Leitzel and Wirth and Colleano—she felt literally on her way to the clouds.

Ella's sister, Sarah, and William Lamont of Bird Milman's wire act, stood by in the empty garden to wish her well. Ella deserved the break. She had no misgivings over street parades under the hot sun, she loved all aspects of circus life, and she looked forward to taking her bows. She was grateful she was "with it."

Ella reached the rigging.

"This is where the blood tingles in your finger tips" program magazines of the day proclaimed in describing such daring stunts.

Ella's two well-wishers down on the quiet arena floor peered up anxiously at her diminishing figure. They could see her leaning toward the trapeze bar, ready to step onto it, nervously making up in willpower what she lacked in experience. Greer had stated it took him six months to master his "trip to the clouds." Ella was determined to set new records . . .

That never happened. Sometimes the odds, ladies and gentlemen, are not in your favor and all your great dreams are shunted aside in the darkness of a deserted circus lot . . .

Briefly after taking her position on the trapeze, Ella slipped and fell fatally to the stage below. The aspiring starlet never reached the clouds on a whirling swing, never lived to make another spec, ride in the hippodrome races or walk once more to the red wagon on Friday wondering if payday was still on.

7
Your Money's Wirth

IN the Ringling Museum of the Circus, where history comes to life, among the precious photographs of past glories is a picture of a rider standing nonchalantly atop her horse with exquisite aplomb. A touch of youthful daring underlies her placid posture. She seems posed on the peak of a mountain only she has scaled; in the durable attire of a faithful trouper she exhudes the arresting grace of a beautiful princess who has just conquered the world.

May Wirth, circa the golden age.

She rode during a day when you could not say no to the circus, a day when the stars of America's big tops were the most celebrated live entertainers of all. Their faces on gaudy twenty-four-sheet lithographs were splashed across barns and store fronts, their fantastic feats exploited by press agents promising the public more than it had ever imagined possible.

Circuses transported from town to town a world of "glamour and romance and beautiful people" in the words of John Hurdle, museum curator and like many of us an incurable circus fan, "sights and sounds which were totally foreign, exotic animals, men and women doing wondrous things."

Before talking pictures, radio, and Sesame Street started devouring harmless live entertainers, ordinary life stood still while the ageless delight moved in. Its command was undisputable. Young boys deserted their beds at the break of dawn to greet the arrival of elephants and horses and wagons loaded

with enchanting objects at the train yards. Cows were left unmilked, unloved, school rooms abandoned. Important business appointments were neglected by grown men. Who cared? There was only one place to be—down on Main Street with everybody else, waiting for the jubilant sounds of sunburst wagon wheels, the roar of lions and tigers from their gilded cages, and the band's robust fanfares orchestrating the "Grand Free Street Parade."

Nobody said no to the country's grandest amusement. "The circus was *the* entertainment," sighs Hurdle.

Special excursion trains whizzed families from outlying hamlets and farmlands into the city. Anxious crowds formed where giddy banners galloped in the wind high over billowing white tents. They stood eager-eyed at the images of strange wonders painted on shimmering canvas, listened with rapt attention to barkers spieling the marvels contained on the other side. The language and lure of the big top was universal. In Texas, indians erected their teepees on the showgrounds the night before circus day and patiently waited for their first glimpse of a wagon with long white poles lumbering into view through the misty dawn.

The spirit of Yankee competition gave rise to three-ring holidays. Americans spoiled themselves on heady overdoses of action; while the circus was victoriously in vogue, audiences would settle for

May Wirth. RM.

Gaudy lithographs heralded a world of wondrous delights.
RM.

Those were the days . . . when boys flocked to railroad yards to greet the arrival of circus trains. RM.

nothing less. Give them donkeys in one ring, trained mice in another, educated rats in the third if necessary—but give them something! The quest for novelty was unreal. Christie Bros. crowded into ninety minutes an ark full of animals that included goats, geese, pigs, elephants, horses, baboons, lions, and lambs, not counting Grecian wrestlers and other unorthodox features—every one fully trained and domesticated.

In 1917 the Ringling brothers offered patrons a rare display of industrial fortitude: two rings were given over to a wood-chopping contest between "Australia's mightiest axemen"; in a third ring "speed mechanics" assembled the "intricate parts" of a motor car; if that did not tickle your fancy you could view "a remarkable exhibition of orange packing by the Californians." Something for every nut, at breakneck speed.

. . . when towners judged a circus by counting the number of elephants it carried. RM.

. . . when teams of rosinbacks moved wagons, tents, and
incredible people across the main streets of America. RM.

. . . when sunburst wagon wheels clattered over flatcars
and down the "runs" to cobblestone pavements below.
RM.

. . . when the stupendous forty-horse hitch pulled a wagon of gold tableaus and trumpet-blarring windjammers. CW.

So staggering were the three, sometimes five-ring presentations (with other attendant action on intermediate stages as well), reviewers often walked out of the tent cross-eyed and copyless. There was so much to see, nothing got seen. *Variety's* natty founder and publisher, Sime Silverman, who made annual trips to Madison Square Garden with pencil and paper, one year got smart. Or perhaps he felt a headache approaching as he faced another opening night ordeal. Silverman's cavalier integrity prompted him to dispatch along with himself, two of his staffers. A three-man task force from the bible of show business would descend on the "big one." Once and for all the parts of this mind-boggling puzzle would be identified and justly appraised. Each man was ordered to stand watch over one

. . . when F. Beverly Kelley wrote, ". . . gray morning sees me unpacked, laced together like a giant's shirt and hoisted on tall spars and guyed to earth. At dusk, I am an anchored dirigible, shadowy, with soft light leaking through. Midnight sees my titan ribs removed and finds me billowing to earth. And there I lie like some great mushroom, waiting to be loaded into circus wagons rumbling in an endless cycle from show grounds to trains and back again. I am the Big Top." CW.

. . . when thousands watched a Hagenbeck-Wallace Circus parade. cw.

. . . when flappers and fun lovers jammed Christy Bros. Circus midway, in 1924. cw.

. . . when Sells-Floto Circus, in 1928 at Chicago, turned them away by the thousands! cw.

specific ring, simple as that. The 1909 edition of Ringling Bros. Circus was explicated, investigated, and adjudicated by the three-headed critic from *Variety*—Sime, Dash, and Rush!

Circuses roared through the roaring twenties, living out their last days at the forefront of entertainment with herculean hoopla. They were "in" events on everyone's calendar. Racy flappers had money to spend and a wide open penchant for riotous diversions. Big name big tops cashed in. Al G. Barnes kept five rings alive with continuous action, the lines at its red ticket wagon were long. Charles Sparks jammed seven thousand paying customers into a tent that was considered small for the era; none of today's traveling tent shows approach such capacity. Sells-Floto, the "circus beautiful" turned away during one performance alone at Chicago in 1923 six thousand dejected souls. Yankee fun seekers reveled in fast and furious happenings under canvas arenas. Speed and still more speed was the order of the day. They knew a would-be from an established pro, could appreciate a fine aerialist with unashamed enthusiasm and over an exceptional performer went wild.

Practicing old-timers claim those were the heyday years, when superstars like Leitzel and Codona brought to the center ring a flawless grace and breathtaking vitality. How could one say no to Clyde Beatty or Mabel Stark, to the exciting Flying Clarkonians or the great Hanneford riding family? To Con Colleano or Bird Milman?

They created a world of dizzyfying excitement, a world of olympic-like proportions. When young Karl Wallenda stood in the wings of the Garden on his historic opening night, he got the jitters watching many of these great artists perform. "My God," said the self-assured performer, "We gonna flop here!"

That the Wallendas received a standing ovation was a testament not only to their greatness but to the greatness of audiences during the twenties.

Ringling's famed bandmaster Merle Evans, who played for all the top acts then and has scored every important one since, remains bedazzled by the times. "They had the greatest circus I think I ever saw."

The Maestro's recollection of that glorious era paints a vivid picture of the American circus at its highest plateau: "They had *Lillian Leitzel, May Wirth, Bird Milman . . . Poodles Hanneford*. All the big stars. And *Codona . . .* the best looking man in tights I ever saw. *Showmanship*—you just *had* to

like him, he did it so easy. And the Clarkonians, and they had *sixty-nine* acrobats, and they'd march 'em down that track and we'd give a chord and they'd all go in the rings—*sixty-nine* of them. You tell that to people and they don't believe it. They had one or two good acts of every description. They had head balancing acts—they had five guys that used to stand on their heads up on the trapeze . . . five perch pole acts on five different stages . . . and Hillory Long . . . he used to skate down a thing as high as the ceiling on his head—a platform on roller skates. *That* was the *twenties*.

"Bird Milman was the best act I ever played to. They'd give her a thousand dollars a week, just to walk across the wire and back again. That's how good she was—a beautiful woman, and showmanship. Clyde Beatty was a great showman. They'd have a guy with fifty horses in the ring—that was Christiansen. He'd have some ponies here, and some camels there and some zebras up there running around. That was *some circus*."

Others speak for the stars of that era with comparable conviction.

Tommy Hanneford recalls, "my greatest thrill was to see Uncle Poodles do a side somersault off the horse."

Of Con Colleano, Karl Wallenda exclaims, "the greatest—he was fantastic."

John Ringling North, interviewed some years ago, reminisced, "The spectacle of the dainty and lovely Lillian Leitzel, twirling like a human pinwheel, high in the top of the tent, may never find its equal as long as there is a circus anywhere."

F. Beverly Kelley, then a promising young press

. . . when Poodles Hanneford stopped the show. cw.

agent, once asked John Ringling what he thought all these marvelous artists had in common.

Answered the sage circus king, "Fire."

No single performer epitomized better the showmanship of the golden age than May Wirth. The incredible 125-pound equestrienne marvel packed everything into one ring—dazzling looks, a swift sense of the nonstop magic that audiences craved and a package of tricks atop a circling horse that may never again be matched in any sphere, anywhere...

Around and around she rode, never leaving her horse without design, dancing the Charleston one season and the Blackbottom the next, prancing over banners, crashing through paper bags, leaping onto her steeds with baskets tied to her dainty feet, somersaulting through hoops of fire, bounding from one horse to another, reversing her position and whirling backwards, shattering the odds against perfection with bewildering energy. In less than nine minutes *thirty* tricks, and while her horse traversed the ring but once, she turned seven complete somersaults... *seven!*

"Hit 'em up jacks" they called her. May Wirth was a three-ring production all in herself.

Like most great American circus stars, May was not born in this country. She woke up one day in Australia and discovered herself to be the child of a show family. Better get cracking, little May had just seven years in which to become a bubbling contortionist good enough for a solo spot at Her Majesty's in Adelaide. From the beginning, flowers and candy flowed regularly from charmed fans. Well, almost. One evening the ravishments were missing, and our up-and-coming acrobat boldly refused to go on. A forceful relative delivered May to the spotlights and she contorted under protest, without candy. A trouper must learn to endure.

At ten, May was riding horses with professional ease and had mastered wire walking, tumbling, and other assorted skills. By her twelfth year she worked five different acts in the Wirth Circus. In between shows she appeared as one of the darlings in the children's circus, a midway attraction. Clearly, May Wirth had little time for being anything other than May Wirth. Horses and cheering crowds were threatening to claim her soul, a destiny her parents did not resist.

Ordinary romance? Who needs that? May's childhood boyfriend Frank Wirth (not a blood relative) told her when she was twelve that he would someday marry her. Perhaps the young equestrienne nodded in agreement to pacify poor Frank while she removed her tumbling slippers and slipped a feather into her pretty hair for the family riding routine, coming up next. See you later, Frank!

May's heart was set in a hard, wooden forty-two foot ring. Therein she pursued a crash course in how to become a circus star overnight. Or was she writing the course? May turned the Wirth family into a feature with Ringling Bros. Circus and herself into the first performer ever to be awarded a solo spot by the Ringlings. In 1912 at the Garden, the entire arena was "surrendered over" to the fresh Australian marvel. John Ringling billed his new discovery as being eighteen years old because he feared that nobody would believe the "world's most remarkable equestrian star" was actually fifteen!

Circus goers got their money's wirth. *Variety* acquiesced to Miss Wirth's blazing achievements and followed her career with unwavering awe, a sampling of which follows: "... it's (Ringling Bros.) two features being the Cinderella spec and May Wirth.... the feminine marvel of the tanbark... perhaps the best individual attraction under the big top today.... no man or woman bareback star has ever approached her acrobatic achievement atop a circling horse.... the wonder girl of the circus ring.... she seems to be in even better form... her equestrianism is beyond compare.... May Wirth is the greatest of equestrians.... There never has been her equal and maybe never will be.... There is no question that May Wirth was the star of the performance."

Andrew Downie, in 1921 wooed away the Wirth family from the largest of circuses for a guaranteed sum of $1,000 weekly plus percentages. Downie was expanding his Walter L. Main Circus and feared impending competition from the bigger Sells-Floto show. The show-wise trouper knew that May Wirth *was* the greatest show on earth, that to get her under his canvas would make him a formidable box-office contender. Sure enough, out came the customers in droves; the Australian rider pulled more than $20,000 a week into Downie's red wagon. Quickly, the original contract was augmented to eight more weeks. The wonder girl of the center ring was a solid box-office sensation. By the time John Ringling rediscovered his runaway star, May had given Downie two solvent seasons.

May enjoyed all the luxuries of a circus celebrity, the Wirth family occupied an entire car on the train,

*. . . when the crowds cheered May Wirth and her horse,
inseparable partners in a display of nonstop magic.* RM.

had their own private dressing top and ate at the
executives table in the cookhouse, an honor they
shared with only Lillian Leitzel.

Success did not distort May's zeal. She continued
practicing as if true stardom was still down the road,
a habit that daily irked her brothers-in-law whose
pinochle games were jeopardized whenever May
needed them to rig and work a safety mechanic while
she rehearsed.

Each time May appeared between shows, the
pinochle players steamed.

"There she is again!"

"I was bored," explained the lady genius of
bareback riders, looking back over the golden days.

"I wanted to do something and not thinking that
my horse had been standing up all night, traveling
from town to town, that wasn't a kind thought."

Reluctantly the brothers followed May into the
big top, cursing her "up hill and down dale." And
she rode and rode and rode. . . .

Her favorite horse was Joe.

"Was he temperamental. He'd shy in and throw
me off, that's why I had so many accidents."

Why not change horses?

"I loved him too much."

The affections and loyalty of a rider for her steed
are irrevocable constants. May at twenty-two years
of age finally accepted Frank's lifelong proposal. She
married her ardent admirer, though soon afterward
Frank left the act and settled into work for an agency
in one immobile city. The couple remained formally
faithful. One might conclude that Frank understood
his exuberant spouse had priorities outside of wed-
lock.

One was Joe.

"I love him to this day. When I lost him I lost my
pal."

Another were the crowds. Unshakable was her
devotion to them. In 1927, opening night on Ringling
Bros. and Barnum & Bailey in New York, May
slipped while performing her highly popular basket
leap, bruised her back badly and lost her wind.

May and "Petsy." The star equestrienne practiced between shows. "I gave my whole life to riding." RM.

Refusing valiantly to forgo her reputation, she tried the trick again, this time solidly well, and proceeded with inspiring determination to the completion of her routine. May received the evening's top plaudits.

"I gave my whole life to riding. Because I loved it so, I think that's why I improved in other things that other people couldn't do. I tried to do everything. I used to stand up on the ring curb, as I'm only five feet, I used to get a kick out of that, if I thought the audience was pleased . . . that's a big satisfaction."

Probably the saddest year in May's life was her return to Australia following her third triumphal season in America. It was May's great ambition to again appear in her beloved homeland, and doubly disappointing, therefore, when on opening night and for the rest of her twelve-month stint, she failed to receive anywhere near the enthusiasm she had experienced in the United States. It was a stunning blow, as recorded by George Wirth in the *Australian Life Magazine:*

"May got as far as her dressing room before she broke down. She cried pitifully, poor girl. This was her great reception from her beloved Australians! . . . They had looked on coldly and indifferent. . . . But May has a mightly heart. All the time that she was in Australia she never complained. That one outbreak on the first night was all we heard. Night after night, she gave of her very best, and went through the same routine of wonderful riding, smiling at her audience at the end of her act just as though they had applauded her to high heaven."

When the Wirths appeared at the Olympic Theatre in England one winter, they were honored by the presence of Queen Anne and Lord Longsdale. The royal party included the Prince of Wales, who was officially confined to a state of mourning over the recent death of his grandmother. The Prince was escorted to a special black box, the curtains drawn. The first family were about to be diverted out of their well-studied decorum and the young prince out of his doldrums.

May Wirth was on the bill.

The Queen proved to be "a very lovely audience." She passed a compliment discreetly to the star equestrienne "to say she enjoyed the Australian rider very much."

The Prince of Wales was not so reserved in his behavior. Frustrated in a state of deprivation, he floundered in his box of mourning to see what was stirring the audience. Restlessly the heir apparent squinted through the dark curtains. The vague outlines of America's foremost rider tantalized him. What *was* she doing . . . somersaulting? . . . with her back to the horse's head?

"Leaping, no. She's jumping through hoops of fire! Are those baskets on her feet? Good grief," sighed the Prince to himself, "what jolly momentum! Does she never fatigue?"

The Prince's nose pushed against the curtains. His official sorrow abated. What *was* going on up there?

"I don't believe it!" he murmured, straining to get a glimpse. . . .

Oooops. The curtains flared aside and out popped the Prince's noggin, his eyes dialated with excitement. At last, a dandy nice view. The young man was entranced.

"What a bloody good rider!"

The house rang with wild applause. May took her final bows and graciously backed out, careful not to slight members of the royal party, while somebody pushed the Prince's protruding top back into his box of deep mourning. The forceful move was not effected with the finest etiquette.

In blushed disarray, Queen Anne, Lord Longsdale, and their party had been entertained to the point of ruffled impropriety by the celebrated star of the great American circus.

They backed out, too.

8
Life, Liberty, and the Right To Be Hoodwinked

LITERARY giants and lesser known scribes have all succumbed during one fit or another to the awesome aura of tented cities that move by night. Some never return to their senses; they go on to become successful press agents—the virtuosos of vitriolic verbosity. While their wages vary considerably, their sins are all the same: in a word, adjectives.

For openers, consider the following description, penned by a famous turn-of-the-century publicist, Tody Hamilton, of Barnum & Bailey's somersaulting automobile:

> "The Limit: Le Tourbillon de la Mort, Where Chuckling and Expectant Death Meets Disappointment and Chagrin. A Turning, Twisting, Twirling, Tossing, Tilting Transportation; the Thrilling, Terrifying, Tremendous Tumbling, Tantalizing Triumph of All Time!

> "Absolutely The Extreme Limit Of Human Daring and Intrepidity. The Veritable Cap Sheaf of the Incredible, Closely approaching a Marvelous, Maddening, Mechanical Mystery and Miracle."

The driver in this admittedly thrilling stunt possessed unusual nerve; in Hamilton's rhetoric, he was hopelessly heroic. Man needs his symbols of courage and adventure, and the circus has been a

Americans at the ballyhoo. There are no limits. RM.

85

prime provider. Hamilton's syntax reflects an era of unstinting magnificence in big top history . . . that era when you could not say "no" to the circus . . . when red and silver trains crisscrossed each other in the night, racing onwards in a never ending struggle to be first in the next town—first to empty the pockets of circus-hungry Americans.

The abrasive marketing techniques of rival big tops as practiced through the early twentieth century—before the onslaught of movies, radio, TV, and rock—can be attributed as much to the press agent as to the big boys at the top who hired him. A good showman, after all, *was* a press agent. He faced his competition much like today's television executives deal with each other in the perennial battle for rating supremacy. Press agents then were a nervy bunch—concocters of notorious tales and fabricators of the most bizarre attractions. At stake was a piece of the action in a booming industry.

Circus consumers then seriously compared the relative merits of shows competing for their dollar. The "sacred white elephant war" is a superb example of a profitable controversy waged with devilish attention-getting skill by master showmen. On the one side were Barnum & Bailey with Toung Taloung; on the other was Adam Forepaugh and his Light of Asia. Whose bull was truly "sacred" or the *most* sacred? To the great amusement of the public, the competing entrepreneurs produced documents signed and attested to by leading authorities certifying the authenticity of their respective pachyderms. The conflict sputtered on through charges and countercharges until the sham lost its lure. As it turned out, Toung Taloung was believed to be an authentic imported bull, though only grey in color (with a few pink spots "here and there"), while Forepaugh's the Light of Asia was declared a fake, though he enjoyed overwhelming public acceptance with his whiter complexion (achieved by having been "sandpapered and calcimined"!).

The feuds among today's sports and TV figures and their agents and producers, resulting often in the dissolution of contracts and the switching of affiliations, are similar to those waged between big-top celebrities during the golden age. The separation of Dan Rice, America's foremost jester, from his sometimes employer Doc Spaulding, turned into a nasty quarrel over ethics, staged for maximum publicity. The two once-allied partners were now hurling insulting "rat sheets" at each other in full-page newspaper adds. Doc Spaulding engaged Clar-ance Chester Moore, an Albany printer and a fledgling writer of calculated neutrality, to fashion deflamatory (and entertaining) slurs against Rice. So brutally arresting were the Moore-instigated insinuations concerning the character of the prominent buffoon, that Rice hired Moore *also*, to retaliate for him! The ambidextrous, totally amoral Albany author satisfied each of the rival clients, collected a small fortune out of the deal and helped give a petty squabble whopping commercial value.

The hoopla that preceeds any event is what Americans love the most. We come alive at the ballyhoo—be it a political rally, a championship prize fight, or the entrance to a spangled wonderland. It's the pitch that turns us on. Give us a spiel worth remembering, and we'll go away reasonably satisfied, even should the offerings delivered "on the inside" bear scarce resemblance to the promises made out front. A nation of expectant consumers are we; once the sale has been made, more than half the fun has been consummated. Knowing full well the barker's appeal is a gross distortion of the facts, innately we desire to perceive life in the same way.

The apostles of alliteration addressed themselves to this one simple fact. Through the power of words alone, they inspired the men who employed them to greater heights. Thanks to such press agents as Willard Douglas Coxey, Major John Burke, Tody Hamilton, and Dexter Fellows, literally we talked ourselves into three-ring madness.

Those dapper publicity specialists have gradually vanished from the scene, like so many things that were once vital to a thriving circus operation. The redoubtable Floyd King was one of the last of these great advance men of the old school. Six months before he would take his last mortal breath, I chatted with him on the craggy outskirts of Macon, Georgia, where he dwelled in cheerful semiretirement.

Truly a golden age figure, Floyd King preceeded every show he ever represented with a cataclysmic cascade of amazing, alluring alliterations and ephocal, eye-engulfing exaggerations. Born the son of a preacher, in his latter years Mr. King waxed strong in a prose that gave the circus world a sanctified ring. It is a lingo I have not encountered anywhere else and it suggests a Shangrila under canvas. The various sentiments about the basic purity of trouping, as contained in the essays he penned for his own King Bros. Circus program magazines, stand like beatitudes of the big top:

"As pilgrims with no abiding city, leading a life of

*Let there be trumpets and drum rolls, acrobats and flyers
fast and furious. Let there be clowns and elephants. Let
there be circus!* RM.

multiplied activities and varied fortunes amid scenes of din and turmoil, hurry and agitation, our platform is courage, ambition and energy governed by honest purpose and tempered by humanity . . . The voice of joy and health resounds through our ranks; we are united in a fraternal good-will unbroken by dissension, our life of weal and woe is ever invested with peculiar delightful fascination, and boisterous relish transports itself from town to town.

"The elevated standard of morality among circus men and women is a revelation to one who lives with them from day to day and is their close companion. The atmosphere seems charged with health and happiness, virtue and vigor."

Down the road, spaketh the pastor of press agents, ". . . we will pass sunny hours on meadows enameled with violets and daisies and goldened with buttercups and dandelions where the circus is passing the day." One can almost hear the Hallelujah Chorus at the back door, waiting for the ringmaster's whistle to signal it down the hippodrome track!

Twenty-five years earlier Mr. King had brought to my hometown the first tent circus I ever saw, and I had a special feeling for this endearing gentleman of slight dimensions and sprightly ways. There in Macon, I found him as friendly as a button ready for another hundred years. Here was the man who had routed shows in, placated fire chiefs fearful of burning canvas, charmed city editors from shore to shinning shore with choice seats (free, of course), the man who had fronted the biggest of big tops, and played top dog to a few of his own while he watched his money and dreams trickle down the drain and the creditors appear. He'd been up and down, and over and under, as they say. Well, when you plan for a life of "multiplied activities and varied fortunes," you are subject to the occasional feeling of owning absolutely nothing.

His spirits were untarnished from it all. And what were his first words to me?

"Sit down boss," he said, putting me instantly at ease. You might have happily mistook my humble, animated host for Snow White's cobbler or Jimminy Cricket's Godfather.

"Now, what can I do for you? Just go ahead, ask me anything you want."

We conversed about the life of "peculiar delightful fascination." Theologically, Mr. King never opened up, nor did meadows enameled with violets and daisies roll trippingly from his tongue. There were crisp tales to be told of intrigue along the trail—rival agents in sereptitious battle, saboteurs in the shadows . . . . entrepreneurs on the move. Blowdowns and foreclosures. The master's voice intoned each date and place like a dependable old Victrola record taking me back to another time: I heard in my mind the sounds of steam sputtering

Soft-spoken Floyd King effectively heralded every show but his own. CW.

A typical billposters' war. In this case, Ringling lithos dominated the old warehouse. RM.

Note billposters on the roof's edge, who seem to have claimed victory over Buffalo Bill. RM.

During heyday years, competition among rival big tops was fierce, each show being represented by several advance crews of billposters. RM.

from a locomotive sloshing through a small town on a hot afternoon . . . . the rumble of wagons clattering down the runs of the flat cars to the cobblestone pavement below . . . . the blaring crescendos of trumpets and tubas blowing over perspiring crowds. . . .

". . . . the first section went on the way down to Gary, and they got to a place called Ivanhoe, and they had a hot box. They were pulling into a siding to repair this hot box and I think most of the train except five or six sleeping cars had got off the main line into this side track. Long came on the main line this Michigan Central train, they had flares out back, torpedos on the track to stop the train, but it never hesitated, the engineer evidently was asleep and they ran into this first section right down through the center of the cars. In those days they were heavily constructed wooden sleeping cars, and over a hundred people killed."

I asked Mr. King why he joined the circus?

"All that moving around. Everyday you got to see new main streets and new courthouses."

In his eighty-seventh year on this earth, the King was still perched tentatively on the edge of a chair like a man in a train station waiting for the next local out to tomorrow's stand. I found him the spitting image of the Yankee salesman—a smile on his lapel, shoes buffed and ready, a worn briefcase full of hope in hand, sagging a little under the weight of fresh letterhead, recycled optimism, a score of contracts, press passes to appease every city editor extant. The word lovable comes to mind.

Through the late 1960s he reigned supreme as general agent for three shows—Clyde Beatty-Cole Bros., Sells & Gray, and King Bros. Mr. King never stopped treating the circus like a circus and refused to relinquish the grandiose style of promotion to which he had grown accustomed. He ticked on like a stubborn grandfather clock. No detail escaped his ubiquitous zeal. He coddled all three enterprises lovingly across the land, masterminding each route, christening promotional crews, directing lithographers and public relations men via a stream of telephone calls from various hotel rooms in key cities. The circuses fronted by Floyd King moved day in and day out with unbroken spirits. Associates to this day speak with great respect for his grasp.

What is the key to a successful circus?

"Routing and good towns," said the general agent who moved through the twentieth century like the old country doctor. As other men dinned high in the air or sped over turnpikes in sleek automobiles, the Clyde Beatty-Cole Bros. specialist continued shuffling aboard pullman cars and gliding pristinely down steel rails. From station to station he lugged a battery of trunks, typewriters, boxes of unusable lithos, unwrapped roles of tickets from another year—each time routinely enlisting the services of an attendant and rewarding the man with his customary, "Thank you, son" and a twenty-cent tip. The advance man breezed through inflationary periods totally noncommittal to progress.

The expertise of a seasoned trouper does not become obsolete overnight. Circuses are traditional rather than revolutionary, and the men and women who have served them well can count on years of viable employment within the industry. In 1956, when the Ringling show was stumbling through its last days under canvas, it became obvious that the policies of modern thinking businessmen had failed to revitalize the show against continuing financial losses and organizational inadequacies. Management called for the man. Floyd King came aboard too late and at the wrong end. He should have been verbally in front of the show, not trailing it with second-guesses.

A circus that fails to ballyhoo its forthcoming arrival with brazen authority—as Ringling failed to do that ill-fated season—may roar through town unnoticed. Enthusiasms must be generated, images of grandeur constructed. The excitement created before circus day is perhaps more important than circus day itself. Any show that Mr. King headed up was automatically the "Sensation of The Amusement World," whether it had fifty silver railroad cars or a couple of broken-down wagons and a few feeble goats.

When Zack Terrell and Jess Adkins in 1935 took over the Cole Bros. title, one of their best decisions was to engage Floyd King as chief publicist. Working to depression era audiences, King portrayed Clyde Beatty as "the poor baker boy who rose to international fame and riches." The master of adjectives embellished the circus itself with a royal background, announcing that Cole Bros. only recently had returned to America after "conquering conquests of continental Europe." *Variety* noted, "Cole is giving its customers a small booklet issued by Floyd King telling all about its European tour and other things it didn't do. It's good reading nevertheless and may help to enliven the name."

Actually, the Cole Bros. name had previously

Floyd King's Gentry Bros. title, on the skids in 1930. Commercial tie-ins failed to keep the show solvent. cw.

been held by King himself, who managed the show through defeats suffered in continental North America—head on into the skids of 1929. Far luckier was he at touting the fortunes of other men than was he at establishing his own. During the twenties, Floyd and his brother Howard acquired show titles and railroad cars. In a few years they were operating with ease two shows—the fifteen car Gentry Bros. Circus and the ten car Cole Bros. Circus. Canvas experts proclaimed Floyd King a "crackerjack" showman.

His reign of greatness lasted for a short spell. By 1930, the enterprising King brothers were grappling to keep their precarious assets intact. Business plummeted from two thousand paying customers on the average day to a mere four hundred curious souls. Howard telegrammed Floyd: Gentry Bros. is losing money. Floyd wired back: Better close the show. Floyd, in charge of Cole Bros., had problems of his own. Already the King's debts were nearing the twelve thousand dollar mark. Opening day in Walade, Texas, had grossed $154. The brothers were stymied.

"It took me a lifetime to get those two shows together. I felt the circus was a dead issue. I said, 'to hell with the circus, I want no part of it.' They got me broke quick and fast."

Wanting "no part of it," what did Mr. King then do? He promptly reinstated with the Hagenbeck-Wallace Show in the press department, a job he held before rising to the fortuitous heights of circus owner. Again he was ballyhooing another man's shindig. A sense of confidence returned. Mr. King

began tinkering on the West Coast during winter months as proprietor of a traveling animal conglomerate. Desirous of reasserting his autonomy, he boasted twenty cages filled with squirrels, racoons, badgers, a wolf, and assorted bears. It was a mild diversion for those willing to pay the modest price of admission, a deeply personal satisfaction to the man successfully in charge, and a formidable addition at train stations to his usual collection of trunks and briefcases. Good enough, still, for the customary two dimes into a redcap's hands.

Good enough, also, to convince Floyd King he was again a future tycoon. Our advance man advanced once more to the throne of managerial majesty, throwing his earnings and energy into another bid for distinction—KING BROS. CIRCUS.

". . . THE COLOSSUS OF ALL AMUSEMENTS, THE GREATEST EXHIBITION OF MAMMOTH ENTERTAINMENT OF ANY AGE OR COUNTRY. TRULY THE PEER OF ALL INSTITUTIONS, EVER PROCLAIMED THE YEAR'S BEST HOLIDAY WITH ALL ITS WEALTH OF NEW AND MIGHTY WONDERS GATHERED FROM EVERY PART OF THE WORLD, SETTING A PRECEDENT AND CREATING A NEW ERA IN THE WORLD OF ENTERTAINMENT, WITH ITS COUNTLESS INNOVATIONS."

Fate did not agree.

When King Bros. Circus came to Santa Rosa in 1950, our virtuoso of vitriolic verbosity was in the throes of troubles. The press agentry had been arriving on time, while the circus that followed was a straggling rumor of underpaid performers, mechanically defective trucks and torn banners moving in fragmentary leaps and bounds, none of them all ever showing up at one place at one time.

". . . ACRES UPON ACRES OF WATERPROOF TENTS HOUSING THE COURTS OF HAPPINESS, BRIMING OVER WITH INNOVATIONS AND WONDROUS SURPRISES AND A MYRIAD OF UNPRECEDENTED AMAZING FEATURES FROM ALL STRANGE LANDS. A NEW ERA IN THE CIRCUS WORLD!
700 PEOPLE FROM EVERY COUNTRY ON THE FACE OF THE EARTH.
300 HORSES—THE FINEST AND MOST BEAUTIFUL EQUINE SPECIMENS IN EXISTENCE.

3 VAST CONVOYS OF DOUBLE LENGTH
CARS LOADED WITH WONDERS
20 CAGES OF WILD ANIMALS, AS
COMPLETE AS A FULLY ILLUSTRATED
NATURAL HISTORY.
20 CLOWNS—THE WORLD'S MOST
FAMOUS JESTERS IN CONVULSING
CONVENTION.
5 HERDS OF PERFORMING ELEPHANTS,
INCLUDING AN ENTIRE TROUPE OF BABY
ACTORS.

From a distance the King Bros. big top—the first I
had ever seen—sent tingles through my blood. Up
close, the fantasy was in trouble. In fact, the "Courts
of Happiness" were undergoing some last minute
emergency alterations. We were informed by a
somewhat emaciated voice emerging from an even
more emaciated sound system that the afternoon
performance would be delayed "some." The seats to
the King's pagent were not yet within the city limits
of Santa Rosa.

We waited in the hot sun with mayflies and
mosquitoes. A sideshow barker appealed to the
crowd for their patronage. About an hour passed and
finally we were admitted into the big tent, where
makeshift chairs—borrowed, I surmised, from a
local church—had been arranged in haphazard rows
over the lumpy terrain of grass and weeds. It all
seemed glorious, just being inside at last.

The show finally began. I had a sneaking suspicion
that some of the performers were stranded in
another town. Still, it was enchanting. Was I too
young to know better? I am not sure. . . . Off the end

The King Bros. clowns evoked a few scattered chuckles.
cw.

Floyd King's biggest problem as a show owner: mechanically defective trucks crimped the "Colossus of All Amusements." cw.

King Bros. Circus, 1950. The opening spec was hardly a "marvel of rainbow magnificence." cw.

When all the trucks showed up on time, King Bros. Circus looked like this. cw.

Believing customers crowd Floyd King's red wagon for a ticket to "The Courts of Happiness." CW.

of a springboard some virile acrobats leaped over elephants. High in the air a daring man stood on a swinging trapeze with one foot. Another man juggled flaming torches, some ladies dangled rhythmically from ropes. I recall the magic of childhood—the most precious time to be at a circus—when the people who performed under big tops were special people no matter what they did. I had not seen many circuses then. I was enthralled.

Anyway, how could Mr. King ever live up to his own syntax: ". . . A CONTINUOUS, EVER VARYING, ALWAYS CHANGING KALEIDOSCOPIC MULTIPLICITY OF ALL-STAR ACTS BY ALL-STELLAR ARTISTS, EMBRACING A FLOOD OF FOREIGN TALENT NEVER BEFORE SEEN IN AMERICA, THE GREATEST NUMBER, THE HIGHEST PAID AND THE MOST ASTOUNDING ACTS EVER CENTRALIZED. . . . A MARVEL OF RAINBOW MAGNIFICENCE . . . GORGEOUSLY DECORATED, LAVISHLY DRAPED, GEM STUDDED, MAGNIFICENTLY CARVED AND BURNISHED TO THE GLORIOUS BRILLIANCY OF THE SUN"

Press agents are almost never around when the wonders they allude to are unveiled before human eyes. I suspect the experience is too traumatic. Poor Mr. King, he was right there in the middle of it, though, witnessing in detail another one of his own circuses slowly biting the dust. Whenever he cast himself in the role of chief executive officer, invariably he confused muddy lots for soggy buttercups, could not understand the verities of starving artists and believed with all his heart in the good humor of

his trucks to forge endlessly on with or without water in the generators or drivers at the wheels.

". . . Underlying the pomp and glitter and the odor of sawdust is a system of government and management whose scale and scope are stupendous and staggering. No human institution, we think, is more perfect in operation and direction."

Floyd King was going broke in a stupendous and staggering way. No big thing. He became properly addicted to the tenuous nature of show business at an early age. The crackerjack trouper sprang vigorously to life in Hickman, Kentucky, 1891. That was a time, mind you, when Barnum & Bailey laughed off the ambitiously rising Ringling brothers. A time when circus wars flourished—when Chilly Billy Cole and the Sells brothers fought to convince the public they had the greatest shows. Press agents were perilous. Possibly baby Floyd heard from his crib in the mellow bluegrass country the dissident sounds of clashing calliopes and bludgenous barkers . . .

"All that moving around" began at age one, when the King family relocated at Memphis, Tennessee. Young Floyd was a star pupil, winding up his academic days at Duke University. He landed a job in a small newspaper office. Sitting behind one typewriter at one desk, the cub reporter quickly felt ill at ease. Cherokee Ed's Historical Wild West Show came to town one day. A willing recruit was waiting. King hopped aboard the train and felt a marvelous sense of security and fulfillment on the open road. The illusion lasted for several days.

". . . Everything was moving along nicely with the circus. We'd been on the road a week or ten days and I woke up one morning and I noticed the train wasn't moving. The sun was nice and bright outside. Must have been about seven o'clock. So I got up and dressed, and I walked out of the sleeping car and there's four or five circus people sitting on the side track on the cross ties reading the morning *Herald Advertiser* there in Huntington, West Virginia. And one of them was reading a story, it was about almost a half a column size story and the head of the story read, 'Attachments Big Feature of The Wild West Show.' "

Cherokee Ed's was making history fast. "It wasn't able to move out of town."

During King's brief tenure with the outfit, the seeds of true vocational desire were planted. "On this wild west show, I saw a feller hanging around the front door, nicely dressed and I never saw him

93

do any work of any kind. I asked somebody, 'What the hell does that fellow do?' 'Why,' he says, 'he's the press agent!' "

That suited the jaunty Kentuckian just fine. A couple of years later and King was nicely dressed and hanging around the front door on the Al G. Barnes Circus. The first-of-may learned fast and his natural skills blossomed. The next season he talked his way into a better position with Hagenbeck-Wallace: fifty dollars a week plus expenses. Harvey Wallace, impressed with the teetotaling lad during an interview, put him immediately in charge of his press department. Floyd King, in return for the favor, hesitated not from that moment forward in joining the scheming ranks of compromising literary types and swashbuckling billposters. Every man was out to bolster his boss's image. Rugged advance men did not then report to polite Shrine potentates.

Our fearless trailer blazer saw around him the symptoms of a healthy American circus: billposters spilling blood over coveted display space on innocent barns; Walter L. Main nailing down exclusive rights to the Long Island Railroad, thereby shutting out his biggest rivals; John Ringling conspiring with the Erie in a like manner; Secretive agents delivering to the highest bidder the secretive route of the in-the-chips Sparks Circus.

In trade journals, King could read of sixty billposters saturating Augusta, Georgia, with "Wait For The Big One!" lithographs or such gleeful projections as this one in *Variety* concerning the 1910 season: "Consideration of the fall campaign portends the greatest series of opposition fights dixie ever witnessed. The battle ground of the confederacy will become war scenes between bucket and brush brigades and local billposters and the printing plants will wax financially fat."

Mr. King was primed to prove that he, too, could make life interesting for his cohorts. At the forefront of one of Barnum & Bailey's thorniest competitors, he did not anticipate humbly standing aside while its agents careened forward unchallenged. At any train depot anywhere, the little King could alight with ammunition in the form of contracts, ample complimentary tickets, fly sheets, specifying unprecedented wonders, twenty cent tips, and his own unassailable manners.

Into the *Journal* offices at Sioux City, Iowa stepped the pressman with the sun-kissed smile of a preacher. When you have youth and inexperience on your side, why not exploit them? The apprentice-

ship of Mr. King was marketed for all it was worth.

Suggested the Hagenbeck-Wallace toutmaster to the city editor of the *Journal*, why not conduct a circulation drive and offer your carriers free circus tickets for so many new subscriptions sold? He just happened to have some passes handy. Would fifty suffice? Oh, and by the way, might it be at all within the realm of possibility to obtain, in return, a half page advertisement?

The city editor gazed for a moment at the slight young man before him, meek yet determined. The look of hope and honest ambition moved him.

"Mr. Wallace is back with the show," explained Mr. King, "and we'll be in here a week after the Barnum & Bailey show, and I'd sure like to get a good representation before we get there against Barnum & Bailey."

The king of Kings glanced poignantly into the eyes of the man in Sioux City who could move mountains.

"If you could run that big cut it would tickle the old man to death. It would put me in a very good humor, too."

The editor grinned warmly, did not commit himself, said he would consider. The two gentlemen shook hands; Mr. King departed with his fingers crossed.

Barnum & Bailey's representative Willie Wilkins checked into town the following Saturday. Confidently he strutted the streets, he was ahead of the "Greatest Show on Earth." Then he picked up a copy of the *Journal*. Wilkins' dapper airs took a nose dive.

"He saw a two column cut of his—five inches deep—and here's this big splash of mine," recalled the culprit.

The Barnum & Bailey publicist in a fit of anger nearly flew through the printed page into the offices of the newspaper that Floyd King effectively courted. Nobody at the *Journal* was in. Wilkins stormed down the street, slammed into his hotel room, and picked up the telephone. Throwing caution to the winds, he called the city editor at his home. The message was clear: Wilkins wanted the *Journal* to act in a grown up manner and recognize Barnum & Bailey by reversing the disproportionate allotment of space given to the "other" show.

The editor did not feel inclined to take orders from a press agent, certainly not at his house. He issued some unpublishable words and hung up. King was off to a scandalously good start.

For your foes you wish only rainstorms and

blowdowns, bad crowds and bum notices. And if you can not conspire with providence for help, there are techniques for twisting fate in your favor. Circus men at war with each other are fiendishly imaginative.

"We will pass sunny hours on meadows enameled with violets and daisies and goldened with buttercups and dandelions." Such landscape—call it King Country—may have been there to behold when Hagenbeck-Wallace passed the day at Fort Collins, Colorado. However, all traces of the promised land were missing as Ringling Bros. Circus, scheduled to appear on the same plot of land a day later, rolled in a few hours after its predecessor big top had vanished into the night. During the dark interim hours the vicissitudes of nature transformed King County into a wretched muddy mess. Had a hurricane descended on the lot? The showgrounds were flooded now, and the Ringling red wagons had to be pushed and pulled to their appointed placements by surplus teams of horses. The tents mushroomed up like giant mud puddles.

"When they got the last wagons off the grounds," recalled my hearty host, referring to the Hagenbeck-Wallace wagons, of course, "one of those fellas turned a water plug on and flooded the entrance."

Mr. King, still perched tentatively in his chair, disclaimed all credit for the man-made act of God.

"I didn't stick my head into someone else's department."

Yet, a reflective glint of victory in his reminiscent eyes suggested a deeper sense of shared responsibility. Whoever turned on the great flood, a meadow "goldened with buttercups and dandelions" was nowhere to be found after the circus of Mr. King pulled up stakes. Either the violets and daisies were squashed beyond recognition under the soggy remains or tucked someplace down the road in the briefcase of the unsinkable little advance man.

9
The Garden or Your Circus

STEP this way, folks, to the story of John Ringling, most colorful figure the circus world has ever known. Prepare yourselves for a rare Shakespearean scenario as we say goodbye to the golden age.

Peek momentarily through the doors of a smoke-filled room at Madison Square Garden, where a tense confrontation between "Mr. John" and the great Jerry Muggivan is in progress. The two arch-circus kings are dickering over rights to the coveted Garden, and Mr. Ringling is about to learn one of the great lessons of life. . . .

. . . from his youth up, Johnny seemed destined to inherit the throne of circus power. The youngest of the five Ringling brothers, Johnny clattered infectiously across tabletops in a pair of big wooden shoes, singing "I'm A Dude!" in the 1883 edition of the Ringling Brothers Grand Carnival of Fun. His cocky airs and bold affectations caused a riot. Fame and fortune smiled in the wings.

"Bring back the dude!" roared audiences in every town. The pretentious youngster was a hit. At sixteen years of age, he sported a high opinion of himself, possessed a witty tongue, and was thoroughly irrational. He never lost the winning complex.

By his eighteenth birthday, John mastered the outward appearance of a sophisticated somebody. In any town other than his own he was taken for a dandy. His brothers called him to the sterling position of general agent. Now in the circus business, they needed a man of convincing demeanor to book successfully into new territory. John loved leading the way. In a stetson hat, frock coat, and permanent black mustache, the debonair advance man in his twenty-third year was a fitting prologue to the expanded Ringling Brothers United Monster Railroad Shows, Great Triple Circus, Museum, Menagerie, Roman Hippodrome, and Universal World's Exposition. John was every bit as impressive as the ambitious title with his tall, striking stance and the quick movements of his deep searching eyes.

"In John Ringling," wrote Earl Chapin Man, "I saw youth and a magnetism which made the whole town feel that a circus was coming!"

The girls noticed other beguiling qualities. Being by far the more rakish of the lot, Johnny preferred for good reasons the incognito status of working comfortably out of the puritan reach of his brothers. He was perfecting the manners of a circus magnet and he did not wish to have his personal freedom crimped.

Into and out of hotel rooms slipped the handsome general agent with the free-lancing eyes of a Don Juan. When he was not signing contracts with hay merchants and blacksmiths, John entered into advances of another sort. The big time city slicker from Baraboo, Wisconsin, entertained a common passion. Should a hotel waitress catch his fancy, our

John Ringling, in costume for an annual Sara De Soto celebration, the most colorful figure the circus world has ever known. RM.

restless Romeo succumbed. If the encounter resulted in a viable infatuation, the pursuer adjusted his routing activities so that he might remain, for as many moons as cupid would allow, in close contact to the enchanted nest.

He went north and booked a town, returning to the same hotel that evening. The next day he advanced south, inking another contract. The following day he went west, and then east. Each night he hurried back to his latest flame, located roughly in the center of his work area. The Ringling Circus moved in curious circular patterns around a mysterious center point. Did the brothers ever have reason to question the highly unique booking procedures of their bewitched advance man?

"It's a wonder I didn't break the damn show,"

John confessed to a friend, "going to some of those little hick places so I could get back there to that broad!"

No success came fast enough for John Ringling. He argued vigorously with his older brothers for expansion into other shows. From James A. Bailey in 1904 they acquired half-interest in the Forepaugh-Sells title. By 1906 they were sole owners. The same year Mr. Bailey died. John Ringling bristled over the Barnum & Bailey title. The more conservative Albert and Otto procrastinated, a lesser flamboyant trait which paid off. When the financial crisis of 1907 followed, the boys were able—still largely at John's badgering—to purchase for less than half a million dollars the "Greatest Show on Earth"!

John Ringling maintained a regal posture in front

Young Johnny Ringling in his big wooden shoes, a star of Ringling Bros. Grand Carnival of Fun. RM.

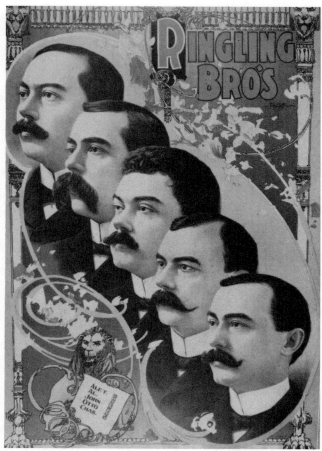

Most powerful circus conglomerate ever—the five Ringling brothers from Baraboo, Wisconsin. John is in center of group. RM.

Charles Ringling, best loved of the brothers, was outdazzled by John's flamboyance when the two survived to share the throne. RM.

of three circuses. He captured the spotlight with the aura of spectacular negotiations and international travels in search of new talent. "The coming head of the circus world" speculated seasoned observers. The assumption was a misleading one; essentially it was a five-man effort that enabled the brothers to outlive, outdazzle, and outzap their competitors. It took far more than the charms of a "dude," and any two brothers would always have been stronger than a single member.

Possibly in order of importance the brothers began passing away: "King" Otto, the financial wizzard, in 1911; Albert, the senior brother, their founding member and guiding spirit beloved by all, in 1916; Alf T., their advertising genius, in 1919.

The house that John built in Sarasota, 1925. The 32 rooms of Ca 'd Zan, outlandishly embellished, cost nearly 20 million dollars, not counting the gardens, walkways, and art museums surrounding the palatial estate. RM.

That split the control evenly (in theory only) between John and Charles. A strange sibling rivalry ensued.

John's kingly eccentricities escalated, and he started acting as if there were only one actual survivor to the throne. He built a palatial estate in Sarasota, erected a stately Naples-styled museum in which he crowded great works of art he had accumulated while touring through Europe. Additionally, Mr. John sank profits into promising real-estate ventures and oil wells. He snatched up short-line railroads like in a game of Monopoly, entertained in his lofty spare moments, with his first wife Mabel, rich and famous eccentrics from the world over—as if he had nothing else better to do.

John grabbed from Charles as much of the limelight as he would relinquish. Naturally, a friction developed. Charlie wanted to make it known that he was also a Ringling, and not yet a dead one.

So he started following the leader. When John built a bank in Sarasota, so did Charlie. When Charlie established a park, so did John. If John could acquire a yacht, Charlie could get a bigger one. John commissioned an army of masons to build him a stately mansion. Guess who laid bricks next door? The two remaining Ringlings altered lavishly the Sarasota landscape with golf courses, Roman archways, fountains, and statues.

Under the big top, their messy in-house feuds continued, although when the brothers collided over policy differences, rarely was it in each other's presence.

Charles adored the swinging ladders. The uppity John protested publically such pretentiousness, and whenever he came on the show ordered Fred Bradna, their equestrian director, to "take those ladders out!"

Once the critic departed—having in the space of

99

several hectic moments asserted his commanding personality—Charles appeared from the wings and uttered the next predictable line: "Where's my ladders?"

Demanded management's softer half," "Put 'em up!"

Dangerous feats were doubly hazardous on rainy days when the tanbark in the rings turned to mud. Because Charles Ringling opted with compassion for the performer's safety, of course John Ringling would not.

"It's a bad ring today. No forward," directed the kindly Charles to their dedicated equestrienne May Wirth. "Don't do anything that'll cause an accident, May. I want you for the rest of the year."

What did John want? Come hell or high water, he wanted "his pound of flesh." Should May please one of the brothers, she was certain to offend the other. Mr. John stormed back to the private dressing top of the Wirth family, having suffered through an abridged display of superb horsemanship, and inquired nervously of the senior Mrs. Wirth, "Why didn't May do a forward somersault tonight?"

Retorted the star's mother, "Would *you* do a forward in there?"

It is not meant as an accusation to suggest that John did not lament for very long the passing of his brother Charles in 1926. The last interference to his authority was removed. Johnny was now a totally free spirit, all decisions were his alone to make. His ideas had all turned to gold; why should his luck not continue? Possessed by a reckless sense of infalibility, John Ringling teetered on the edge of perilous pompousness.

His nose went higher into the air. Unattractive quirks surfaced. He practiced at being inaccessible, his latest social hobby. He stood up loyal circus hands, scheduled appointments he did not intend to honor, scoffed in private at the ordinary individuals waiting in a reception area to see him. No one could question the great and mighty John Ringling. He terminated traditions he did not agree with, flaunted his new autonomy by postponing until late in the year a practice, ordinarily carried out in August, of renewing or allowing to expire performers' contracts. The courtesy had enabled the acts to plan for the following season; now they must wait it out until His Imperial Impudence made up his mind. The man who once cut up in a pair of big wooden shoes was not amusing anybody now.

The smug circus king slept through whatever

"Mr. John," left, *entertains President and Mrs. Calvin Coolidge. Secret service agents look on.* RM.

meetings did not tease his jaded curiosity. One was a conference with officials of Madison Square Garden. They did not look up to the big-top Daddy as a deified being, even though he and his late friend Tex Ricard had built the new arena and for several years held the majority stock. Upon Ricard's death in 1929, the directors seized control and cast a modified attitude towards Mr. Ringling and his circus. Their tenant had never signed a formal contract, and they were anxious to make some changes. Principally, the Garden had been forgoing considerable revenue through the loss of its Friday-night boxing matches to popcorn and lemonade entertainment.

Mr. Ringling was summoned to a second meeting. As fate would have it, he attended. Therein he was invited to ink an agreement that would require him to preempt his circus on Friday nights for boxers and their hysterical fans.

The tenant roared. "*Me* call off the circus for a couple of lousy boxers fighting up there? I helped build this garden! We make as much out of that one night of performing as we make the other six days!"

Rising to his feet for a scathing exit, he threatened

Ringling's arch rival: Jerry Muggivan, head of the American Circus Corporation. CF.

to take his circus elsewhere, even open in New York under canvas. Mr. Ringling was gone.

The landlords did not court their tenant any further. Instead, they gave the green light to the Sells-Floto show, the starring property of a syndicate of circuses supervised by an equally obstreperous circus king, Jerry Muggivan. John Ringling had met his equal. The Garden was in the balance. . .

The aspirations of Jerimiah Joseph Muggivan never phased the Ringling brothers. "Oh, Mr. Muggivan," one of them was reported to have cracked, "he came out of the small wagon show class, and sooner or later he'll go back into that humble occupation." The slight was an issue that Mr. Muggivan never allowed himself to forget. While the Ringling boys chuckled, Jerry turned a "humble occupation" into a sober threat. It's amazing what will spur an ambitious man forward. History at some favorable juncture may accord to the devout Catholic showman due credit for a couple of adroit accomplishments. One was deciding, at an early age, that he someday might own a circus. The other

was deciding, later in life, that one circus was not enough. Mr. Muggivan accumulated show titles with the fervor of a stamp collector working off a Rockefeller grant.

Jerry started in the business selling tickets on the Sands & Astley Circus, circa 1900. There he met another ticket man, Bert Bowers. The chaps formed an invincible friendship that carried them far. Barely able to muster the resources, Muggivan and Bowers invested frugally in a small railroad outfit which they toured as The Great Amburg Shows. Not a single pachyderm graced their inaugural caravan. Sympathetic Cedar Rapids, Iowa citizens, all 700 of them, in a farewell jest the day that Jerry and Bert came to town, placed a tin elephant alongside one of the wagons—as a facetious hint. The boys got the message and progressed far by being in touch with what today is called market research.

In short order there were live elephants, more tumblers and jugglers, aerial nuts, a swelling inventory of rolling stock, tent poles and stakes, water buckets and decomposed roustabouts to tote them. By 1920 the partners boasted ownership of six bona fide show titles (most of them slightly withered): Howe's Great London, Gollmar Bros., Yankee Robinson, Dod Fisk, John Robinson, and Sells-Floto. The title scouts were running out of names, so the next one they added was that of a new partner, Edward Ballard. Little did Jerry suspect the balance of power would ultimately shift against him. The triumvirate incorporated into a game plan called the American Circus Corporation. The corporate title was far from wishful thinking. The three industrious

A Sells-Floto toast to the new season. General manager Zack Terrell, left, *shakes hands with Chicago Coliseum officials.* CW.

101

The American Circus Corporation at its height owned 11 shows. Sells-Floto Circus was the group's prize property. CW.

Madison Square Garden, the showplace of circus kings coveted by Jerry Muggivan. RM.

producers had in mind—on most days—the eventual domination of the entire American circus field. I said on most days.

While John and Charles Ringling fought over swinging ladders and yachts, Messrs. Muggivan, Bowers, and Ballard vacillated between the urge for total conquest and a lesser, more cowardly desire to sell off their holdings, take the money and run. In 1922, then operating five shows, the syndicate boys made an offer to buy the circus with swinging ladders and May Wirth. They were listened to at length by Charles Ringling and politely turned down. (The dominant Ringling, John, was lost somewhere in a French art gallery.) So the American Circus Corporation reversed its outward strategy. If its directors could not buy the Ringlings out, let the Ringlings buy them out. In 1928 they cajoled Mr. John into taking out an option on a possible purchase of their properties. At first, he did not take the matter seriously.

The "Big One" (Ringling-Barnum), circa 1930, center of John Ringling's circus empire. RM.

None of the principals involved seemed committed to a set path. A greater need to resolve years of rivalry and declare someone the winner prevailed. It was inevitable that sometime, somewhere John Ringling and Jerry Muggivan would come to blows in an executive showdown. The decisive moment approached when Muggivan landed the Madison Square Garden contract. The testy transaction set into motion a grizzly battle of wills centered around the survival of John Ringling's ego.

"I've got the contract," purred the triumphal Mr. Muggivan. "I've got the Garden."

Mr. John was shocked out of his normal preoccupation with Rembrant originals. Well had he reason to be. "If you didn't show the Garden you were a dead duck," as Floyd King put it. "That would be building Sells-Floto up tremendously."

John was a dazed and seemingly defeated man, vulnerable now to any number of intriguing plots. Telegrams ricocheted between the Garden's new occupants and the evicted impresario. A conference was proposed and Mr. Ringling set his alarm clock. All parties arrived on time. John Ringling's gallant airs were not in evidence. Only did the gravity of the situation reveal itself on his taut, worried face. The participants gathered like back room moguls over a table of shifting fortunes. The smoke of nervously held cigars spun around them. Two rival circus monarchs faced each other head on. They had reached an impasse. Each had his eyes on the spangled throne; neither was willing to share it. One must give way.

Somebody calmly proposed the only way to settle the tiff would be for one of the parties to buy out the other. John Ringling knew it was either the Garden or their circus. Suddenly the option he held seemed like a possible ace in the hole. Moreover, John's autonomy gave him an edge over Muggivan, who must share his decisions with two equal associates.

"How much do you want for it?" queried John.

Into their last official huddle went officials of the American Circus Corporation.

"Two million."

"Sold," said the haggard monarch.

On 6 September 1929, John Ringling amassed the largest conglomeration of sequined paraphernalia ever held by one man—11 shows, 275 proven railroad cars, hundreds of tents. There were six thousand employees he could stand up, fire and rehire as the spirit moved him, including for $10,000 a week Tom Mix. The inheritor of this vast frivolity loomed over it all with blasé confidence. "My kittens," he called his new shows. For the privilege of keeping the prestigious Garden contract intact (and on his own terms, without boxing matches), John Ringling laid down $450,000 in cash and signed two notes totaling $1,550,000. That was not all he paid.

Jerry Muggivan was the loser, a defeated man overruled by his partners. Muggivan reported to the meeting fully intent on buying the only title that he could never have. Instead, Ballard and Bowers, weary of trouping and eager to end the exhausting conflict, outvoted Jerry and accepted Ringling's offer. They knew best. Jerry, soon afterward, announced plans to return to the field with a new set of show titles. He was moving forward like a reborn man on the trail of a brand new career. A few months after the historic sale, a double hernia sent Jerry into a Detroit hospital. A day following an operation, blood clots formed and on 22 January 1930, Jerimiah Joseph Muggivan died. Eulogized *Variety*, "There has been no greater figure in the outdoor world."

John Ringling's demise was slower. In the face of the great depression, his luck turned. Surrounded by an estate valued at over $23 million—a mere fraction of which he refused to liquidate—Mr. John had scarce funds to support his epic life-style. He remained unaffected. Under his wings, his "kittens" all slipped uniformly into the red. Charles Sparks Circus registered its first losing season ever.

In January 1932, the circus king par excellence suffered a coronary stroke. The summer following he carelessly defaulted an interest payment on the circus notes. One or two of his paintings would easily have produced the funds necessary to stave off the creditors. Would he part with a couple of masterpieces?

"I only *buy* paintings. I don't sell them!"

While the budding comic tragedian recouped from his illness in the Half Moon Hotel at Coney Island, his old friend, the hotel owner Samuel Gumpertz, was off in New York mutinizing the sagging Ringling ship. The "Gump" had supplied the circus over the years with numerous freaks, and he was turning into the most curious of them all. Slyly the traitor gained the backing of Edith and Audrey Ringling, widows, respectively, of Alf T. and Charles. Together the ladies held sixty percent of the circus stock and they had little endearing affection for their autocratic brother-in-law, John Ringling, especially in the wake of his recent excesses. The Gump arranged with a group of New York businessmen to buy up the outstanding notes,

Sam Gumpertz, for whom friendship became less important than the lure of circus power. CW.

104

In the end, John Ringling was brought down by his own reckless arrogance. RM.

and through a complicated series of contractual maneuvers he was able to connive his way into the manager's seat.

The ailing Mr. John was retained in a figurehead status only, losing virtual control of everything but his own disgruntled house servants, who bickered with him daily over back wages, and the constant attention of Internal Revenue agents building up a case against the circus for massive tax frauds.

Nor were Mr. John's troubles lightened any by his ill-advised second marriage to Emily Haag, a woman at the outset of some means. Whether Mr. Ringling when he met her was in search of a new wife or supplementary petty cash is debatable. On the day of their nuptials, the veteran "dude" exacted from his bride-to-be a loan in the amount of $50,000 shortly before saying "I do."

Emily, in John's eyes, was a pitiful replacement for his first wife, Mable. Emily hated the circus, and she entertained guests in a flightly manner, bobbing about the room vivaciously like a fickle fly. John once insulted her royally in the presence of company. "For God's sake, Emily, light somewhere!" The intimidated spouse threatened legal action against back payments owed her for the wedding day loan. John countered with a bid for divorce. Amicably, both partners dropped their respective charges and resumed, not by moonlight shores, their mutually infuriating union. Its duration was brief.

The deposed circus king added to a swelled head a colorful stiff neck and puttered on oblivious to reality, refusing to act like anything but the mythical giant he portrayed so well. Mr. Ringling made unobtrusive appearances at the circus, quietly posing as its aloof Lord. He spoke with foreign performers about future contracts. Sam Gumpertz took offense. The new chief operating officer dispatched a caustic telegram to his old "friend" warning him to keep his nose out of the circus or the new directors would throw him out altogether. The blow was devastating.

Crippled and disheartened, the last of the Ringling brothers could not believe what had happened. His brothers had all died at the height of their usefulness to the circus. John was stranded on the sidelines, powerless and ignored.

Onto the balcony of a small hotel in Pensacola, Florida, Henry Ringling North wheeled his aging Uncle John. Cole Bros. Circus had come to town, and a parade of spangled acrobats and gilded wagons would soon be streaming down Main Street. Eagerly the old circus man waited for the first strains of the calliope, waited for a glimpse of eternal magic. Did he feel as he had in his childhood when with his four brothers—Albert, Otto, Alf T. and Charles—he stood anxiously on the misty riverbanks of McGregor, Iowa, anticipating the arrival of Dan Rice's Great Floating Paris Pavilion Circus?

Without his brothers now, John Ringling was very much alone. Tears streaked down his confused face as the parade passed by. It never returned.

10
The Curse of Blacaman

OUR next exhibit, a strange tale of animal hypnotism—Blacaman versus Howard Barry on the Hagenbeck-Wallace show, farewell tour of 1938, considered the worst season in circus history.

Bushy-haired and mystic-eyed, Blacaman's face formed a foreboding portrait of the occult and beyond. On a southern California street you might take him for a struggling junkie or for an assassin waiting for the next presidential motorcade to pass in review. In the hands of circus illustrators, Blacaman became a true demonic threat: a disquieting figure

Crowds rally to one of Hagenbeck-Wallace's last unloadings. The tale of its 1938 tour portended the ultimate demise of major American big tops. CW.

with the afro hair spread of a Harlem pimp, torturous pupils piercing the grizzly resistance of a lashing lion, sharp white rays denoting rare mental faculties—ten fingers extending downwards from a chin of dark wisdom with cunning precision.

From Mexico he surfaced, he and a horde of crocodiles and lions. No, Blacaman did not coerce them through flaming hoops of fire with a whip and a chair. He hypnotized each by his seemingly supernatural powers. It was an act that had greatly impressed Howard Barry, the ambitious new operator of Hagenbeck-Wallace Circus. In Blacaman, Barry saw a great box-office draw. Not realizing that mystics who keep company with crocodiles are subject to fits, Barry signed the trainer to a contract he lived to regret.

The Mexican "Hindu Animal Hypnotist" arrived at circus winterquarters on a cold February morning in Peru, Indiana. At the outset, he shook Barry's hand cordially and acted civilized. A baggage car filled with Blacaman's charges followed. This being the Frank Buck inspired "Bring 'Em Back Alive!" era, Barry and his staff planned to exploit the new act to the hilt. Already, Blacaman's image was everywhere to behold—on fresh lithographs; streaked brazenly across the advance advertising railroad cars; and on the sides of the ticket wagon:

Grand Stand Seats
First Time in America
BLACAMAN

The "Hindu" animal hypnotist was seen as a top box-office draw. Eventually, Blacaman cast a "spell" over the entire show. CW.

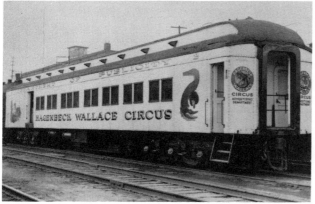

Blacaman's demonic image got prime treatment in circus advertising. CW.

Hindu Animal Hypnotist

Facing Death!

With Jungle Lions and River Nile Man Eating Crockodiles

Unprotected—Bare-Handed

The ticket wagon did not advertise the unforseen twist of events that lay ahead to plague the circus. Barry had in mind the successful operation of his show over a depressed American landscape. If he could cut the nut and show a little profit, fine. The young manager had the previous year acquired control of the Hagenbeck-Wallace title. Before that he was a world-wide scout of strange features for circuses, as well as a press agent of some note. Show ownership now preoccupied the determined trouper; during Barry's first season at the helm he developed the reputation of a "mad man." Partly, it was his inability to direct employees diplomatically. Partly, it was the frustration of the times that any showman felt—a depressed economy and drastic new shifts in entertainment tastes away from big tops. A clever invention known as television was now being enjoyed in the homes of a few rich families. Movie houses were drawing long lines of satisfied customers.

Barry dispensed his advance department loaded down with photos and stories of the great Blacaman, sensation of the center ring. Weeks before the show's official opening, members of the press were treated to a special private performance wherein the animal hypnotist threw into a trance not only a cage filled with assorted creatures but an audience of awed newspaper people. Poodles Hanneford did not that season receive anywhere near equal attention. Hanneford could not cast a spell over a moth; he was only the country's leading equestrian comic.

The Hagenbeck-Wallace wagons embarked on one of the strangest seasons ever in Indianapolis, Indiana on 16 April. Opening-day crowds hushed the moment Blacaman entered atop an elephant. A dozen female attendants, costumed like disposable outer-space stewardesses on a disco flight, adorned

107

the man who was to face death "bare-handed." Blacaman rode in on a howdah, frilled in white billowing garb, his heavy chin resting soberly on one wrist as if he were deep into meditation.

Suddenly, down a ladder off the sanctified pachyderm he alighted. Curiously animated, he gazed tentatively over all three rings while his exotic assistants lugged onto tables cranky crocs and liberated into the caged arena wild lions. Blacaman flashed his eyes through a series of warm-up moves. Howard Barry stood by the performers' entrance, mesmerized. The audience sat motionless.

The pock-faced sorcerer scampered from one subject to the next like a magician on the run. He stared into the eyes of a seething crocodile. The reptile yawned dizzily then froze, its dentures exposed in a rare holding pattern. Blacaman stalked another crocodile, glancing at him menacingly. The creature was stilled. Barry chuckled with obvious delight, convinced the act would attract huge crowds.

Blacaman transferred his penetrations to the center ring for the ultimate showdown: the hypnotist pitted against jungle-bred lions. He provoked the brutes into chaotic movements. Then he turned on his clairvoyant powers and reduced them to a heap of rag dolls. Surrendering precisely on cue, the tough guys lay absolutely quiet while their master kicked and caressed and tossed them about by their limp, submissive tails. The audience loved it.

By the commanding snap of his right finger, Blacaman returned the beasts to the innocent state of nature. The charismatic crocodile charmer basked in wild applause and exited.

Barry viewed the opening day as a good omen. He was too optimistic to estimate soberly the odds against trouping in 1938. There were the crippling spells that Blacaman might cast over anything that stood in his path, including if necessary the circus itself. And there was another potentially constricting force that was preparing to stalk the edge of Hagenbeck-Wallace lots. That force was Robert Whitehead, a disruptive union organizer who had been curtailing the profit factor of circuses with an army of pickets. Whitehead had instilled common workers with an unprecedented desire for decent salaries. Around every major show he and his lackeys hovered, committed to the consolidation of shiftless come-and-go canvasmen into the formidable ranks of the *American Federation of Actors*.

It did not matter to Whitehead that Shakespeare was rarely performed under the big top, nor that most circuses were melodramatic only in the sense of approaching bankruptcy. In 1937, the arch unionist cornered Sam Gumpertz, general manager of the Ringling show (alias friend of John Ringling), into signing an agreement that doubled the wages of the workingman.

What had stake drivers and water boys in common with Broadway huffers? Above and beyond dragging canvas across muddy lots and sleeping beneath shady wagons on rickety flat cars, these drifters lended occasional support to the circus specs. Robbins Bros. once fitted a group of black canvasmen in hula skirts and had them parade around the track in a Mother Goose pageant. Gumpertz, in a frugal mood on the Ringling show, created an enormous dragon for the grand-opening parade by draping a hundred feet of painted dragon material over a line of subjugated roustabouts. Tote that plume! Lift that feather!

Gumpertz was extremely civil to Whitehead's demands. That hospitality proved fatal for American tent shows. For the first time ever, all the hoopla and the hundreds of men who for years had pushed it down the road for three meals a day and a flophouse on wheels became very, very expensive.

The paths of Whitehead and Blacaman were about to cross-polinate.

Hagenbeck-Wallace pursued a sorry rendezvous with the misfortunes most shows were facing that year. A recession in the late 1930s left Americans with little money to spend on amusements. Healthy crowds congregated at the switch yards to watch the arrival of Howard Barry's thirty-car train, gaily decorated in orange and lettered in silver and blue scroll. The unloading was a grand free event.

Hagenbeck-Wallace elephants parade onto another precarious lot. CW.

The depression brought out crowds to view the circus set-up. CW.

The side show ballyhoo, another free event, drew large crowds. CW.

Thousands of well-wishers stood by as the big tents went up, waved at the elephants being paraded to their appointed positions on the grounds. Then, as the barkers on the midway concluded their afternoon ticket spiels, everybody went home. The free show had ended.

More often than not, two shows were presented before nine thousand generally unoccupied chairs. It being the nature of a true showman to exhaust his options before throwing in the towel, Barry trudged forward through the worst season in circus history with a fierce, almost psychotic determination to hang on. His profits from the 1937 season were slowly being swallowed up in a large number of hapless stands through Pennsylvania, Maryland, and Illinois. Yet Barry remained certain that if he could pilot the show to California, there would be crowds at the ticket wagon clamoring to see a feature so bizarre and trendy as Blacaman. He was banking on salvation at a well-known circus lot in Los Angeles located at Hill and Washington Streets.

At the start, Blacaman responded constructively to some critics who cited him for lack of showmanship—if that was possible—by adding to his collection of subjects chickens and rabbits. However, the Hindu Hypnotist from Mexico resented conducting his art in a vast, empty tent and he was not prepared mentally to accept less than the full wages he had contracted for. As the days grew longer, he began skipping certain shows. One Friday payday was called off. Blacaman exploded. Drawing a deep breath and cursing his unsavory plight with what appeared to be a doomed enterprise, sagacious troupers claim he started a jinx from which the circus was never fully able to recover.

Meanwhile, Robert Whitehead was intensifying his own destructive spells. His wrecking crews enveloped Barry's tents like a flock of hungry ravens. Pickets went up in ominous formations at Allegheny, Pennsylvania on May 7.

HAGENBECK-WALLACE UNFAIR TO THE AMERICAN FEDERATION OF ACTORS!

"What the hell do those sons of bitches want with my canvasmen?" shouted Barry. "People want jobs. They don't want to lose them!"

Showmen praised Barry for his forceful stand. A local court of appeals judge extended support, shutting Whitehead out of Pennsylvania completely. At the state border the professional mob waited to resume their harassment. Thus, Barry was freed for the next few days to deal with internal problems. There was a blowdown on 12 May, and Blacaman around this time started performing only when the spirit moved him. How to handle an intermittent hypnotist became the paramount subject of Barry's staff conferences. The producer was trapped in a paradox: which would hurt him the most—letting Blacaman go and losing a box office gimmick, or suffering the consequences of trying to retain him? Barry decided he needed Blacaman, even with his sporadic temper tantrums.

The show slipped out of Pennsylvania, and the union protesters went back to work. Naturally, two weeks later the circus train miraculously escaped going up in flames when a nearby boxcar was set ablaze, allegedly by one of Whitehead's men. Given

The privileged few—those who could afford it—stayed on to buy tickets for a visit to the menagerie and a seat at the actual circus performance. cw.

Trouping with a winner: spirited performers on the Al G. Barnes and Sells-Floto Circus, one of the few shows to survive the 1938 season. In mid-tour Al G. Barnes was augmented with acts from the Ringling show, which closed early in Scranton, Pennsylvania, following a labor dispute. cw.

the daily ordeals that Howard W. Barry faced—bum houses, mounting debts, the unpredictable behavior of Blacaman, numerous trips to courts of appeal (he went into and out of receivership four times in three weeks)—most other managers would have ordered the show back to the barns in a hurry. Circuses were falling like mayflies in a September blizzard. Tim McCoy launched a modern thirty-car wild west extravaganza and saw it fall to pieces abruptly in Washington, D. C. on 2 May. Downie Bros. (fronted by the redoubtable Charlie Sparks, a

man who had never failed before) called it quits on 31 May. Sells-Sterling and a host of other shows followed the same early demise. Ringling Bros. and Barnum & Bailey ceased operations in Scranton, Pennsylvania on 12 June. The biggest of circuses was unable to effect a necessary twenty-five percent pay cut among its newly unionized work force representing the American Federation of Actors. Ringling sent its best acts to join the nonunion Al G. Barnes Circus on the West Coast.

Howard Barry's ghost train moved relentlessly forward, closer each day to California. The company saw big crowds form in Des Moines, Iowa on the Fourth of July. Its hopes soared. By now most of Whitehead's shills had given up. Unfortunately, Blacaman had not. The "Hindu Fakir" was fighting for his own right to be paid. His brooding spirit infected the show, old-timers argue. Even one of the elephants, Mable, became militant. Mable turned on her handler, forcing him fatally against a railroad car on Independence Day. This pushed Barry to the breaking point. Up to now he had demonstrated admirable calm and control in contrast to his own outbursts of temper during the previous tour. He could not restrain himself indefinitely.

The boss summoned his performers to a special meeting. He reaffirmed his pledge for a full season and offered to honor a committee appointed by the performers to oversee all financial expenditures. The magnanimous proposal was gratefully declined. The artists were satisfied with an excellent cookhouse and adequate sleeping quarters on the train. That constituted, they believed, ample remuneration during current hard times.

Poodles Hanneford wired the *Billboard:* "There is no strike here. Performers and workingmen all satisfied. We are all very happy trouping under very fine treatment and looking forward to a long and successful season."

Blacaman did not. He snubbed the harmonious conflab between Barry and performers and refused suddenly to appear at Des Moines. Tempers flared in the heat of a sad Fourth of July. Barry's big top was jam packed with anxious celebrants. They must not be disappointed. How many of them had come in good faith to see the animal hypnotist? Backed by the overwhelming mandate from his company, Barry flew into a rage of his own. Blacaman got a bitter taste of another man's fury.

"You get in that tent and work those damn crocodiles, or I'll chop all that goddamned hair off your head, you son of a bitch! You won't have that beard, either, when I get done with you, mad man! Damnit, get in that tent!"

Blacaman was dumbfounded. He fled for his car, bolted off the lot in a blaze of dust, and roared uptown to the police station. His hands were sweaty and his face shook with the fear of emasculation. He ranted and raved to a local judge, combining his powers of persuasion with the bellyache of an abused child. Blacaman swore out a warrant against Barry for threatening to inflict upon him an unsolicited haircut.

Demanding $2,000 in back wages, the mad Mexican secured an attachment against the show's lighting system and ticket wagon. He declared a desire to be released from this transcontinental ordeal. And he sought, as well, the release of his pets from the show-owned cage wagon that carried them.

For Howard Barry, Des Moines was but another dreary day. Shortly after midnight, he and Blacaman and their respective attorneys emerged from court in pragmatic agreement. The circus posted a $2,000 bond guaranteeing the Hindu Fakir a positive judgment in his pending back-wages suit. The attachment to the lights and ticket wagon was lifted. The show moved temporarily out of darkness.

Four days later, at Lincoln, Nebraska, Blacaman still had not resumed work. The crocs lay untranced, and the lions reclined lazily in cage wagon number 25. Their master, still haunted by his hair-raising encounter with the boss, sat morosely in his private auto on the edge of the lot. Barry spent that morning in a federal court authoring a countersuit against the bearded guru, seeking $62,540 in damages for repeated refusals to perform and for discrediting the Hagenbeck-Wallace name.

"People come out to see Blacaman. Where is he? Off somewhere sulking," exclaimed Barry. "I've sunk thousands of dollars to advertise this man. We've based our success on him. And we never know when he'll perform! People come out of the tent and ask us, 'Where was Blacaman?' What are we to tell them? They take me for a con artist and a liar. How will I ever bring the circus back to these towns? Nothing like this, your honor, has ever happened to me!"

Rather than face a judgment against him, Blacaman started performing again. A couple of days later he went back on strike. In Kearny, he threatened to free his animals from their cages unless Barry forked over a substantial sum of money. The morbid

Hagenbeck-Wallace billposters with a litho for a stand the show would never reach. CW.

ultimatum threw the town into an uproar. A few brave citizens dared visit the circus grounds. Most of the town's population enjoyed behind closed doors the frightening episode.

Thirty plasters went on the show for back salaries. Several performers tried throwing the show into receivership. Barry thwarted every legal obstacle with heroic stamina, filling out affidavits, filing countersuits, genuflecting to the appropriate authorities. In Topeka, Kansas, a canvasman complained to a district judge of being brutally attacked by a circus official when he approached him for seven weeks back pay. The show left Topeka three hours late, escorted by two deputy sheriffs.

Barry allowed his disgruntled acts to walk. The performance deteriorated to a one-ring presentation. Blacaman astonished everyone by appearing for several weeks with regularity. This was followed by another lapse into temper fits and no-shows. To

111

The circus train—its doomed status symbolized by Blacaman's foreboding image—rattles in to Long Beach. cw.

Californians greet the shaky enterprise with ominous curiosity. cw.

the *Billboard,* he wired a telling lament:

". . . Tired of the North America and the hour can not come to soon for me to leave."

Hagenbeck-Wallace reached California on 24 August. Salvation did not loom at the golden gate. In Glendale, a young boy was ravaged by a lion in the menagerie tent. At the Los Angeles stand, wire walker Phil Esclante fell to the ground and suffered severe injuries. A roustabout was struck by an automobile in Hollywood, succumbing shortly afterwards. During a matinee performance in the movie capital, an aerialist plunged from a swinging ladder to the lap of a twelve-year-old girl. At the same show another wire walker, Bill Crowson, lost his balance and fell to the sawdust twenty-five feet below.

Where were the Whitehead pickets? They had long given up their vigil, convinced the circus needed only Blacaman to destroy itself. The jinx troupers claim he began plagued the show through its final engagements in southern California.

The great mesmerizer of wild animals classified himself "ill" during the early dates, including the extremely crucial premiere showing in downtown Los Angeles on the Washington and Hill street lot. The patrons who flocked to see Blacaman were left to wonder if they had been hoodwinked. A sour word-of-mouth quickly dubbed the Hindu Hypnotist a fraud. Patronage dropped. Although Blacaman showed up for most of the following shows, it was far too late. For a circus not to deliver at each and every performance on a feature attraction so aggressively billed, it is box-office suicide.

I find it difficult to slight Howard Barry, a man who clung to the last threads of hope that things would come together somewhere down the road; that the great days he had known were not gone forever; that long ticket lines, packed houses, and green bills strewn in piles over the floor of a red wagon besieged with customers were yet within reach.

The resilient young operator coaxed his fading caravan to its last stand with undefiled faith. On 20 September 1938 at Riverside, California, residents stood by in somber fascination while the thirty tarnished cars of Hagenbeck-Wallace jerked slowly from side to side down the tracks. They gazed with uncertain wonderment upon a ticket wagon which bore in ornate lettering the words:

Grand Stand Seats

First Time in America

BLACAMAN

An air of dark finality hung over the train. It had come a long way, from Indianapolis and Peru? No, from all the warm summers before, from the cities of another age when Main Streets hummed to the clattering rhythms of horses and calliopes and bright, brassy bands, when young boys believed with all their hearts in big tops . . . it had come from a day in the vanishing past when you could not say "no". . . .

. . . The circus had reached the final stop of its final tour. Eight major circuses closed early that season; only two of those would ever again return to the road. Gone forever from the tanbark trail were the names of Sells-Floto, Tom Mix, Robbins Bros.,

After a sudden closing in Riverside, California, the cookhouse was kept in operation to retain workingmen while Barry scrambled to finance a second tour. CW.

The final zinger: Riverside sheriff attaches the big top, attended by tentmakers Baker and Lockwood. CW.

Roustabouts crowd the pie car for their last stipends. CW.

Sells-Sterling, Gentry Bros., and Hagenbeck-Wallace.

Everybody loves a circus until it can't pay its way. Baker and Lockwood, the tent makers, repossessed the canvas. Ringling Bros. and Barnum & Bailey, from whom the train and rolling stock were leased, ordered them returned to the Baldwin Park winter quarters of Al G. Barnes. A few hundred workingmen held fast to Barry's expressed hopes of reopening on a smaller scale and touring eastward. To accommodate these loyal hands, the cook house stayed in operation for a couple of weeks. But on 8 October, Baker and Lockwood repossessed that, too. Blacaman took possession of his animals and sent them to the Goebel Lion Farm. Cage number 25 was empty. Show officials realized too late it was not the crocodiles or lions they should have kept behind bars.

The First-Time-In-America animal hypnotist walked off the lot with his beard intact, his pockets drained, and his faith in the great American circus badly shaken. No doubt he departed with a surplus of small ammonia tablets—the key to his "magic." For when rubbed between his fingers, they broke up into vapors and subdued the animals quite satisfactorily.

The hindu fakir did not learn the true meaning of showmanship as once practiced in this country under gaudy, freewheeling big tops. Nor did he ever return to reexamine his doubts. It was Blacaman's *last* time in America.

11
Le Sacre Du North

GEORGE Balanchine, ballet master, was on the telephone chatting with Igor Stravinski, a well-known composer.

"Igor, would you like to write a little ballet for some elephants?"

A pause at the other end.

"How old?" queried the austere musician.

"They are young elephants, Igor," assured the dance man.

"Well, if they are young elephants," answered Stravinski, "perhaps so."

Thus, one of the boldest spectacles ever conceived for the big top, "Ballet of the Elephants" was born. The culprit behind this creative madness was John Ringling North, a man who believes a circus should be crafted by the finest artisans available. North visualized a "choreographic tour de force" to feature his most reliable pachyderm, Modoc. He wanted her tutored by an internationally recognized ballet master and he desired a vigorous original score commensurate with the indestructible dynamics of thirty mammoths on the move in vinyl-reinforced tutus. The wild strains of a Stravinski original seemed just right.

North was delighted when George and Igor agreed to work on the ballet. Being the sort of chap who comes around every other century to turn all known traditions upside down, North relished the thought of having two eccentric artists on his, if not exactly on Modoc's, side. He loved dazzling circus goers with innovations so bizarre and beguiling they could not leave his shows simply entertained.

John Ringling North has shown us how limitless are the artistic possibilities of an open big top. He is probably the greatest creative showman the American circus has ever known. To have seen a circus produced by him was to have been enchanted and challenged in the same breath.

With his brother Henry ("Buddy"), John kept the teapots whistling and a bartender hopping around the clock with ice at Ca d'Zan, the mansion built by his late uncle, John Ringling. Deep into the night, distinguished New York artists gathered in suave merriment on a lush carpet over costume sketches, scenarios, lead sheets—diagrams specifying North's latest version of paradise in three rings. A puckish grin on his face, the avant garde producer chaired the proceedings with kingly delight, dividing liberally his interest between his staff's exquisite brainstorms and a bottle of Taittinger. A new circus produced by John Ringling North was in the works. Have another drink, world. . . .

After gaining control of the circus in 1937, Mr. North promptly initiated a program of vast modernization. He joined forces, in 1941, with Norman Bel Geddes, who redesigned the tents in rich blue and red hues and decorated the midway in modern decor. Geddes engineered a futuristic sus-

Strangest collaboration ever—elephant man Walter Mc-Clain, left, with dance master George Balanchine, at work on a ballet for elephants. RM.

John Ringling North, artistically courageous above all others. RM.

pension pole big top (intended to eliminate all of the interior poles). In prospectus form, the giant triangular structure looked like Atlantis being pulled out of the ocean by a thousand cables. The actual date it would be implemented was not specified.

A young Broadway designer of future fame, Miles White, was appointed by Geddes to sketch his costume ideas. White suggested John Murray Anderson might be the ideal director to implement North's lavish production concepts. Anderson, once hired, got in swift communication with Balanchine who, in turn, rang up Stravinski. The elephants were never consulted.

Only was Stanislavsky missing from the fold (a gross oversight). Already on the payroll were a gorilla named Gargantua and a celebrated aerial director named Barbette. Peter Arno, New York

North engaged Norman Bel Geddes to restyle the circus midway and big top. CW.

Geddes designed this suspension-pole tent (for the exhibition of Gargantua) as the prototype for a big top of the future. CW.

cartoonist, joined the conclave with a portfolio of satiric illustrations for the new program magazine. Sarasota for a spell replaced Gotham as the capital of revolutionary art. On what other forum could all these precocious adults disregard Aristotelian principles of form without recrimination?

They decided that "gaiety" would theme the 1942 edition. A wise decision that was, considering that to handle the ballet of elephants in more serious tones might constitute artistic suicide. Arno held up his cover design for the program—a whimsical sketch of two flirtatious pachyderms, the suitor clad in a scant tutu with one arm shyly touching the waist of his demure sweetheart, she in a longer Victorian gown.

A chorus of chuckles signified approval.

Another Arno cartoon portrayed a graceless flyer clinging inelegantly to a trapeze bar, his female partner frantically clutching his bony ankles. The circle roared with delight.

Reportedly, Barbette was the only "serious" person present. Lost in the throes of a new aerial ballet, he found the thought of elephants in tutus far less funny than the vision of his aerialovelies going near them in toe shoes. Casting himself in the role of a martyr—which he played very well—Barbette cursed this unsavory undertaking against which he must compete. Under contract he had promised to have fifty girls on web by opening night. Now, he was biting his lips and declaring dramatically, "and that's what I'm going to deliver!"

In a corner, Henry North mulled dutifully over dozens of small wood blocks layed across a table, each one representing a wagon or flat car, train-loading strategy stuff. In context, the exercise seemed terribly dull, although someone must tend to details. Afterall, this fantastic undertaking would soon be thrust on the open road.

Johnny North suggested a clown wedding to solemnize the union of Mr. and Mrs. Gargantua The Great.

"Brilliant idea, Johnny!"

Composer Henry Sullivan provided memorable melodies for several editions of the circus. RM.

116

"Give it to the producing clown," said Murray Anderson, diverting John's attention to another matter. A musician was seated at a piano and it was time to hear Stravinski's "Circus Polka" composed for the elephant ballet. The buoyant circle subsided to a hush. Intently and obediently, they listened to the rush of dissonant harmonies emanating ruthlessly from an overworked Baldwin. A string quartet by Schonberg would have elicited greater response. Fortunately, the composer was not present.

Murray Anderson spoke of the daring tonal qualities of the piece.

"Oh well," offered a simpler mind, "it'll make us a load of publicity."

"It will, indeed," added North, who wisely declared the meeting adjourned. He did not want the group to linger over Stravinski's obstinate contribution. The bohemian big-top tycoon desired a sniff of fresh air before retiring. Gallantly he trotted away on a horse to another make-believe world.

There were more appointments to grace: North might chat on the telephone with the deposed King Farouk of Egypt and arrange to forward him a cartload of American cigars or autograph invitations for a party to be given in Manhattan toasting a new Vanderbuilt. He might fly off into the night, like a restless big top, for tea with Ernest Hemingway or an alternate literary chum, or simply go to the John Ringling Hotel in Sarasota and jam with the boys in the Mlle. Toto Room. North loved playing his saxophone, the instrument upon which he composed many melodies for the circus production numbers.

His wind exhausted, Johnny might then roam the moonlit streets in search of a beautiful damsel waiting to be discovered by the bon vivant of the big tops. When he chanced upon her, quickly he conceived in his mind a great pageant in which to feature her—be it Alice in the center ring or Dorothy down a yellow sawdust road. Rarely did these lyrical offers materialize. Most of the "discovered" Alices and Dorothys, after reporting for stardom at circus headquarters, were routed routinely into the clutches of Barbette, there to be immortalized as "Aerialovelies." Or they could remain mortal, return to a different street corner, and hope to be rediscovered.

At dawn, the circus king retired to his private railroad car, the "Jomar," requesting not to be disturbed during the "night." Around nine hours later, he rose fully refreshed, about 5 P.M., to continue his collaborations with Proustian society, twelve tone composers, and photogenic gorillas.

"He has the charm of the world," says Miles White, the man who designed North's greatest shows. "I adored him. I still do. He is one of the most enchanted men I've ever known . . . his whole makeup, a great flair for theatrical pizzazz in everything he did. It was calculated to be in the grand manner of the great impresario.

"He wanted the most beautiful, the most terrific and extraordinary show that he could produce. In a Sarasota hotel room he locked me until I had sketches for the acts. (I talked him into coordinating all the acts' colors; the performers wore their own costumes before then.) I met with Johnny at the bar and he looked over every sketch. We went to Paris two seasons, for more feathers and more sequins."

Circus press agents did not have to exaggerate in touting North's dazzling costume effects. They needed only to quote such experts as fashion author Rubye Graham:

"If spangles are missing from Milady's wardrobe this year, it's for an obvious reason once you've seen the 1953 version of Ringling Bros. and Barnum & Bailey Circus . . . for more candy-colored spangles, or sequins as they are known to most of the gals, are used in this year's circus than have ever been used in any single production, including the movies. Not a single spangle was left in Paris, and it's a fact that several of the top Paris couturiers were searching all over Europe for these colorful accents for their new collections of ball gowns for the gala events of Coronation year . . . It's because John Ringling North is presenting the most glittering costume pageant ever unfolded."

In 1955, under blue canvas on the barren, industrial outskirts of Richmond, California—a World War II shipbuilding town—I saw my first circus produced by Mr. North. That season he had acquired the largest herd of elephants ever carried on one show. Fifty-five of them! They pranced down the hippodrome track in a charming fantasy, "Mama's In The Park." Clowns cavorted as kiddies mimicking grown-ups. Stately showgirls strolled lazily in turn-of-the-century frills. And, who were the little babies being wheeled about in bigger-than-life buggies? Yes, they were a nursery of junior pachyderms, pushed by mamas in Flatbush bonnets! A lilting melody composed by North (dancing to the lyrics of Irving Caesar) conveyed the images of

Clown Felix Adler portrays Old King Cole in this lavish
spec produced by North for the 1941 season. RM.

a small New England town on the green:

> Mama's in the park,
> Papa's in the park,
> Baby's out to play all day.
> Happy as a lark,
> Happy in the park,
> Mama puts her cares away!

There are some things you can do in a circus that are not possible in other mediums of entertainment and art. That is, I believe, Mr. North's principal message. The 1955 edition of the circus was laden with wondrous spectacles sensitively conceived and beautifully wrought: The "Mama's In The Park" number; "Holidays," a floated pageant of awe-inspiring ebullience; "On Honolulu Bay," a lush aerial spectacular highlighting the strangely unreal talents of Pinito Del Oro, the beautiful head-balancing

Costumes by Miles White gave the rainbow a run for its money. RM.

aerialist; and "Rainbow Around The World," the majestic finale of winged horses and radiant mermaids, rousingly set to music by a march that North composed and which was later adopted by the United Nations as its official theme song.

And what wondrous acts! When the ever-searching talent scout bearing the initials JRN toured the continent each spring in an open Mercedes, typically he returned with a bouquet of new acts (as many as twenty or more). Among the impressive galaxy of outstanding performers, generally of European descent, whom Mr. North honored on American sawdust, there is Alfred Court, the Cristianis, Francis Brunn, La Norma, Rose Gould, Lola Dobritch, Harold Alzana, Unus, Roberto de Vasconcellos, the Zoeppes with Cucciola, Lou Jacobs, Emmett Kelly, Dieter Tasso, Victor Julian's dogs, Charlie Bauman, Mister Mistin, Tito Gaona, Pinito Del Oro, Tonito, Hubert Castle, Josephine Berosini, the Nocks, the Stephensons, Gerard Soules, Elly Ardelty, Gena Lipkowska, Ingor Rhodin, Truzzi—and so many more . . .

Many of the above artists were featured with the 1955 program. One of them was the unbelievable Unus—the man who stood on one finger. He was, according to press agent Roland Butler, "The Talk of The Universe." In the words of Merle Evans, ". . . the greatest man performer I ever played for. He was Mr. Showman himself."

Like Pinito Del Oro and Josephine Berosini, and like the poetic equestrienne ballerina Gena Lipkowska, Unus evoked a mystical, other worldly aura—a quality which sums up the circus as seen through the visionary eyes of John Ringling North. A big evening under the big top should carry us literally out of this world. There was a depth to the performance that one could not fathom in a single viewing. It was at a circus such as that one, I suspect, when Ernest Hemginway was moved to write, "It is the only spectacle I know that, while you watch it, gives the quality of a truly happy dream."

The surrealistic qualities Hemmingway alludes to are found in three rings of constantly shifting images, in the collage of action that splits our focus between fantastic options, like a rainbow dispersing in many directions. North opted for a fantasy of illusive parts that could be savored momentarily. He literally made dreams come true in his eclectic big top.

"Except for Mike Todd, I've never met a producer with the same flair," says Miles White.

Nor, might have he added, with quite the same sense of humor. Rehearsals for the historic "bull ballet" (nicknamed by a facetious water boy) officially commenced one March morning at circus winter quarters. The unassuming George Balanchine stepped into the practice ring and introduced himself to his rookie ballerinas, careful to hide any reservations. Had it not been for the circus subsidizing the untenable aspirations of most of these girls, they would never have made it out of Florida in leotards. Balanchine had Walter McClain, the chief elephant handler, order his huskies through some basic routines. Then the two conferred on minor modifications to transform the traditional massed maneuvers into choreographic patterns projecting grace and symmetry.

The normally severe and uncultured McClain mellowed astonishingly well in the dance master's presence. Circus people are remarkably adaptive. At that point, however, the stolid elephant man was still protected from the Stravinski score. No one had the nerve to break it to him.

The Russian taskmaster directed the girls onto the heads of their mammoth partners and motioned

Young Johnny North and a group of his "starlets." RM.

them suavely through a few simple steps. Like a shelf of Barbie dolls in a tornado, they began falling off their partners—not very esthetically.

Balanchine stood back, paused, and observed with detachment the confusion.

"Try landing on the balls of your feet," he counseled the mangled chorines.

It is to this day argued which of the two groups was more amenable to the Russian's good-natured instructions—the girls or the bulls. Johnny North squinted with disbelief through an opening in the canvas and decided this would not be the time to make an appearance. Suddenly he longed to fly out of town on the first available plane and dine in serenity with whomever he chanced to meet wherever the plane happened to land.

North's artists were left to fend for themselves. Weeks of frustration passed. The bulls did not

respond well to Balanchine's choreography, and the girls seemed hopelessly ill-at-ease. Nobody believed this charade of women dancing on reluctant elephants to alien music would ever come together. Miles White prophesied with trepidation his pink tutu designs turning to inkblot patterns on the first rainy lot. Barbette screamed over the bruises inflicted on his aerialovelies whenever they went near the pachyderms. Merle Evans gazed at the mysterious Stravinski composition like a young student facing calculus for the first time. The charts resembled a battleplan for the pilgrimage of centipedes across central Nebraska. Evans wondered how Souza might have written it had he been a twelve-tone maniac.

The band leader shook his head in defeat. He could not imagine placing these sheets before his windjammers. He had already prepared them for a

Walter McClain watches his star pachyderm, Modoc, in rehearsal under Balanchine's direction. RM.

John Ringling North, right, *and his brother Henry. Bringing the circus back into family hands was their first priority.* RM.

couple of hundred cue changes. The six-minute Stravinski work seemed to contain that many *alone*.

Had this been the Tulsa, Oklahoma, Civic Light Ballet, opening night might have been prudently delayed if not canceled. No, this was Ringling Bros. and Barnum & Bailey Circus, scheduled to open in

New York City on 11 April. The circus trains, therefore, departed for the Northern Hemisphere on time, loaded with mauled ballerinas under sedatives—each one relating how a certain impresario had approached her on a street corner one moonlight evening; distraught elephants ready for the nut house; an elephant trainer asking everyone in sight, "Who the hell is *Stravinski?*"; and the usual paraphrenalia—lions and tigers, jugglers, Gargantua, and Barbette.

The insane high hopes of John and Henry Ringling North carried the company forward to new heights. The Greatest Show on Earth unfolded at Madison Square Garden to marvelous reception. Captivated by the brilliant innovations, the house was ready for almost *anything* by the time Display 16 came around:

The Ballet of The Elephants
Fifty elephants and fifty beautiful girls in an original choreographic tour de force featuring Modoc, premiere ballerina, the corps de ballet and the corps des elephants.

For its daring novelty alone, and in context of opening night, John North's wild creation was a howling surprise. "One of the hits of the '42 tour is the Ballet of The Elephants," wrote the *Billboard*.

Grand slam 1941 headliners included Truzzi. RM.

. . . Count Roberto de Vasconcellos. RM.

122

. . . Elly Ardelty. RM.

"It's a sensation when viewed from all aspects."

The elephants clumsily snubbed whole measures of music, while some of the fledgling ballet girls scrambled just to stay alive during fortissimo and fade out. Yet, judged on its own zany terms, the number was a triumph. Nineteen forty-two audiences and critics were charmed by a circus that challenged the imagination.

Balanchine's wife, Zorina, in a ravishing guest appearance moved with intrepid ease over Modoc's dependable noggin. The duo shared the encores and each was presented with a bunch of red roses. Modoc clutched hers by her trunk and lumbered proudly off.

"The Ringling show this year actually lives up to the 'Greatest Show' billing."

—*Variety*

"Certainly the first and only show in the world ever to collect under one roof four such illustrious showmen as Norman Bel Geddes, John Murray

. . . the Cristianis (Belmonte astride horse). RM.

123

. . . "Ballet of the Elephants" RM.

Anderson, George Balanchine and Gargantua."
　　　　　　　　　　　—John T. MacMans, *PM*

"A show of extraordinary beauty, a circus with the pastel quality of a child's dream. 'Ballet of The Elephants' was breathtaking."
　　　　　　　　　　　—*New York Times*

"It was so impressive," remembers Jane Johnson. "The elephants had on their little ballet skirts, all the girls came in their little tutus, and it was eye filling and it was joyful, it was gay. It was absolutely the most spectacular thing I ever saw."

Miss Johnson, who then took dictation from the North brothers, is now a spirited tour guide at Ca d'Zan. Her vital reminiscences offer a wonderful insight to the past.

"The elephants have their standard acts and dance a little, but with their tutus on it looked like they were actually doing a ballet. People would laugh and applaud and 'oooo' and 'ahhhh'. It was a most joyous thing, one of the greatest happiest things I ever saw in my life."

"The dance step that the girls did was a very simple dance, but how many people who go to circuses don't go to ballet? John brought the ballet to the circus, and many people have never seen girls on their toes. And those pink tutus on the girls and on the elephants, they were just magnificent in the circus tent."

"How fortunate I was to have worked with those North boys for so long. John Ringling North is a genius. I admired so much what he did. John would think things fast and he'd talk to his brother, and Buddy would talk to me. He was most creative, he would have wonderful ideas. His ideas were big and if they weren't practical the boys would work it out together. Buddy used to come in the office and say, 'My brother John is crazy!' That's what everybody all over the lot said."

124

"He was not crazy, he just had more sense than anybody else and he had vision. Buddy was the practical one. The one that could sooth things over. If John went traipsing through saying, 'We're going to do this, and we're going to do that . . . we're going to change this'—performers are like children, and maybe their feelings would be hurt. They would come and talk to Buddy. And Buddy would say, 'That's alright, we'll do this gradually. My brother John has a wonderful idea, this is going to be very good for you.' "

"When people criticize John, I say he's not to be judged by ordinary standards because he's not an ordinary person."

Similarly wrong would it have been to judge "Ballet of the Elephants" by ordinary standards. Nothing like it had ever been attempted anywhere, barring possibly the parting of the Red Sea. What in the vast realms of entertainment was there against which to compare it?

Stravinski's polka was judged by *Variety* ". . . so weird that it does not belong in a circus." Where it did belong remains a puzzle to all but the very esoteric. The musicians never completely unraveled the main beat. "It was the hardest music I ever played," confesses Merle Evans. "One bar was three-four, and the next bars four-four. It came at the last part of the show, and you were blowed out anyway. The boys didn't like that Stravinski thing. And I didn't care much for it. And I don't think the elephants liked it, either."

How well the maestro knew. Accustomed as they were to strong, reoccurring drum rolls, the big brutes kicked their skirts up at the chopped rhythms and estranged chords. Because they could not or would not follow the "beat," the young ruffians with bull hooks who handled them were assigned to effect Balanchine's movements at the precise moments by poking them. Trouble was, nobody knew when to poke the pokers. Any and all unified massed arabesques were purely coincidental.

As succinctly stated by Miles White, "You can't dance on sawdust."

Plato's theory of forms be damned, thousands of hinterland families had a ball. Laughter and joy prevailed. Perhaps too much. Johnny North escaped to Europe to scout for new acts—serious ones. Stravinski never came within splashing range of a water bucket. Balanchine relocated in New York with an unlisted telephone number.

The band did not last very long, either. Due to

Modoc, the ballet's "premiere ballerina," with her trainer Walter McClain. RM.

labor problems that summer, the musicians went on strike. Phonograph records were substituted in place of live music. Fortunately, as Walter McClain saw it, the elephant ballet had never been recorded. He was elated with the thought of being freed from the damn thing at last.

McClain did not get his wish. One morning in Philadelphia, Jane Johnson, while listening to the radio in her hotel room, heard what she thought were the familiar inaccessible tones of a modern composer.

"That's the Stravinski ballet!"

The executive secretary raced to the circus grounds, excitedly reporting to her boss, "Buddy, the radio station played something that sounded just like the ballet!"

They called the station to find out what the selection was titled.

They learned it was a piece composed by none other than Chopin.

A puzzling silence. The two exchanged suspicious looks.

"Chopin?"

Did it matter really? Would the elephants know the difference? Henry North purchased a copy of the record and played it for the duration of the tour. It bore an uncomfortable likeness to the music his brother John had paid Igor Stravinski $1,500 to

125

write. The big bulls continued kicking their skirts up in protest. Modoc plunged gracelessly on, never forgetful of her opening-night triumph when she flaunted a bunch of roses in her trunk.

Rumors spread through the show alleging plagiarism on the part of a famous Beverly Hills atonalist. The subtleties of perception by which one work of art may be delineated from another do not flourish in the minds of men who move fast red-wagon caravans through the night.

"I think North has been hoodwinked very little," concluded Jane Johnson, summing up a memorable season. "But in that instance, I've always had my doubts."

Stravinski dedicated his Circus Polka to "a young elephant." Modoc, not mentioned, kicked her tutu aside and never attempted another arabesque. Exit, finis, the corps des elephants.

12
Gargantua, It's Your Honeymoon!

A SCOWLING gorilla behind bars eyed another gorilla in another cage. One smirked. The other sneered. In anthropoid annals, beauty is in the eye of the beholding ape. Neither Gargantua the Great nor his new bride, Mlle. Toto, were the victims of love at first sight. They had been escorted to the altar of matrimony by a self-appointed primate pastor, John Ringling North. These unlikely spouses spent their first season with the circus in separate, nondestructable boudoirs.

The honeymoon was still in the planning stages. This was a hazardous match in the great tradition of big-top hoopla. He, a tough insensitive sulk; she, the doting, submissive type. North feared the two partners upon first embrace might tear each other to pieces.

Can this marriage be saved?

From the start, Gargantua was a loner. Deprived, so the story goes, of a normal homelife in the suburbs of West Africa, the perky little guy ran away when he was not big enough to scare a grasshopper. He took refuge in the hands of a couple of missionaries. Unable to convert him, they sold the little pet to Captain Arthur Phillips, commander of an African trading ship, the *West Key Bar*. The hairy heathen got a free ride to America. When the ship docked in Boston, a sailor who Phillips discharged took his revenge out on the captain by tossing nitric acid into the young ape's face. Disfiguration gave Gargantua a permanently mean look—the torn upper lip of a prize fighter and the distempered eyes of King Kong, eminently marketable attributes.

Captain Phillips unloaded his pet primate on Mrs. Gertrude Lintz, a fancier of stray animals. She took pity on Gargantua's facial burns as well as internal problems caused by the acid. She called in a dermatologist and considered plastic surgery of some sort. Gradually, the little gorilla was nurtured back to health and happiness, and he developed an affection for his keeper, who resided in Brooklyn. One night, when he jumped in bed with Mrs. Lintz, she decided it was time to seek other lodgings for him. Mrs. Lintz had paid $2,000 for the pet, and she felt he might now be extremely valuable as an attraction with a circus or carnival. She called John North, who was registered at a New York hotel.

The North brothers were highly receptive to Mrs. Lintz's offer. They came out to see the maturing pet and were immediately impressed. John believed they could do with the gorilla what Barnum had done with Jumbo. The boys agreed to pay $10,000 and Mrs. Lintz drew up a contract.

Phenomenal showmanship ensued. In a rare stroke of genius, Henry had the brainstorm for calling their new acquisition "Gargantua." (He may have never suggested this fantastic name had it not been for the fact that the ape's original name was "Buddy," the same as Henry's nickname, and Henry

The selling of Gargantua rivaled P. T. Barnum's handling of Jumbo. CW.

Crowning equestrian showmanship, during a day when
the horse was king. CW.

Dazzling, innovative routines thrived when circuses were
highly competitive. CW.

Truly deserving of every accolade, the incomparable May Wirth. CW.

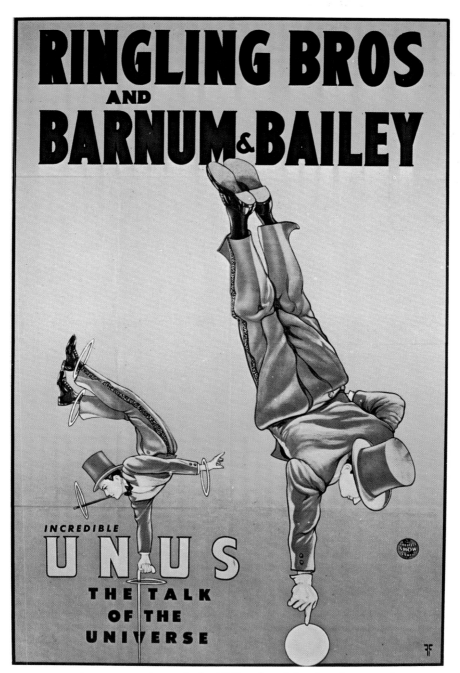

A sensation through the 1950s when John Ringling North imported him to American shores, Unus astounded believing audiences until others began duplicating his extraordinary act. CW.

Lavish circus spectacles, elaborately costumed and choreographed, are not a product of modern times as some critics have argued. CW.

A child's delight, the circus enchants with its beatific rearrangement of reality. CW.

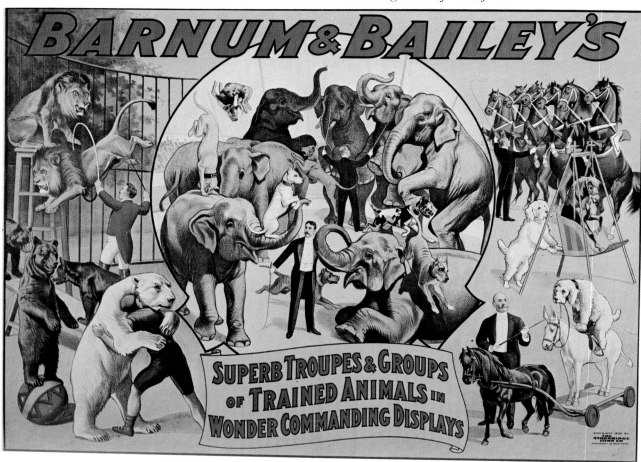

The "Sacred White Elephant"—never so white as when presented by Ringling Bros. and Barnum & Bailey! CW.

All glory to Rome: blazing hippodrome races helped perpetuate the myth of a circus born out of Roman vengeance. CW.

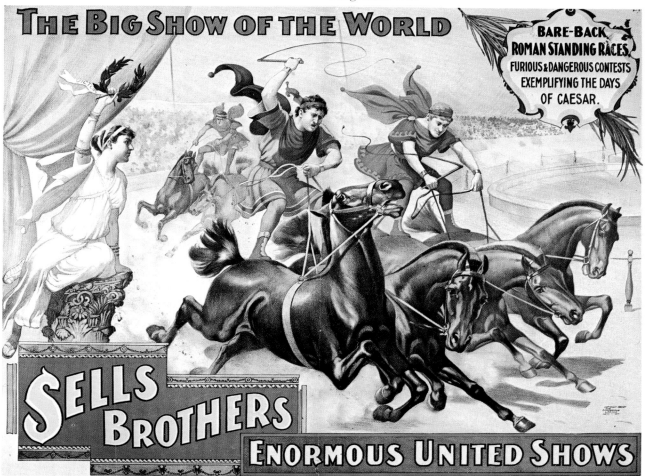

Magnificent circus art set precedents in the advertising world. CW.

The center ring's most famous lady animal trainer, Mabel Stark. CW.

Gargantua was a natural ham around photographers. RM.

"Gargie" never missed a flashing camera. RM.

The gorilla loved tearing a new tire to shreads. RM.

did not wish to share the same title or notoriety.)

John directed the press department to treat their new star with more renown, contempt, and reverence than an impeached president. The half-ton bachelor seized immediate public acclaim and during his first tour with the circus in 1938 became the most feared living thing in the United States. The media in this country has always been quick to recognize first-rate hoodlums.

Behind bars, "Gargie" was a doozy. "A horrifying nightmare vision of what man might have been," declared publicity genius Roland Butler. "With a smirk of cruel calculation and a sadistic scowl on his huge bestial face, this pernicious primate defied civilization from behind heavy steel bars of the strongest cage ever constructed."

Grown men and women with their bemused children gathered in morbid delight around the big beast's air-conditioned wagon to view their ancestral beginnings. Gargantua's keeper, Jose Thomas, boasted his dour inmate could easily free himself by flexing one good muscle or doing a little pirouette right through the door. Thomas added, assuringly, his charge preferred sublime isolation to civilized life as he saw it from his lofty sphere.

The primate prima donna was said to have shown a rare sense of humor. Sometimes he seemed to be laughing at the characters who stared up at him in his glass-enclosed world. A few jaded circus buffs scoffed in disbelief. Grumbled one, "The man who caught that chimpanzee is a liar!" He should have taken the chimp for a walk. Gargantua once grabbed North by the arm. Luckily, North pulled away in

129

Mlle. Toto, Gargantua's prospective wife, flirted proudly with her keeper, Jose Thomas. RM.

time, leaving Gargantua in possession only of his coat.

The ballyhoo attending every episode surrounding the feared cage was tremendously successful. Gargantua made the cover of *Life* magazine. Predicted *Variety*, "If Gargantua the gorilla survives the season, 'The Terror' as he is billed should ensure a fortune to the show. Not that it is the first time such an attraction has been with the circus, although not in this generation, but never with the showmanship of this presentation. . . . He is probably the toughest so and so that ever hit the lot."

It's amazing what pulls 'em in. Millions of circus goers, on their way to a fantastic show in the big top, went first to the menagerie for a thrilling glimpse of the famous terror. And that's where they decided how good the show really was.

At the end of his first tour, King Kong's look-alike was chauffeured in a large vented crate to London for further exposure. Gargie made guest appearances on the bill of Bertram Mills Circus. According to the press agents, he acquired a "British accent."

The primate now cocked his head to the side and slurred his screeches.

John North believed that Gargantua was not meant to live alone. Moreover, the producer envisioned a gaggle of baby gorillas running wild in an air-cooled nursery of terror on wheels. In three season's time, the expansionist-minded North secured a prospective mate.

Gargantua, meet "tantalizing Toto—a winsome female anthropoid of slighter smaller proportions and a much more serene disposition."

Of a multitude of marriages not made in heaven, this one tops the list. On paper it looked promising. Anatomically, the mates were natural complements: He, a fully mature eleven-year old (the equivalent to a man in his twenties); she, ten-years old and ripe for action. He hit the scale at 550 pounds. She tipped it gently at the 460 pound mark. His waistline encompassed seventy-six inches. Hers, an alluring sixty-two inches. (Eat your hearts out, guys.) His arm span outstretched her's by one foot. He stood five and a half feet tall, three inches higher than she. Both hailed from West Africa, he from the Cameroons and she from the Belgian Congo. A decidedly homogenous pair.

In truth, Toto bore a hefty, beer-barrel midsection and the depleted looks of a divorcee on the rebound. The suitor acted affronted. He did not evidently desire a mother figure. Despite the apparent incompatabilities (who says that "love" has anything to do with the success of a marriage?), Mr. and Mrs. Gargantua The Great rose to international prominence. They did not during their first year together share a single embrace, yet the "hairy honeymooners" became overnight the entertain-

The newlyweds' portrait—outwardly they were compatible. RM.

*Actually, "Mr. and Mrs." shared separate, nondestruct-
able boudoirs.* RM.

ment world's most popular couple. He snarled in his
cage. She whimpered in hers.

A nation of disenchanted spouses identified with
two incompatible apes. And to think we humans are
considered an "evolved" species.

If infidelity was their goal, the hairy couple did not
reap the side benefits. In their separate chambers
they remained placidly aloof to each other. Toto
luxuriated on a Beautyrest mattress—one of the
products that was being promoted by the circus. Her
husband, when he was not making faces at the
crowds, pursued his favorite pastime—reducing to
shreads rubber tires (the maker of which was not
advertised).

The sexless abstainers shared one common passion: food. Four times each day both primates

consumed in perfect marital harmony two bunches
of celery, one loaf of bread, a dozen assorted fruits
and vegetables, a half dozen eggs, three quarts of
milk, two tablespoons of liver extract, a half pint of
chocolate syrup, and other liquids not detailed on
their published menu.

Gargantua's endless antics before the crowds may
have drained him of his natural virility. By the day's
end, the super stud did not turn to matters of the
heart, did not heed any of the hints his motherly wife
initiated. Instead, Gargie indulged in another of his
fetishes—the nightly obliteration of a fresh feather
pillow, followed by the shreading of his bed sheets.
Freud would call it subliminal sadism. In circus
lingo, it was a hell of a show.

While an early annulment would have thrilled the

passionless duds, no, argued North, romance would flower in time. One year passed, and North's dream couple appeared not an inch closer to their first volcanic hug. In fact, they seemed, if anything, platonically pooped.

The circus president, growing impatient, ordered an end to the impish impasse. Two cage wagons packed with breathing dynamite were moved end to end. A hint was being tossed in Gargantua's face.

He leaped up, sensing contact with a foreign object.

The intervening steel doors were removed, separating the lovers now by only two thin bars. The masculinity of "The world's most terrifying creature" was on trial. Reporters and flashing cameras crowded around for a sneak preview of gorilla conjugality. Would a tender wink from Gargie send Toto into a dizzy fit of ecstasy?

The newlyweds checked each other out, sniffing and snorting from a distance. A few deliberating moments passed. John North grinned, confident that ravishing violent love was about to commence.

Gargantua moved forward with a mutilated stalk of celery, a gift for his beloved mate. The gesture drew great sighs of expectation from the onlookers. Then Toto promptly threw it back in her "husband's" face!

The big guy was shattered. Toto grabbed the bar and flung herself indifferently against it. Gargantua retreated to his corner. The two ape's had not touched. Their first epocal entente was a bust. North, determined to keep alive the possibility of an eventual union, had his publicists contrive this explanation for the failure of their first encounter to ignite true passion:

The temperamental mates were actually concealing a burning infatuation. Toto's abrasive rebuff was a cunning move aimed at arousing the beast in her husband. By making herself hard to get, Mrs. Gargantua hoped to achieve the irresistible appeal of a cold, hard sex object.

Oh, the games gorillas play!

Gargie suddenly discovered his puberty. The conquest of his dear, sensual Toto took priority over everything else. As the press agents figured it, the uncouth bully showed signs of becoming a real gentleman:

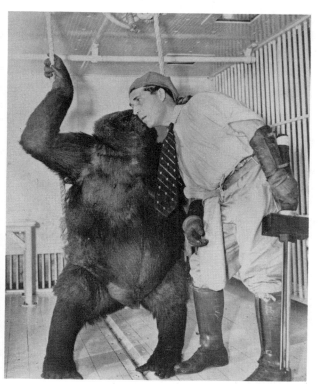

The perfect wife, Mrs. Gargantua demonstrated her domestic talents before an indifferent husband. RM.

. . . Mrs. Gargantua shared her marital doubts with keeper Thomas. RM.

The wife had the heart of a kitten. RM.

"Every day is Saturday night for Gargantua the Great, giant gorilla, as far as bathing is concerned. The famous primate now insists upon tubing daily, using a wash cloth and a basin of water for the rite, one that his bride, Toto, has observed for years. Of course the big stiff started it to please her, and the idea that a gentleman bathes daily seems to keep him at it. . . . the keepers figure it's all in the course of true love, and that in the near future the mating call will sound sweet and low in the great white connecting cages."

Two years of daily showers, good dental hygiene, and a comehither look in Gargantua's eyes convinced his wife that now he meant business. Toto drew closer again. Once more, the barriers separating an erotic pinch were removed. Once more, Mr. and Mrs. Gargantua the Great scampered up face to face. The circus president crossed his fingers. The press department, running low on fabrications, held its breath.

This time around Toto got it right in the face: banana skins and orange peels that Gargantua hurled at her. The spoil sport that he was, Gargie had set the stage for a royal retaliation. Never willing to forgive Toto her first rebuff, Gargie patiently waited out his turn, and when it came he played it like a master sadist. And he laughed. Yes, Gargantua laughed!

"Gargantua spurns his mate's love," cried the ballyhoo boys. "Toto, secure behind bars, does not shrink. She seems to smile as though Gargantua were a big bluff. And she no longer hurls back the fruit showers at him. She, who was so indifferent, is crazy about Gargantua."

Ten loveless years passed. The aging anthropoids lived like a couple of Victorian prudes sharing a bottle of Geritol. You do your thing; I'll do mine. Toto submitted to a strict diet imposed by her keeper to lessen the bulge around her tummy. Beautifully toned, she reclined in singular splendor on her Beautyrest. The husband, in his private chamber, dawned a new coat of silver fur, giving him the look of a fox (another of his shrewd illusions).

North accepted the inevitable. He had sunk $125,000 into the childless couple. Convinced their nuptials were null and void, he ordered the adoption of two young primates from his own congo cradle in West Africa. North engaged anthropologist Martha Hunter to supervise their integration into the quaint family circle.

Gargie fell into a deep depression. His ardent followers surmised he had taken all he could, that somehow he sensed the plans being made to foist upon him adopted offspring. The confirmed bachelor suffered a nervous breakdown at the end of the 1949 season. Gargantua, ironically, lay dying as two youngsters sailed to America to meet their foster parents, a well-known circus couple behind bars.

Gargantua II and his foster sister, Toto, were weaned on a bottle of warm milk. Like so many moppets in modern times, they grew up with only one parent. Their mother gave them abundant affection. They did not experience the thrill (or agony) of seeking affection from their intended father. Gargantua, great showman that he was, held on through the final day of the tour and passed quietly away in Miami.

The press department felt great relief—freedom, at last, from the exasperating chore of having to further justify the indifferent actions of their big, bad bachelor. Wrote program editor William Fields, "The cage which once bristled like a Sing Sing cell-block with the sullen menace of Gargantua and the unfulfilled Toto, is now warm and friendly as the two adorable anthropoid youngsters adjust to their new home."

Adopted "offspring" for the Gargantuas—Gargantua II and his foster sister Toto. RM.

The husband, Gargantua the Great, remained stand-offish. RM.

Study of a grieving widow. Mlle. Toto following the death of Gargantua in Miami. RM.

God bless Gargantua. He was a great showman, and I'll tell you why.

The epilogue to this curious tale is a revelation of dirty work at the altar. My source, C.C., alias Sanitation Department, Ringling Bros. and Barnum & Bailey Combined Shows, Inc., now drives a bus in Sarasota. I jumped aboard for a ride down memory lane.

C.C. talked about the sordid truth. Gargantua simply was not fit for the peculiar calling. It was against his nature. The union was a humiliating hoax. It never could have worked. There were no blood tests, no signed documents. The vital statistics were fabricated. The whole affair was a bloody sham, a crass embarrassment to the primate's pride.

No, this marriage could not have been saved. The husband did not want a wife. The husband wanted a husband.

Gargantua was a lady.

"A *lady*?" I was shocked and amused.

"Yes, a lady!"

"You're kidding me?"

"No, Gargantua was a lady!"

C.C. had put one over on me. We laughed for the longest spell. The unexpected curves down the road jostled only myself. C.C. held the wheel like a pro.

"And not a very gay one at that!"

Now, there are only two ways you can take *that*. In any case, you need not bother asking the press agents to clarify it. They still haven't explained away the missing bathtub in which the world's "most terrifying creature" became a well-bathed lady's man.

13
King behind the Throne

SMALL deals don't interest Arthur M. Concello, the grand master of circus logistics. At present, the former executive director of the "Greatest Show on Earth" is leisurely secure with a cigar, two swimming pools, and a telephone on which occasionally he confers with business associates over his next possible extraordinary move. Unless it involves millions, no thanks.

Back to one of the pools, or to the Gong Show.

When you've turned thousands of triple somersaults through mid-air, presided over mammoth big tops, chaperoned Yankee Doodle juglers and acrobats to the Soviet Union, had Hollywood at your mercy for script consultation on red wagon scenarios, what is there left to tickle your fancy? So you try a new recipe for barbecued frog's legs, change socks, and wait for another phone call.

Concello, the jaded circus producer, lives efficiently well in a sedate white brick house on balmy Sarasota landscape. The spacious arrangement of glass, marble, and leather into clean, uncluttered lines suggests a mind of calculated order. At the edge of a placid indoor pool is a round glass table—clean as a slate—surrounded symmetrically by four canvas chairs, seemingly posed for historic negotiations. A circular driveway delivers you to the impeccable premises, where a vociferous great Dane springs into action, waiting to monitor your every move. If you taxi up in a metered vehicle, you are

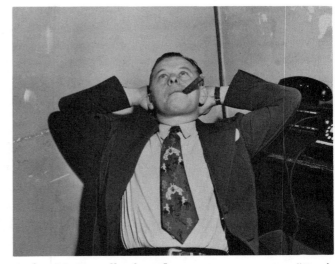

Arthur M. Concello, from flyer to circus executive. "Don't give me the publicity. I want the money." RM.

already safely in the coin-happy hands of your famous host. The trapeze flyer-turned-circus executive counts, among his collection of profitable pastimes, the local cab company.

No, the mastermind of perpetual motion never really retired. He still putters over a fleet of mobile units—thirty yellow limousines. Got to keep a show on the road somewhere, Art.

History will someday discover with a bang that what James A. Bailey was to P. T. Barnum in the

Concello's flying acts on the Ringling circus, 1937. Art is fifth from left, *with Antoinette.* RM.

nineteenth century, Arthur M. Concello has been to John Ringling North in the twentieth—a faithful king behind the throne. Together, North and Concello created a great circus under the greatest of settings, the last truly magnificent and totally impractical big top. Because Concello was around, the unwieldy giant made enough money to perpetuate itself. Like the self-effacing James A. Bailey, who brought operational stability to Barnum's flamboyant exhibitions, Concello conquered Johnny North's epic productions float by float, plume by plume, into managerial work orders. A great theatrical entrepreneur and a shrewd detail man linked in concert may be considered a lucky showbusiness combination.

As the ambitious star flyer of the Flying Concellos, Arthur developed a valuable sense of timing, the key attribute of a circus mover. Counting himself a veteran at the senior age of seventeen years, Arthur established a school for flyers in Bloomington, Illinois, utilizing an old barn he purchased from Mamie Ward. Before the legal age of maturity (as recognized only outside the circus world), Art was a bona fide star who regularly performed a nifty triple while simultaneously managing—on the side—half a dozen other flying troupes. The prolific instructor naturally showered considerable attention on his

wife, Antoinette, who became the first lady to accomplish the triple. At the Garden opening in 1937, *both* performed the triple on the same bill, a feat that has not since and may never again be seen by mortal eyes. Equestrian Director Fred Bradna termed it "the highest peak of team flying ever exhibited." Miss Concello to this day is revered as the greatest lady flyer of the ages, so completely polished was her form.

By 1932 young Arthur, circa twenty years old, shared the spotlight with the renowned Alfredo Codona. Quickly, the sweet taste of applause and glory faded. Concello realized he was serving a short-term occupation and that he was nowhere near retirement age. His superb sense of timing told him he might be useful to the circus in other less ethereal ways. Like most any man not in command, he began finding fault with the management of the show. Late performances irked him. So did antiquated set-up procedures. Art took notes and convinced himself he could update the operation for greater efficiency. It's clear he was an aspiring corporate man in big-top terms.

"He was one of those strange and peculiar people who never had to practice," recalls Jane Johnson. "He was always in condition. He wanted to be in management. Well, he was such a *great* performer,

Air-conditioning the big top was a bold though unsuccessful North-Concello innovation. RM.

for many years people didn't take him seriously. How could a performer like *that* want to do anything else?"

The answer was simple, according to another inside source: "The minute he saw where all the money was up front, he got out of those flying tights and got in the office."

A triple into the red wagon, perfectly timed. John North's star was on the horizon. Concello firmed up his credentials for an executive slot while North, playing to the hilt his status as executor of his late Uncle John Ringling's estate, raised the necessary capital to regain control of the circus for his family. The paths of a couple of crack showmen were approaching the point of profitable union.

In the fall of 1937, North gained operational custody of the show and Concello became a sympathetic supporter. Although still a performer, Art rendered valuable assistance to John from the sidelines. Opening night at Madison Square Garden in 1938, a walkout of striking property hands necessitated embarrassing guest appearances in blue overalls by the new show officials. John, his brother Henry, and Art pushed cage wagons for Frank Buck's animal act. The boys wheeled Gargantua around the track, set props for all the performers, and later hoisted the flying trapeze nets into place. The crowds cheered their involvement.

The North brothers clung to a precarious thread of power in the divisive Ringling family and in 1942 appointed Concello to the position of general manager. The shows they produced were critically

Only those sitting directly beneath the air-conditioning vents were cooled, while others around them sweltered as usual. RM.

acclaimed, well run, and in the black.

North mastered the accoutrements of an aloof impresario. Concello remained always in direct contact with the ground forces, content to assist his friend John rather than market his own formidable name and establish a separate trick. Perhaps Concello could see the writing on the wall. The great depression had sent to pasture a host of major circuses. Union organizers haunted the country's floundering big tops, ready to engulf them, too. Movies had risen to the forefront of entertainment and television's ultimate spell was on the horizon. Three-ring divertissements seemed terribly passé.

Although the circus prospered under the North

Antoinette Concello, the only lady flyer ever to accomplish the triple. CW.

141

Concello cut expenses by replacing horses with tractors.
"They don't eat a thing until you turn them on." RM.

regime, rival factions within his family clamored for their day in the sun. North's principal foes were Robert Ringling, son of the late Charles Ringling, and his circus mother, Mrs. Charles.

"They're going to throw me out," North confided to Concello in 1943 when mother and son got their turn to call the shots. At the board of directors meeting that spring, John and Henry argued against touring the show during wartime without available flame-proof canvas. Tragically, they were outvoted. Robert Ringling got a crack at the throne.

With the flick of one misspent cigar ash, Concello retained his cool. He is not a man to be throttled by earthshaking board-of-directors' edicts. The general manager surmised he'd be leaving, too, and decided he might as well go with another show. Something to

"You couldn't run 'em off and you didn't pay 'em any money," said Concello of the men who moved the big tops of yesteryear. RM.

142

Two views of the catastrophic Hartford fire in 1944. RG.

pass the time while John got reappraised by his greedy relatives.

Art did not find an offer to his liking, so he laid down $50,000 in cash for his own circus—the twenty-car Russell show. He hired Clyde Beatty, printed thousands of reduced-price matinee tickets for school children, and did predictably well up and down the West Coast.

While the Norths and Concello were absent, Ringling Bros. and Barnum & Bailey fell to the most disastrous fire in circus history. As cruel as it may sound, at Hartford, Connecticut, on 6 July 1944 the career of Robert Ringling went up in fast flames. One hundred sixty-eight persons were trapped under burning canvas. Six officials of the show were sentenced to prison. By a strange twist of fate John North's star was rising again.

It was not difficult for a man of North's ambition to look resolutely strong in the face of the Hartford catastrophe. North had operated the circus successfully for five years. His relatives had struck out. North filed a negligence suit against them, and they countered by charging him with "trying to wreck the circus and buy it up as distressed goods."

Wreck the show, North did not. He scouted Europe in the fall of 1946 for new acts and contracted for the show a shattering burst of fresh talent. The 1947 edition was judged by critics a landslide victory in tanbark entertainment. "This circus big-tops them all," penned Walter Winchell. "You've never seen anything like it," exclaimed Robert Williams in the *New York Post.* "The Greatest Show on Earth merely lived up to its lofty label; so much so it left its own press agents groping for words."

The heir apparent to the throne would not be denied his destiny. North's momentum in popular support carried him to the brink of a driving goal; by the fall of 1947 he needed only $250,000 to secure 51 percent of the stock. To Art Concello, then president of Russell Bros. Circus, he turned, knowing the dynamo of do-or-die would deliver. Concello, good sport that he was, friend of Johnny North and his circus, sold his own show to Clyde Beatty for three times the price of his investment, got in touch with his cigar-chumping cronies, and handed over a quarter of a millon dollars to his friend the budding circus king. On time, in a battered briefcase. In cash.

Concello was instrumental in helping John North become, at age forty-four, the first individual ever to hold a controlling interest in the Ringling-Barnum title. Behind the new circus king stood another circus king.

"He could very well have withheld it," emphasized Jane Johnson, "and said, 'To hell with your circus, I'll have a circus of my own.' But he didn't."

Fifty-one percent is exactly what North desired. He reappointed Concello to the general manager's post.

"The smartest move I ever made," said North, praising the inevitable. "At one time or another this show has been mismanaged to death."

Art got the "yes and the no," his own expression for the authority of a top manager to accept or reject a myriad of daily decisions: contract proposals, employee disputes, how to deal with hay merchants and conniving fire marshalls, whether to accommodate or resist the friendly bribes of law enforcement officials. The "yes and the no," of course, gives a man unlimited access to the red wagon, the place Concello coveted the most. "Up where they're counting that money." He wanted his fair share.

The feisty, shrewdly efficient executive exploited the challenges before him. He patented an ingenious folding seat wagon which eliminated the hundreds of workingmen required to erect and dismantle the traditional jacks-and-stringers type of seats. The circus then paid its versatile expediter $20,000

New fire-proof canvas in 1945, tested by Washington,
D.C. Fire Marshall R. C. Roberts. RM.

Concello's ingenious folding seat wagons saved hundreds
of manhours and put the show back on schedule. RM.

Aerial view of circus in rehearsal at Sarasota, in the 1950s, shows the seat wagons in use. RM.

annually in royalties alone for the use of his sacred invention!

"I don't want publicity," he told me. "I want money."

Another of Concello's clever innovations were the illuminated side show fronts he implemented in the early fifties. These, along with other refinements to midway decor, enhanced the entranceways. Roland Butler critiqued the embellishments thus:

"This year's new sideshow fronts, banner lines, and ticket wagons, painted by Bill Ballantine, were a screaming riot of color, while his eye-seizing paintings of the sideshow attractions, in huge Victorian rococo shadow box frames, originated by Art Concello, were like nothing ever before seen on this continent.

"Extending across the tops of the brilliantly bedecked ticket wagons at the main entrance was a highly ornate fifty-foot scrolled panel, peaked by pennants.

"This striking midway innovation, emblazoned with every hue of the spectrum, made circus-goers' eyes pop and warmed the welcome to Wonderland."

There is no question that Concello moved the circus with impervious precision through hell and high water. Profits soared—enough to settle by 1952 over three million dollars in claims, which North inherited, arising out of the Hartford fire. On top of that there were sufficient returns—believe it or not—to ensure the perpetuation of North's unstinting production budgets and to stock the bottomless billfold of the zealous dollars-and-cents man in the red wagon.

Workingmen settled for a few lousy bucks and the

145

Stunning midway magic. The illuminated shadow-box sideshow fronts were conceived by Concello and painted by artist Bill Ballantine. RM.

deep satisfaction of pushing the ageless delight down the road. "You couldn't run 'em off and you didn't pay 'em any money," says Concello, whose pursuasive charms with tough itinerants, neer-do-wells, and winos were far reaching. Nena Evans remarked once to the boss, "You can work a person longer hours for less money and make them like it more than anybody I ever knew."

The general manager inspired the humble forces with his classic carnie face—a portrait of wayward heroism and sundry adventure. Concello would not ask of a man anything he himself would not do. There he was, up in the rigging testing the tension of a wire; behind a tractor fiddling with a locked clutch; under a flat car inspecting a hot box. The lovable gruff guy was thoroughly akin to mud, grime, and guts.

What is the key to running a circus well, I asked the logistics expert.

"Good bosses," he answered.

Concello granted to each of his subordinates solid autonomy. A complaint of stale coffee was referred to the head cook. French acrobats bemoaning Merle Evans' right to score their routine with a Spanish march were amiably requested to speak with the bandleader. "He's in charge."

Somebody scoffed a lingering bad odor coming from one of the new portable restroom facilities.

"Don't tell me about it!" retorted the man at the top. "Talk to the sanitation manager!"

The perennial question of what constitutes an ethical circus operator does not escape the rugged Concello administration. To some he was *the* king. To others, specifically the ones who had reason to fear him, he was "little Caesar." The power he accumulated behind North's back some observers have called "frightening." North loved the limelight; Concello craved greenbacks bound in fat stacks. North dined with costume designers on Park Avenue, he graced the continent for new acts and new

146

girlfriends. Concello followed the show from Sheboygan to Kalamazoo and made his daily rounds, exacting fees for in-house gambling privileges. Card tables and poker games thrived.

Right or wrong? A pragmatic approach to the survival of a tented caravan must involve the motivation of a horrendous work force. The sleazy pack of men who moved the big show in those days did not respond to genteel admonitions from white-collar types. The same holds true today for the few remaining so-called "mud" shows. What drives these shiftless characters forward to the next stop, rather than permanently off the train, if not the lingering hope of a jackpot at tomorrow's roll of the dice?

James Anthony Bailey was a teetotaler and a strict gentleman. It's unthinkable, however, that he rallied his razorbacks on by reading to them each morning from the bible. When most American circuses had fallen by the wayside, Ringling Bros. and Barnum & Bailey continued its optimistic journey into modern times under the stringent command of one Arthur M. Concello. Seldom did North suffer a losing season. Defeat was out of the question.

Concello moved the show. Clouds appeared in foreboding formations over a lot already saturated with mud.

"Shall we set her up, or blow the town, Art?"

The manager glanced at the firmament, sighed a little and bit hard into his cigar.

"Yes, set her up."

"Hey, Art . . . what about that busted dishwasher. You want it replaced?"

"Go ahead," said Concello.

"Billboard Bertha wants back on concessions. . . ?"

The chief executive turned abruptly and walked off.

"*No.*"

It was a rainy day in Cedar Rapids, Iowa. A well-known film director was traveling with the show, at work on plans for a movie about circus life. That morning he walked down to the lot, surveyed a dreary quagmire of mud puddles and speculated the date would be skipped.

"They'll *never* put the tent up on *that* mess," he concluded and returned to his suite aboard the train.

He heard a knock on his door shortly after lunch. Concello queried the celebrated filmmaker.

Cecil B. DeMille on location for the filming of The Greatest Show on Earth. cw.

"Aren't you gonna go down and see the show?"

"There's going to be a show *today*?"

"That's right," answered the one and only Art Concello.

The tent was up by 1 P.M. Straw had been laid over the soggy hippodrome track. The house was packed.

Cecil B. DeMille could not believe his eyes.

One of Concello's greatest favors to his boss, John Ringling North, was the right "no" to the wrong director. DeMille's award-winning motion picture "The Greatest Show on Earth" would not have been made had another director gotten his way. The circus had inked a contract with Paramount for the flick and held final script approval. David O. Selznick first took out an option for the screen rights but in six months time failed to produce a treatment. He pleaded with Concello for an extension. Concello said "no."

DeMille stepped forward with a proposal, although he did not have a script to present, either. Yet something about the director's attitude impressed the man representing the circus.

Concello said "yes" to DeMille. The rest is history.

One sequence called for Cornel Wilde to fall from

Actor Cornel Wilde in a scene from DeMille's The Greatest Show on Earth. RM.

Actor James Stewart played a runaway clown in DeMille's award-winning movie about circus life. RM.

James Stewart, left, *Dorothy Lamour, and Emmett Kelly* in The Greatest Show on Earth. RM.

the flying trapeze. DeMille was stymied for a way of staging the scene.

"Well, *I* can tell you how to do it," proffered Concello.

Anxious to know, the filmmaker invited an explanation.

The circus boss hesitated. "But, it's gonna cost you."

Management by that time was sickened over the contract it had signed with Paramount, which gave the studio so much for so little. Thus, additional advice on-the-set became costly, and DeMille agreed to pay Concello ten thousand dollars for the answer. Art passed most of the money along to loyal hands—to the people, as Nena Evans, one of the recipients, puts it, "that worked their tail off around there that weren't getting much money."

How did the big-top executive solve DeMille's problem? Simply, he dug a hole beneath the trapeze rigging under the tent, spread a net over the cavity

149

and covered that with leaves. Then, before allowing Wilde to take the fall, he took a test dive himself.

"That's Concello," testifies Evans. "He wouldn't ask you to do anything he wouldn't do."

There is a touching scene in the movie that captures the enchantment of a great era. A trio of trapeze troupes, one over each ring, are all in motion, the flyers costumed in angelic white. The deep blue canvas around them embellished with red stars forms a lyrical frame. Over the center ring the lithe, exalted form of Antoinette Concello swings radiantly over the crowds. It is one of many wonderful moments actually shot on location. On film forever is a three-ring masterpiece.

True to his nature, Concello stayed in the background, refusing to appear in any of the minor sequences which focused on management figures. Art gave those chances to his assistants, Frank McClosky and Tuffy Genders. North, in typical contrast, hosted an entire scene early in the movie, playing himself the dashing circus magnet.

Although he never sought it, Arthur M. Concello deserves comparable recognition. Millions of circus goers were assured a seat at the edge of excitement and wonder, on time with rare exception, thanks to the man whose name they may never know. Among show-wise circles, obscurity is out of the question. As Merle Evans puts it, "DeMille knows about him."

14
The Last Great Big Top

I HAVE never found myself in agreement with those who contend that John Ringling North is "a damn good business man." I think on Mr. North's restless mind were higher priorities.

One was showmanship. Miles White assures us, "Money didn't mean anything to Johnny. Style meant everything to him." The circus, according to Mr. North, speaks a mystical language. If it dazzles the multitudes, purpose accomplished. Show a profit? That's okay, too.

Another of North's keen concerns was keeping the sun out of his eyes. The all-night celebrant, spending time with the circus during an engagement in Havana, suffered insomnia while trying to sleep one afternoon. He wandered downstairs to an adjoining swimming pool at the Hotel Nacional. There he bumped into some ordinary souls gathered in harmless social merriment. Among them was columnist Robert Ruarke, who reported North's bizarre entrance.

"What is that awful thing up there?" asked the bohemian night owl, pointing to a yellow object in the sky.

"That, Mr. North," someone is reported to have said, "is the sun."

North squinted curiously. "What do they need it for?"

Of the many curiosities exhibited then with the circus—from Mrs. Gargantua The Great to the seven-year-old "pint-sized wonder" xylophonist Mister Mistin—North himself ranks high. Ruarke, perturbed by an inopportune telephone call from the gregarious producer, to his readers wrote, "the day I decided that Mr. North belonged in his own circus as an exhibit, preferably caged, was when he called me at 4 A.M., after I had snatched a few hours of sleep, and demanded brightly that I come and join him at tea. He had inverted dinner and breakfast, all without sleep, and now was clamoring for companionship at tea."

"Listen . . . I'll tell you about him" begins Nena Evans (North's former secretary), "he knows how he wants to live and it may be crazy to you and me, but he can afford it so he does it that way. The first thing the hotel did when he'd come to New York, was to get the big picture window draped because he didn't like the morning light."

Neither did North care much about budgetary matters. The circus was making money. Claims resulting from the Hartford fire had all been settled by July, 1952. DeMille's movie took off, providing the show with loads of added publicity and lucrative royalties. Johnny North reveled in the spotlight of success. Given the winning circumstances, he listened less to Art Concello.

"Actually, when they'd get on their feet and get a lot of money in the bank," recounts a top aide, "then John wanted to be Mr. Circus. At this point all Art

Impractical fantasies on the edge of oblivion: the circus cookhouse dispensing 1,400 meals daily. RM.

. . . Arrival of the circus train in a new town each morning. RM.

Ignoring the inevitable, John Ringling North assembled 55 elephants (the largest touring pachyderm contingent ever) for the 1955 season. RM.

Director Richard Barstow, right, *with another mandate from producer North for unstinting splendor.* CW.

In high preseason spirits at Sarasota, from left to right, Tuffy Genders, Ernie Burch, Robert Dover, and John Ringling North. RM.

was interested in was balancing the sheet at the end of the year."

North's extravagances were difficult to control. He continued packing each new edition of the circus with a staggering array of "First Time in America" performers from Europe and presenting a lavish new set of eye-popping production numbers. The show carried then roughly twice the number of artists who are seen with it today.

Art tried to compensate for John's excesses by cutting back on the number of exterior frills. He moved the menagerie to the front end of a slightly enlarged big top. He replaced teams of horses with tractors. "They don't eat a thing until you turn them on."

Concello's arch frugality posed a threat to North's arch imagination. Heated conflicts erupted. At the close of the unspectacular 1953 tour, Art pressed John for further reductions.

"Let's cut the show a little smaller so we can operate this thing with labor conditions."

John took offense at such rational nonsense. Abridge the ageless delight? Who says we're not making enough money, and who needs to show a big fat profit anyway?

The meeting was short-lived. Art swallowed his pride, John went back to sleep. Robert Ruarke kept his phone off the hook.

Art had accepted what John could not bring himself to face: the tented days were numbered. Hard-top arenas and auditoriums would eventually claim the circus. As far back as 1950, the progressive-minded Concello had tinkered with some trial indoor dates—in St. Louis and San Antonio—"to see how fast you could get in and out." How much longer, Concello was asking, could the show support a traveling hotel on wheels, a complete restaurant, a huge portable exhibition arena, and half the country's wino population?

Unions at the door ruled out the continuation of cheap labor, so essential to the operation of one-day stands. And good accessible lots big enough to handle forty tents were being plowed under by the bulldozers of progress.

"Who wants to drive to Minnie's pea patch to see the show?" argued Concello.

The two giants in control of the nation's biggest big top reached an unofficial impasse. On Art's mind was a nasty little thing called the daily nut. On John's was the very opposite. He yearned for a separate and larger menagerie tent as in the golden days of yore, and for a longer, more impressive circus train. Ten more cars, at least.

Art faced the immovable wishes of the man from whom he derived his authority. He threw up his arms in exasperation.

"If you want to make it bigger, *you* come back here and *you* operate it!"

Lavish New York premieres. In 1954 at the Garden opening, left to right, *actor Henry Fonda, Emmett Kelly, and Ringling radio-television publicist F. Beverly Kelley.* RM.

154

Superior European stars: The Rixos. RM.

. . . *Alexander Konyot.* RM.

. . . *Gena Lipkowska in the "Holidays" spec.* LP.

. . . *Pinito Del Oro.* RM.

. . . *Albert White on a float from "Dreamland."* RM.

. . . The Nerveless Nocks. RM.

. . . Dietter Tasso. RM.

North accepted the invitation, simple as that, and the two boys dissolved their association.

If hiring Concello to be general manager back in 1942 was the "best move" North ever made, was letting him go his worst? Throwing caution to the winds, the undeterred circus king proclaimed the dawning of a new era in showmanship. The Norman Bel Geddes suspension-pole big-top designs were dusted off and now seriously considered. Orders were placed with Westinghouse for streamlined heating units. North instructed his jungle liaisons to scout scores of baby elephants. He wanted fifty pachyderms, the largest herd ever to be presented!

Outsiders with convincing showbiz credentials were swooped up to help the circus redress itself. Modern marketing techniques were employed. From Los Angeles came Milton Pickman, an agent who negotiated several one hour TV specials with General Foods for $100,000 each. North created a post for Pickman as special promotional director. One of Pickman's memos urged the immediate abandonment of traditional outdoor billposting brigades. North, a man to try anything once,

. . . "American, U.S.A.," 1953 finale. RM.

Concello put the menagerie in the front end of an expanded five-pole big top, an economy move that North later resisted. RM.

approved the recommendation, and thus began a series of drastic moves that made him a very unpopular figure.

The daring policy changes made dramatic press copy. "Moving to meet today's challenges with modern methods," wrote North's new publicity chief Edward Knoblaugh, "John Ringling North carried out a thorough reorganization of the big show from top to bottom. He conducted a shakeup of many executive departments and streamlined others for maximum efficiency . . . many new faces appeared in key positions as Mr. North proceeded with his reorganization plans. Outmoded practices were discarded and a fresh approach to the multiple problems of administration undertaken."

Take hiring, for example. How did North select the man to replace Concello? While dining in a Paris

Precarious management changes: Art Concello resigned as general manager at the close of the 1953 season. RM.

John Ringling North dabbled for a spell at the manager's desk. RM.

North later turned over the executive reins to Michael Burke, a newcomer to the circus world. RM.

café with his brother Henry's wartime buddie Michael Burke, it suddenly flashed through North's mind that the circus could use a modern style corporate man to coordinate the strange faces swarming through the show with their graphs and memorandums. Burke seemed personable and young, and his credits were glowing: All-American halfback, sports writer, P.T. boat hero with Henry—both earned a silver star.

Burke had then landed free-lance writing assignments in radio and Hollywood. Not bad, thought North. And now he was discussing his recent adventures as a special advisor to the U. S. Commissioner in Germany. North wondered if he needed a special advisor himself.

Why not? Another sip of wine and the charmed impresario, ever searching for unusual attractions, tilted the conversation in the favor of continuing a decidedly pleasant association.

"Michael," he asked, "how would you like to be with the circus?"

Insiders say it was in a weak moment that North made the rash offer. "Without Art, he was lost; he didn't know where to go."

Burke, unfortunately, answered yes to the question and kept answering in the affirmative to most everything his new boss wanted. The executive director-elect brought to his job sincere administrative intentions. (Later, he would go on to become president of Madison Square Garden Center, a position he still holds.) Not knowing a wagon tongue from a quarter pole, he complied cheerfully with all orders: His attitude was admirable and his wardrobe impressive. Burke strolled the lot with a briefcase full of plans for a "Circus of the Future": The big top of tomorrow would be octagonal in shape with its three rings formed in a triangular pattern. Heat-reflecting Dupont fabrics were to envelope the immense 12,000 seat structure. The canvas dome, free of interior poles, would be strung from the tips of hydraulically-operated telescoping towers. Giant rolls of aluminum would be spread across the midway and canopies erected overhead to shelter patrons from the elements of life. The mechanically controlled empire, according to Burke, would be push-buttoned into place in a matter of hours by a sedate squad of *twenty men*. First, the highly skilled technicians would dash off the big top. Then, flick twelve thousand chairs into position. After that, assemble in a few minutes the cookhouse. Finally, they would make themselves available to the man-

160

agement at its "discretion."

Twenty men.

Burke's "Great Prospectus" as it was called by doubting Thomases revealed startling faith in technology. The utopian circus world on the move might have seen the light of day under different circumstances. Michael Burke simply was not the man to make it happen.

"A great big tall good-looking guy," says Nena Evans. "And he couldn't stand up in the office wagon. Bumped his head."

Literally, Mr. Burke was too tall for the task. The football hero did not feel readily comfortable around circus people, and suspecting them to be mainly of the con-artist type he instituted measures to audit their activities.

"This was the time," recounts a firsthand witness, "when they had decided everybody on the show was a crook, when Burke was brought in to clean up the joint. Mike had John convinced that maybe all the money didn't get into the red wagon . . . the treasurer spent all his time watching the thieving, but never got anything else done."

In further efforts designed to protect the flow of cash from the people who counted and recorded it, North ordered that it be immediately converted to cashier's checks. He appointed himself the sole signer of all expenditures including the signing over of the cashier's checks as payment to local venders. A splendid decision, deemed his paranoid advisors. Only one problem; the check authorizer was rarely at his post during normal business hours.

Came the iceman with a delivery. To the red wagon he reported for payment. A voice from over the high, almost unreachable counter told him, "You'll have to wait. Mr. North's not up yet, and he's the only one who can sign your check."

"I'll take cash," said the iceman.

"We don't pay in cash anymore."

"When's Mr. North get up?"

"Sometime around five o'clock."

"It's already noon!"

"Mr. North gets up around five o'clock *this evening.*"

The merchant could not believe the indifference he faced. He drew back in anger.

"I don't have to wait at all!"

And with that, he gathered his cold blocks and drove on to a more cooperative client.

"An explosive renaissance of high ethical standards," wrote the press agents, describing these unusual practices. "Turnstiles were placed at the entrances of the big top and sideshow to facilitate accurate checks on ticket sales . . . overloaded staffs were slimmed down . . . new horizons of thrills, chills, and laughter await the millions of circus goers on this continent."

Though good press copy it made, North's reorganization was a sincere attempt on his part to straighten out the ranks. Getting rid of the bad guys, however, threatened to deplete the show of qualified help. Under the guidance of Concello's reliable assistants who stayed on after Concello left—men such as Frank McClosky and Tuffy Genders—the show remained deceptively indestructible. Burke moved in his own theoretical world, tinkering over the Great Prospectus. He conferred with engineers and textile manufacturers, substituted one fabric for another, posed knowingly with a cup of coffee over preliminary design drawings.

As long as it was on paper, Burke's grasp of the Circus of the Future was superlative. Out there in the real world, the circus of the present suffered. Crowds dwindled. Press agents resigned in protest over the gross curtailment of complimentary tickets alloted them. Dissension between key officials over North's controversial policy changes caused heated flare-ups and eventually triggered a mass exodus of experienced department heads. McClosky and his top assistants, Walter Kernan and Willis Lawson, directly under Burke in authority, all were fired in a mid-August masacre during the 1955 season. Loyal underlings followed them off the lot. North's gran-

Striking pickets infested circus grounds during 1955 and 1956 with unreasonable demands, sabotaged trucks and equipment. CW.

diose managerial blunders—mistakes perhaps never before equaled in circus history—were beginning to backfire. The new order of things had not materialized.

North seemed strangely unmoved by the problems tearing his show apart. In France he met with famed artist Vertez, designated designer of the next edition of the circus. Back in San Francisco, where pickets intensified their harassment of the show during its engagement at the Cow Palace, North smiled amiably for reporters and photographers gathered at the St. Francis Hotel. Did the good-natured showman address himself to the pressing labor problems? No, he talked about tap dancing and saxophone playing, his two favorite pastimes. Displaying unbelievable cool in the face of adversity, North reiterated, "Rain or shine, movies or television, it's still the Greatest Show on Earth and everybody loves the circus."

Surmised a former employee, "Johnny may have thought the show had been managed so good for so long it would just run itself."

Came the telling winter of 1956. More veteran troupers turned in their resignations. The walkout of Ringling's celebrated music man Merle Evans jolted North's cavalier composure. He telephoned Evans at three in the morning, pleading with the maestro to rescind his withdrawal. No, said the master musician, sensing an eerie season ahead. His decision was final. The tormented circus president was forced to find a replacement. After much delay, he finally accepted Izzy Cervone, a man of debatable qualifica-

tions. Cervone added stringed instruments to the bandwagon and championed a shrill commercial sound of extreme plasticity.

Following a tepid run the next spring at Madison Square Garden, the show hit the canvas circuit like a leaking ship on stormy waters. Understaffed and poorly managed, the consequences could no longer be ignored. The big top is a grueling world of survival, and it requires a firm taskmaster to motivate and ride herd over the unorthodox characters who will sling water for elephants and lug back-breaking tons of canvas across desolate lots for piddling wages. It is a sub-society of drifters and dingbats, of rogues and runaways on the move, They are drawn to the dark, demonic excitement of uncertainty; to the unspoken life styles that flourish in the shadows between shows. They crave the tingle of strange crowds, cling to the quasi-security of continual hoopla. Card games on tables propped against wooden poles under flapping torn banners turn them incessantly on. So do the crashing rhythms of rickety railroad cars clattering recklessly down the tracks through blurred crossings in the night. They are driven relentlessly forward by the elusive, unresolved sensation of being nowhere and yet everywhere. For them, the circus, forever on the move, *is* the ultimate escape. . . .

This precarious caravan was starting to crack. Michael Burke with every good intention to his name could not fathom what made it tick, nor what magical formula would keep the diverse parts of the puzzle intact. No more prepared than he were his bright-faced associates, relative newcomers to the tented city that moved by night. Without the Concellos and the McCloskys to show them the way, they stumbled.

A skeleton crew of confused workers struggled with a new suspension-pole menagerie tent—a prototype of the big top of the future. After several frustrating weeks, the avant garde structure was declared impractical and sent back to Sarasota. Back to the drawing board for Burke's prospectus.

North slept through derailments and injuries and through the first seatless performance in the show's eighty-six-year history. The top man fought off insomnia at two in the afternoon while disgruntled truck drivers removed sugar from the gas tanks and electricians sulked over sabotaged winches. Pickets were ravaging the faltering enterprise. They offered a two dollar stipend to every workingman who would leave the show. The surly roustabouts staged several

The "Greatest Show on Earth" nearing the end of the line as an under-canvas enterprise. Technology had dulled the magic. RM.

walkouts daily, each time rejoining the queue for another couple of bucks.

Most matinees were delayed by hours, others skipped altogether. One wise guy dubbed it "the latest show on earth."

The ageless delight limped into Pittsburgh, Pennsylvania, on 16 July 1956. When John Ringling North woke up to the realities, it was too late. Too late to turn back and too late to bring effectively to pass the Circus of the Future. Michael Burke was baffled and defeated. North was morosely resigned to the inevitable. He had lived through it all so many times before. Back in the thirties he had watched great circuses fall with irrevocable finality. Twenty years later, now his was the victim. In a somber, momentous declaration to the press, he wrote "the tented circus, as it now exists, is in my opinion a thing of the past."

Twelve thousand souls jammed the big top to witness the last under-canvas performance of "The Greatest Show on Earth." Small, eager-eyed boys looked on with sadness as a wonderful day drew to a close. Grown men shed tears. Editorials protested the sudden closing. Claimed an astute trouper, "We could go on giving farewell performances for at least a whole year. The circus would clean up!"

Who was the culprit? North's incredible mismanagement colored far deeper problems—skyrocketing costs; the unreasonable demands of organized labor; a dearth of good lots to play on; television and radio and the movies. The twentieth century had caught up to the circus of circuses. Pity progress.

North was denounced as the man who strangled Santa Claus. He rode the circus train back to Sarasota in brooding seclusion. His car was carefully guarded. For weeks he spoke to no one save for a few close friends. His dapper spirits deflated, he searched his soul for a way out of the crisis. There was only one man who could pull him out, and he needed that man desperately—Art Concello. After days of painful indecision, North made a humble overture. Art agreed to talk. They would meet at the Plaza Restaurant.

. . . Shades of a Barnum & Bailey reunion? James could not handle P.T.'s enormous ego and withdrew from the partnership. A couple of disastrous tours followed. Barnum eventually conceded Bailey's importance; the two reunited and thereafter Bailey dominated the managerial affairs of the famous team. . . .

Was North setting the stage for a similar reconciliation? This would be the appointment at which hopefully he and his former general manager would get back together. Concello would consent to operating the circus as an indoor venture. Johnny knew Art's thinking about the future of tented exhibitions on Minnie's pea patch. He realized that Art might bicker for increased authority and a cut of the action. Could he afford to refuse? His debts were nearing the $2 million mark, and a mismanagement suit had been filed against him and his brother Henry by the "49-ers" (the Ringlings who held the minority stock).

John needed King Arthur. Behind the throne again? No, let him sit in the driver's seat if need be. The gentlemen convened at the Plaza, where they were seated by a window in broad daylight. John looked a little ill-at-ease. Suffering from the sun in his eyes? Embarrassed? Or maybe apologetic? Nervously in his mind he prepared to make his offer: "Art, you were right. I want to make a deal with you. I want you to take the circus and operate it." To which, if all went right, Art would reply according to the game plan, "I'll organize it, take it out. We'll get this million, nine paid off."

John Ringling North faced Arthur M. Concello, the man who had helped him achieve his greatest goal. Concello the aerialist, the master organizer, the inventor, the fund raiser and backer, fixer and contract shark, the patron of great cigars—the friend. Concello had enjoyed a two-year sabbatical from big-top lunacy. Surely he was the more refreshed of the two.

Coyly pretending not to know the dialogue planned for the historic dinner date, Concello immersed himself in a cup of coffee and looked

Final stand for Ringling Bros. and Barnum & Bailey under the big top, at Pittsburgh, Pennsylvania, July 16, 1956. CW.

supremely satisfied. His classy carnie face grinned with self-assurance.

Johnny looked sick.

The king behind the throne lit up a big smoke and broached a delicate subject, placid as a perfect stranger. Casually he inquired of his distraught dinner guest, "What's your problem?"

15
Jackpot Season

THREE small tots giggled restlessly in the back seat of our car as it shot down one freeway and merged into another. Their mother guided the wheel. Their uncle, a circus addict, peered up at the signposts cascading past us. We were on our way to the Los Angeles Sports Arena, situated somewhere down the network of maniacal expressways and interchanges. We had heard glowing reports of a great extravaganza being presented there. "In all the world there is no show like a circus," reported the *Los Angeles Herald-Examiner*, "and in all circuses in the world there's nothing better to be seen than the

A contented crowd exists the big top following a performance of James Bros. Circus, 1968.

Circus springs eternal. Bill Rhodes letters up a new John Strong circus truck. JS.

Dobritch International Circus."

One hundred years ago, an overland coach would have shuttled little Debbie, Jeff, and Lisa to the dusty edge of a meadow graced with billowing white tops. Tonight, they were being transported to the world of incredible feats in a fast-moving automobile,

165

twentieth century style. And from a padded seat in a great steel-domed arena they would view equestrians and funambulists performing ageless delights. Each new generation discovers the circus on its own terms.

Man's natural passion for mystery and awe has not succumbed to the age of technology. Circuses seem likely to endure in some form or another. Fifty-five seasons earlier, Floyd King sat on a quiet southern porch with his boss, Harvey Wallace. The two discussed the future of their business. Predicted Wallace, "I'll tell you, Floyd, there always will be circuses as long as you live under canvas. But mark my word, the time is coming when they'll have these big circuses in auditoriums and coliseums where a fellow will have a nice cushioned seat and can observe the circus in comfort in January or February."

True to Wallace's foresight, the big tops of a rich bygone era are heaped in museums, and gilded horse-drawn wagons clatter down the cobblestone streets of our memories. Silver and red trains have vanished. The statistics do not point to a renaissance. Earl Chapin May recorded in 1930 that during the 1870s, some forty odd shows trouped Dixie. By 1893 a dozen of those institutions moved by rail, competing for top territory, and less than twenty years later the number had tripled! Nineteen hundred ten marks the high point in red wagon activity. Three dozen shows traveled on a combined total of 675 railroad cars. An equal number of smaller outfits traversed highways and back roads.

By the outset of the great depression, the numbers had dwindled drastically. Following the devastating 1938 season, thirty shows persevered with

Three twentieth-century legends—the late Karl Wallenda, left, *the late Clyde Beatty, and Emmett Kelly all performed during the 1960s.* RM.

Tomorrow's stars may emerge from such student-oriented shows as Circus Kirk. CK.

166

precarious high hopes through the war years. By 1956 there were a couple of dozen tenters, and all but two now toured by trucks.

The decline, I regret to report, continues in our own time. Our Bicentennial era saw a dozen regularly touring shows. Impressive circus directories listing hundreds of names of so-called shows simply do not reflect the realities. Add to this frail number a healthy multitude of annual Shrine Circus dates in over 400 North American cities and you might optimistically conclude that all is far from lost.

Is the road doomed? I don't believe so, not at least for exceptional artists who hurl themselves gracefully through the air and scamper daringly across high wires without nets. The statistics are deceptive. Americans still flock to circus performances, although a majority of them are either the smaller one-ring tent shows or the independently produced Shrine events. The Ringling show has now two separate units. There are always openings for good clowns and for elephants who will mind their manners in public.

I see too many outstanding new performers on the horizon, and occasionally a super performance. Old-timers pin their loyalties to the Codonas and the Leitzels. Are they tradition trapped? Who would dare dispute that today's Don Martinez, with his 3½ revolutions from the flying trapeze and his ethereal, bird-like grace is not every bit the equal to the greats of yesteryear? And who could deny a place in the sun to the marvelous Tito Gaona, now on his way to completing the quadruple! The triple, during the "golden age" a coveted feat executed by the chosen few, has recently become a staple among many flyers. Youngsters are doing it.

Today has its share of superstars. When they are excitingly presented in a threatrically satisfying manner, crowds will form. Tampa-born Cookie Arturo on the single trapeze is a fine example of a youthful personality soaring to the heights. Arturo's sweeping arcs and his stunning toe suspensions while in full motion are unprecedented. Like a good number of his peers, Arturo is keeping alive a great tradition by adding to it his own unique flourishes.

Elvin Bale has attained heights usually dominated by foreign artists. HT.

Princess Tajana (Struppi Hanneford) with Dobritch International Circus. HC.

When only seven years old, Arturo was influenced by another modern-day star, the beautiful Struppi Hanneford.

"She did a most unbelievable trap act," recalls Arturo. "The style and the way she worked . . . with such comfort and ease."

Struppi astonished the fledgling aerialist. He was left convinced that "the most important thing is getting in and out of a trick with preparation and ease, like a dancer on skates. The blending of movements is what is most important."

Thus, genius transmits itself from one artist to another. Struppi, before she inspired Arturo, was herself inspired by the dazzling La Norma, who many performers I have spoken with believe to be the greatest ever. "My idol," says Struppi, "and she always will be."

. . . . somewhere backstage at the Los Angeles Sports Arena on that wonderful night, Struppi was preparing for another performance as "Princess Tajana." Out front, loftily reclined over an enchanted setting of red and green sawdust, Jeff and his sisters Debbie and Lisa munched on popcorn and peanuts and gawked at the antics of some preshow clowns warming up around the hippodrome track. My sister and I seconded the feeling,

sharing between us a pink cloud of cotton candy. Crowds steadily flowed in through the entrance portals. The house began surging with expectations. The chaotic blend of exotic smells and strange foreign sounds swirled around us.

Suddenly the lights are off. It is pitch dark. A spotlight pierces the black void, searching out a man who is falling in a horizontal trance from the upper reaches of the auditorium to the floor. He lands on a small pad and a cannon shot explodes. The spotlight zooms to catch a lady diving recklessly towards a trapeze bar. She misses!

The starlet plunges downward and is stopped a few inches short of bare cement by ropes attached to her ankles. She dangles upside down in wild directions, the crowd gasping.

The shaft of light races to meet a parade that is now in progress—ebullient clowns, feathered ponies and showgirls, sprightly jugglers and tumblers, all crisply in motion. The house lights come on and the arena is ablaze with color and animation. A stately gentleman in red articulates in a gust of fervor: "DOBRITCH INTERNATIONAL CIRCUS!!!"

The show is on, and what a show it is! A splendid progression of artists swinging and jumping, bounding and leaping, holding on and letting go, catapult-

Struppi Hanneford with Ed Sullivan, following an appearance on his television show. HC.

168

The Hannefords, Struppi, far left, and Tommy. HC.

Tommy Hanneford, in the style of his late Uncle Poodles. HC.

ing and retracting, soaring over horses and bouncing off trampolines. Speed and agility, balance and bravura, they have it. The zany riding Hannefords, the Rodriguez Brothers taking to the high wire like two beavers adrift on a floating log. The Stebbins and their slap-happy dogs, the Nocks treading the dizzy tips of their swaypoles. The Flying Palacios and the tumbling Canestrellis. . . .

. . . and wonderful, wonderful Emmett Kelly, hovering helplessly at the edge of this dreamy happening like a tramp in paradise, penny-poor and bedazzled forever . . .

. . .and Princess Tajana, star of the haunting aerial fantasy "Indian Summer." Princess Tajana, the world is hers to beguile, so serenely at peace with herself is she above the center ring. The enchanted trapeze ballerina, once the "little acrobat," German trouper, Mama's shining hope out of poverty and routine, Jack Mill's discovery, Barbette's favorite, Tommy Hanneford's wife and partner, American trouper, mortal, immortal, human, angelic. . . . butterfly free, Tajana gliding like a silver sail on a tender breeze, the mistress of cosmic grace, Tajana, tantalizing Tajana on the single trapeze, flawless and poetic . . .

. . . it is a flawless and poetic circus. Dobritch International, symmetrical and fluid, exhilarating. Computer-perfect lighting effects. Vitally assured announcements from ringmaster-director Paul Kaye. Inspired music from Jack Cervone's band weaving a hypnotic spell over the action. Balance and counterpoint. Tension and release. The circus *is* the music of infinity set to motion. It is a spangled crimson doorway to all that lies beyond. . . .

. . . and you celebrate quietly, in the exalted dizziness of the evening, the Colleanos and the Leitzels, the Wallendas and the Clarkonians, the Ringling Norths and the Hannefords, Barbette and La Norma and Princess Tajana—all the insane mortals who, each in their time, strove to lift a misunderstood art form and substantiate the hoopla that Barnum began.

For whom are such masterpiece performances fashioned? In colonial times under small one-ring tents, did patrons look for esthetics in tanbark entertainment? I suppose the more discerning ones did, yet I fear that by and large American circuses have paid too little attention to the artistic aspects of a performance.

I give you the thoughts of Struppi Hanneford on the showmanship of Dobritch International, real *or* imagined:

169

*The Zacchini double cannon act, with Dobritch Interna-
tional Circus.* RM.

"We were asking that question many times. Was it Paul Kaye or Al Dobritch? Paul definitely had that certain talent to know how to put a show together. He was Dobritch's right hand. Things do happen if you have experienced acts and good acts. You have less problems with all great acts. It means you don't have to fight for that moment. So this helps. But when it comes to putting a show together, to space it right—each act to follow which act and to give a good flavor to the show, that not all comedy is right there—the spacing of the show, I think that was Paul Kaye's talent. We all do give a lot of credit to Paul. Dobritch was the man who had the guts to go right to the top. That man was about the fastest rising person in show business I ever heard of. Paul with the talent, this made the show so unique."

After whom did you pattern your own act, Tajana?

". . .that style I created on my own. I always wanted to be ballet, to be prima in the air. Torn between dance, performing, or physical education. Could have been in other places. Ice skating, that was a dream of mine. I used to sing and dance and run on ice. That would have been *something*. I would have enjoyed roller skating, too. Tried many things. Already had knowledge of circus life. I decided this is gonna be my career, I gonna stay with it and make something of it.

"The aerial act is a combination of all the things I wanted to do. I love good music. In Toronto, with a band of sixty and violins, I was one of the features on the stage. Listen to the music and it was like a dance. Great experiment. All musicians stood up the last day, hit violins with little sticks to applaud me. I had tears in my eyes."

Sid Kellner, right, *in heady command of James Bros. Circus, 1968. Kellner poses with a local sponsoring official.*

171

Finally, Tajana, what makes a good circus performance?

"When you've got to the finish, when the show is over and you say, 'What, it's over *already?*' And you got that hot, feverish feeling in your body. You know that was an exciting show. It was a great show."

The "hot, feverish feeling" continued with me that season of 1968. I saw many fine circuses. Three of them rated four solid stars each, they all presented masterpiece performances.

Paul Kaye's brilliant direction and pacing (aided by the optimum technical facilities available at the Sports Arena) was mainly responsible for the magnificent Dobritch International Circus. Later in the spring, James Bros. Circus, showing off its first big

Webber demonstrated equal flair in a fast-paced low-wire routine.

Veteran Herbie Webber, as the Great Huberto, thrilled James Bros. Circus audiences with his stand-up "slide for life" following a dramatic ascension up the inclined rope.

top, lumbered like an irresistible pied piper through San Francisco Bay Area communities, met everywhere it went by happy crowds. It's no puzzle why audiences jammed the tent beyond capacity, overflowing up to the ring curbs. Owner Sid Kellner had assembled a rollicking company of first rate flyers, jugglers, and animal stars. Impromptu showman that he is, Kellner by a stroke of good fortune engaged Tom Fewless to pilot a lively seven-piece band. More than any other hand in the soup, it was Fewless's spirited direction from a wobbly bandstand that paced this charming show to victory.

For name-dropping appeal, count among Kellner's 1968 roster the flying Gibsons, the juggling Houcs, Sonny Moore's delightful mongrel revue, head-balancing troubador on the trapeze Senior Antonio Morales, Woodcock's Elephants, a brigade of boisterously corny çlowns, and the unflagging veteran Herbie Webber sliding down an inclined rope with powerhouse impact—bang, crackle, and boom! Loads of laughs and salient chills lovingly orchestrated.

Circus fans went wild over the James Bros. formula for fun. "The tenting sensation of 1968," wrote former *Billboard* outdoor editor Tom Parkin-

172

son in the *White Tops*. Unfortunately, the result was a fleeting one, and before it fizzled Kellner was viewed as the most promising mogul on the western continent. As it turned out, the exciting little crackerjack show was more of a fluke than a conspiracy to impress circus critics. Kellner's successive editions, though charming to a point, in quality unfolded like a roller coaster on its last legs. Regretfully, Mr. Kellner lacks a sense of long-range planning, in fact he can't see much beyond his next two or three telephone solicitation grinds down the road. Another of the producer's downfalls was assuming prematurely the arrogance of an accomplished impresario. This sorry exercise in bad manners has only hindered his relationships to key personnel, whom he invariably alienates. Circuses are not one-man magic shows, no matter how infallible the boss may act.

Having since served time for Mr. Kellner in his one-man press departments, sadly I convey these unpleasant impressions. Why? Because they tell an important story about the decline of many promising shows. Kellner, striking out at one point on a clean slate, stirringly retitled his show "George Matthew's Great London Circus." Moved by the jubilant imagery of nineteenth-century showmanship, I billed the show accordingly:

Peerless Performers From Piccadilly!
The Buckingham Brass Band!
Under The King's Big Top!!

My syntax more accurately reflects the old James Bros. Circus of 1968, Sid's brief convergence with greatness. Most certainly, folks, wonderful three-ring productions can happen by accident. Anything is possible in the realm of sawdust, spangles, and heartache.

Three's a charm. In August, came another breathtaking delight—Ringling Bros. and Barnum & Bailey's sixty-eighth edition. It was the last one virtually produced by John Ringling North, and I can happily verify it to be one of the King's finest. Twelve seasons had elapsed since North and Concello shucked aside the cumbersome canvas trappings and retooled the circus for indoor presentation. Utilizing some sophisticated hardware, Concello devised a flexible rigging scheme adaptable to any setting; decreed that a trio of illuminated ring curbs would be in order; and in a rare clinical mood replaced sawdust with flat dull green rubber mats (ugh). The uncontrollable variance in production quality caused by muddy, weed-infested lots was now eliminated. The show that opened to heartwarming notices in Manhattan did not, by the time it reached the Golden Gate, resemble a shadow of past alleged glories buried beneath Texas terracotta and Alabama grasshoppers.

North, who never lost sight of the great organization, continued combing European shores for astounding new crowd thrillers. The producer's latest penchant for fast gyrating action was further enhanced by the acquisition of eighteen imported acts, including foot juggler Ugo Garrido, aerial gymnasts The Lavrenovi Duo and the inventive Hergotti Troupe who performed from a "challenging carousel centrifuge."

Among the holdovers, Zdravkos Big Swing—highly popular with American audiences—and the incredible Stephenson's dogs were as potent as ever. Antoinette Concello conceived with Andre Prince an aerial ballet of marvelous novelty. The success factor was a specially designed track rigging, peddled by bicycle riders on high, from which thirty-six ladies moved in circular patterns through a shower of bubbles. Ringmaster Harold Ronk sang appropriately "Love Makes The World Go Round." The overall effect was stunning.

The performance had balance, depth, and a breezy exultant pace. Director Richard Barstow intoned the upbeat proceedings with a mod

Fantastic Fudi, with Ringling-Barnum. WT.

173

Superb dressage rider Ingeborg Rhodin graced the "Greatest Show on Earth." RM.

elephant romp, "Carnaby Street." Merle Evans waved the band on through a score as varied and exciting as the circus itself. Three families of "teeterboard terrors," with the eight Faludis in the center spot, piled up simultaneous four-man highs. The merry andrews and the funsters—most of them seasoned jesters from the old big top days—held down the arena while the big nets went up. Then came the "first family of the air"—The Flying Gaonas. More than for his fine triple somersault, Tito Gaona took top plaudits for a nifty climactic trick—falling to the net, bouncing back onto the vacant catcher's bar and landing smugly in a perfect upright pose! Audiences roared with approval.

A rousing fanfare, no doubt composed by Maestro Evans, tuned up our spirits for yet a higher plateau. Showgirls in silver flashed down the track banging on tambourines to the music. Harold Ronk boomed out:

> When you're down and out,
> Lift up your head and shout,
> It's gonna be a great day!

Early retirees, heading for the exits, were stopped in their footsteps. Long-haired customers rose to their feet in honest adulation. "Bravo!" they shouted to a circus patriotically inclined. This one's not over yet.

"There is a brotherhood of man!" sang the melodious ringmaster, and in rushed Hugo Schmidt's herd of performing pachyderms. The entire house was transfixed. The big bulls threw their massive weight skyward into a long mount. The star-spangled

174

Ringling's mad, mod elephant shindig, "Carnaby Street."
WT.

spectacle drew a thunderous ovation. Some stood there for moments in awe.

My jackpot season had come to a close.

Memories set in so fast, and the ongoing struggle for survival takes its toll among the wizards of sight and sound—those daring men who are torn between art and commerce at the red wagon. Al Dobritch, without Paul Kaye the following season, teamed up with a European impresario, Francois Bronett, to produce the Dobritch & Swedish National Circus, a distinctly disappointing venture. Well into its second week at the Sports Arena in Los Angeles, the show resembled scarcely more than a disjointed first rehearsal. Dobritch darted nervously about the performing area, waving his hands in an effort to direct the hodgepodge. Clearly, he lacked Kaye's finishing talents.

Several years later while managing Circus Circus in Las Vegas, the Bulgarian-born showman jumped to his death from the seventh floor of his hotel. Suicide? Dobritch was heavily identified with underworld figures to whom his unpaid obligations were mounting, and nobody in the business believes he precipitated the fall. How strange are the destinies of master showmen.

Paul Kaye, without Dobritch, went on to create

Henry Ringling North, left, *his son John Ringling North II*, right, *and grandson John Ringling North III, along with clown Frankie Saluto and circus veterinarian "Doc" Henderson. Ringling circus sale in late 1967 ruled out the possibility of future management by the young Norths.* RM.

Circus Maximus, a critically acclaimed production that was not effectively promoted. All Mr. Kaye has to show for the ill-fated gem is a scrapbook full of rave reviews. Since those idealistic days he has settled down sensibly as a producer of Shrine circuses. Without a regular string of annual dates, however, Kaye is unable to sustain a solid ensemble company so necessary in the making of a great performance.

Mr. North has suavely retired to picturesque regions of Europe. Sid Kellner is now promoting sports and magic shows, unable to make the transition from phoneman to showman. Kellner may be pinning his hopes on two promising sons, George and Matthew.

I have recounted the wonderful season of 1968 as evidence that the American circus in modern times has some great moments to be proud of. Admittedly, the days when a tented treat could attract long lines without really trying are over. Today's entertainment world is too competitive for the consumer's dollar. The circus will endure mainly on one commodity: talent. The selling of big-top nostalgia—"See the elephants at dawn!" "Watch the great tents rise!"—has limited box-office punch. We are left with the artists who can create performances worthy of the public's favor, a fact many circus men have yet to recognize. The future depends on exciting shows.

In the year 2000, how will the performances of the sixties be remembered? Will Debbie, Jeff and Lisa—the three eager-eyed children who attended with me the memorable Dobritch International Circus of 1968—turn their backs on revolutionary ideas being introduced by circus kings George and Matthew Kellner, Sandy Dobritch, or John Ringling North III? What *then* will be "the good old days"?

The arguments over jackpot seasons never end. I can hear tomorrow's moppets enthusing about elevated ring curbs, telescreen closeups individually controlled at each and every reserved seat, earphones offering a choice of musical accompaniment and intergalactic aerial light shows. All very synthetic. I'm sure today's tots will rise up in defense of the glorious, never to be forgotten past. *"I'll tell you about Dobritch International at the Los Angeles Sports Arena,"* I can hear them saying. "The cotton candy was not simulated. All of the performers appeared *in person, not on video,* they had a *live* band, not some stupid moog synthesizer throwing the Beatles at you in reverse. That was a *real* circus!"

16
Mysterious Great Traditions

"... All that is wonderful, all that is mightiest, all that is novel ... it is the standard circus, the all satisfying circus."
　　　　　—Ringling Bros. press agents, 1932
"... Circus predicated to quality rather than quantity and presented amid the safety and comfort of auditoriums ... Gone are the discomforts of mud and dust, of wind, rain or broiling sun, and of makeshift seats ... here the *circus* is the thing."
　　　　　—Polack Bros. press agents, 1956
"... The real American circus, under the big top!"
　　　　　—Circus Vargas press agents, 1976

SO who needs another definition of the one true circus? To the many myths already perpetuated, new ones are continually added, such as the current claim by Cliff Vargas of "a return to the rich tradition of the circus as it once was in America."

As it once was, *when*? No specific date is given. Has Mr. Vargas in mind the day when George Washington viewed from a private box a one-ring thriller provided by his equestrian friend, John Bill Ricketts? Traditions then were scarce, our inaugural touring companies had little to go on but their own innate sense of entertainment. Whatever worked became a viable part of the program. Horseman Ricketts circled the ring with a small lad on his shoulders and danced a hornpipe from the saddle of his horse. President Washington applauded generously.

Ricketts augmented his tanbark skills with other

Cliff Vargas, most promising showman under the big top, proclaims a revival of the circus "as it once was in America." CV.

crowd-pleasing treats: comic dancers, songs, slack-wire troubadours, and pantomimes. Pantomimes at a circus? Yes, they flourished in the eighteenth century. The transplanted riding star and instructor—a contemporary thinker not bound by sacred customs—interspersed hair-raising dramatic vignettes through his programs. One of Ricketts' most popular offerings depicted a grizzly whiskey rebellion—General Alexander Hamilton in a brawl with some moonshiners. Customers in attendance cheered the dust blazing melodrama. By popular demand other novelties were mounted. So authentically did Mr. Ricketts stage a scene from Don Juan enroute to hell that the realistic flames of damnation literally consumed his mighty Amphitheatre—$20,000 worth. The daring producer fell to a deep depression and sailed for his homeland. In a storm he and his vessel were permanently lost.

When will Producer Vargas present Don Juan in Hell?

Our early American circuses were basically vaudeville in-the-round. They did not originate under romantic tents trimmed with stars and stripes. The traveling tent show was pioneered in the early nineteenth century by men like Aaron Turner, primarily for lack of permanent theater facilities in small towns along the road. Our first producers adapted ingeniously well to changing conditions. The programs they assembled had great flexibility; there were fancy trick riders, fiddlers' interludes, talking clowns, black-face sing-a-longs. Minstrel shows were born in a circus ring.

No signs yet of the "rich tradition" alluded to by Mr. Vargas. One century later, in fact, when John Ringling North nudged a five-year-old xylophonist, Mister Mistin, into the spotlights, straight-laced critics and buffs raised their eyebrows. Likewise, the traditionalists could not justify a troupe of Scottish bagpipers on Polack Bros. Somehow, they seemed as out of place in the twentieth century as do talking clowns and the "Grand Historical Pantomime." Evidently Mr. Vargas does not favor vaudeville in-the-round. Count that tradition out.

Were it not for the absence of an equestrian on his bill, "Big" John A. Strong would be our purist link to the past. The buoyant talkative ringmaster is a decidedly nineteenth-century figure—a Yankee Robinson type. Tall and fatherly, Strong dotes over a performance of humble, almost pristine ingredients. His stars are his own two daughters Sandy and Carol and his extraordinary son, John Strong, Jr. The

The circus as it once was in America: a rich diversity of acrobatic and theatrical treats staged in-the-round. RM.

178

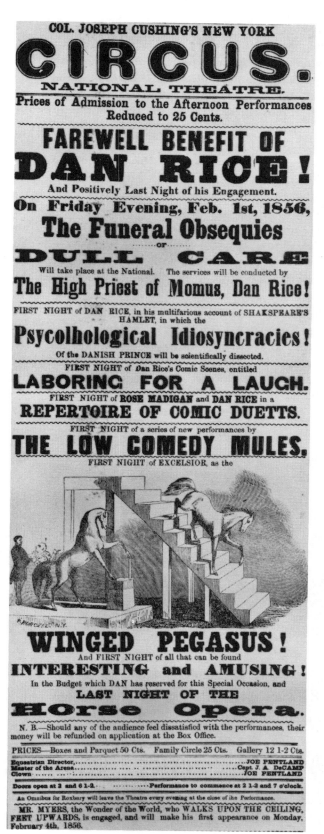

*Col. Joseph Cushing offered New Yorkers a wide variety
of entertainment in this nineteenth-century ad.* RM.

Big John A. Strong, our most authentic link to the past. RM.

vibrant lad is a little whirlwind of versatility, there is
nothing in the realm of sawdust that he will not
attempt and probably accomplish. A motley of
assorted animals of the friendly variety—all home
trained by loving hands—share the ring with one or
two family-oriented acts.

Big John, resplendent in red tails and mature
silver whiskers, in high spirits pushes an index finger
rhythmically back and forth towards his one-man
band. Seeing the circus through Big John's eyes is
the essence of its appeal. He coaxes through their
gingerly paces a trio of peace-loving goats; keys the
audience up to new heights of enthusiasm with the
golden tongue of a press agent and cue-card man.

"Got a nice hand, goats!" Strong exclaims, solicit-
ing solid reception from the little audience.

"Wasn't that great, they love you Sandy!" he
shouts, and the crowd comes through with cheers.
All around a cozy ring—simple, intimate, highly
personal.

John calls his show the "1869 Circus"—a title not
far from the truth. Should he feature a few crack
horseriders he'd have an authentic early American
tent show. After all, both Ricketts and his English
counterpart, Philip Astley (the acknowledged
founder of our modern circus) were top riders. The
roots of our greatest shows on earth lie in the circular
excitement of agile acrobats dancing and somersaulting, vaulting and leaping over galloping stallions.
Horses were the focal points of the primitive touring
companies. They pulled the red wagons by night
over dirt roads, and by day they pranced in feathers
before rural Americans capable of appreciating a fine
horse and a talented rider.

Messrs. Astley and Ricketts might consider Circus Vargas something less than their idea of propriety in view of the handful of liberty horses that comprise its equestrian compliment. How traditions change. You can sit through an entire three-ringer today without seeing one single rider!

Astley and Ricketts might also turn their noses up at the Circus Vargas band—an all-brass contingent. Not one violin or fiddle! In the days of the old mud show, the spirited routines of our top entertainers were accompanied by bugles, clarinets, bass violas, drums, and violins. Dixie's beloved jester Dan Rice, posing merrily within arm's length of his fans, warbled out ditties of his own making—raucous ballads such as "Blue Eagle Jail" and "Root Hog or Die." The irascible cutup spent his professional years being thoroughly mischievous even if it meant breaking a few "traditions."

Clearly, these simplistic shindigs were not scored in a manner that today's fans could easily accept. Purists argue in favor of "true" circus music—the stirring gallops and marches for which Merle Evans is noted. No single musician has defined "circus" music more persuasively than Evans; yet his avid followers misrepresent him when they fail to ac-

knowledge the preponderance of popular melodies that have always dotted his scores. When he assumed the Ringling podium in 1919, Evans was regarded as something of a radical. Unlike Karl King and other classically oriented conductors before him, Evans tilted his music partially in the direction of Broadway and tin pan alley. He added to traditional tanbark sounds the songs that Americans were singing—the charleston and the blackbottom, "Just One of Those Things" and "All Alone."

Larry Pissoni, who founded San Francisco's charming Pickle Family Circus, and whose goal is "to satisfy everyone's preconception of what they think circus is, and then go beyond that and show them what can be done with the form," points out that originally, the music played at a circus *was* the music of the day. Contends Pissoni, his seven long-haired musical makers—a group of mellow jazz rockers—are very authentic, indeed. They create sounds that are currently in vogue. Would Mr. Vargas in his search for "the rich tradition" opt for a bugle and a fiddler, or for an electric bass guitar and a bongo drum?

Circuses have never been orthodox despite what

Youthful rock musicians provide contemporary sounds for San Francisco's intimate Pickle Family Circus. PF.

you may read from a press agent. In contrast to today's merchants of nostalgia are the bold, imaginative showmen of yesteryear who competed vigorously to outdazzle each other in sheer novelty and innovation. Consider the full page ad taken out by the Ringling brothers in St. Louis in 1895, in opposition to a day-and-date battle with the Barnum & Bailey show:

The Up-To-Date Show! It has Arrived!
The show that stands on its own merits. Does not divide—Uses no other name than that of its proprietor. Sails under no false colors—Borrows nothing from the past—Gives you the energy and results of the actual living present—Is too big—Too Modern—Too generous—Too broad—Too liberal—Too prosperous—Too great to seriously notice the petty insinuations of concerns that cannot keep up in the march of progress, and disdainfully holds in contempt the ridiculous, ill-tempered, undignified, fearbegotten, whimsical prattle of disgruntled, outclassed, overshadowed and overwhelmed would-be rivals.

"When you go to a circus," explains ringmaster Harold Ronk, "it's that expectancy of seeing some things that you *know* will be there, and then being surprised by the *other* things." Ronk should know, for the role of a singing-ringmaster which he fills so well has been the center of controversy. There are certain stodgy critics who have carefully defined concepts of what a circus should be and are highly offended when their strict expectations are not met. Let a ringmaster sing, for example, and you are sure to irritate these self-appointed experts.

Wrote Gerald Nachman in the *Oakland Tribune*, "Regarding Harold Ronk, who contrary to the program is not everybody's childhood notion of what a ringmaster should be. Not with those curly blond locks, not without a moustache and certainly not singing "Fascination." Ringmasters are suppose to be tall and lean and dark and look as much like Mandrake the Magician, not blond and paunchy and sing like Mario Lanza."

Presumedly, Mr. Nachman has a Mandrake the Magician complex, or the only circus he ever saw was one directed by Fellini. No doubt he would be appalled by the abundance of vocal selections that flowed from the lips of singing clowns and announ-

Singing ringmaster Harold Ronk argues for innovation as well as for tradition. HT.

181

cers before circuses became "traditional." John Bill Ricketts, not then considered a radical, engaged William Sully, a fully accredited member of Sadler Wells, London. Between tumbling acts and horse-riding displays, Mr. Sully brought down the house with a comical rendition of "Four and Twenty Periwigs." Yes, at the show that George Washington patronized.

The first President might have felt out of place under the immense orange canvas of Circus Vargas, where the sense of intimacy he enjoyed is strangely lacking. The huge Vargas big top suggests a three-ring marvel of the heyday era, so are we wrong in expecting a hippodrome track full of "boisterous buffoons" now and then? Yet when the announcer cries, "Here come the clowns!" only three funny faces appear. Not very important, evidently, are the populated walkarounds of yesteryear, in the considered opinion of Cliff Vargas, self-heralded preservationist of the "good old days."

The circus "as it once was in America" according to the aspiring California showman has nothing to do with quantity at all. And theatrical touches are taboo. To quote his literary sages, "When Mr. Vargas dreamed up his now famous idea for Circus Vargas . . . he vowed to strip away the bogus trappings of Las Vegas and Broadway and to refocus the spotlight where it belonged: on gifted performers and amazing animals."

The message is a rib at the Ringling organization where "spectacles sublime" are still being cranked out as they have been for over half a century by our biggest shows. Is that not a tradition? The big pageants, splashy costume affairs, began in the late

Jupiter, Barnum & Bailey's ascending "Balloon Horse," 1909. CW.

nineteenth century. The original themes were biblical and patriotic—measures taken by circus men to offset the public's low opinion of outdoor show business. Lithographers went wild:

Tremendous, Patriotic, Triumphant, Educational, Moral, Glorious,
Lavishly Costumed 1000 Character Spectacular!
Ringling Bros. World's Greatest Shows
Last Days of The Century or
The Light of Liberty

Barnum & Bailey canvasmen, 1903, outfitted for a biblical pageant. CW.

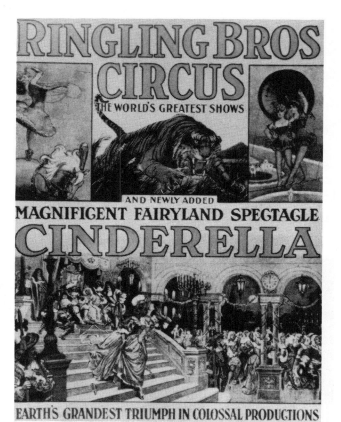

The program cover for Ringling Bros. 1916 spectacle "Cinderella." CW.

The elaborate, time-consuming productions have never met with unanimous approval. On occasion, they have taken a critical beating. Barnum & Bailey's 1914 opener, "The Wiz and Prince of Arabia" moved to tears the *Billboard* reviewer. It did not impress the scribe from *Variety:* "Lord knows what it is. The show starts off with a 50-minute 'Oriental Romance' that drags along to a dreary dirge of the same length of time played by the band. No one knows what it is all about and no one cares, besides wishing it had never started."

The fastidious journal found much to praise, however, in a four-scene pantomime offered by the Ringling Bros. that same season. "The costuming and staging of this production, for which credit is given to Al Ringling, is particularly commendable. A ballet of 50 short-skirted skippers gave the spectacle the necessary classic blend and the addition of the Apollo Trio (bronzed) helped make it an impressive success. Within, it added an unexpected air of progressiveness to the circus."

Many showmen sought directorial imagination. The "unexpected air of progressiveness" made their

programs more appealing. In 1922 John Robinson showcased sixteen lovely ladies on swinging ladders. The band played a popular song while they swung in unison and the crowds loved it. "The piece de resistance," reported a New York notice. "Probably the biggest flash on any outdoor outfit."

The Hagenbeck-Wallace show drew loud ovations from a spec themed after the holy war, "Arabia." The climax was marked by the sacrifice to a cage filled with beasts of a youthful harper—none other than Clyde Beatty in drag. The wild animal trainer was not yet famous enough to avoid "spec." He, excuse me "she" was a knockout.

The Al G. Barnes Wild Animal Circus was not too straight to sugar coat its programs with culture and flesh. Consider the following entries from the 1930 edition:

Display 14. Beauty blended with music. When Miss Blossom Robinson, the gifted soprano, sings, doves and pigeons alight upon her snow white arabian stallion.

Display 20. Fifteen comely and shapely maidens, possessed of pulchritude, trained by Madam

High-stepping strutters, stylishly attired for an Al G. Barnes Circus production number, 1935. CW.

183

Cole Bros. Circus Mother Goose float. CW.

Cole Bros. Circus ballet girls, season of 1943. CW.

Mister Mistin, Jr., a unanimous crowd pleaser with Ringling Bros. and Barnum & Bailey, 1953. CW.

Cherie, in a series of living pictures.

Display 26. Thirty-six singing girls and three dozen dancing horses.

So successful were the garnishments, show manager S. Cronin signed George Cunningham, a revue stager, to embellish future editions. Cunningham dangled the girls from ropes, had them dancing with the elephants and making themselves generally attractive. All the major circuses enhanced their programs in similar ways. Yet when John Ringling North took his spectacles seriously and utilized people of the stature of John Murray Anderson and Norman Bel Geddes to stage them, critics accused North of selling the circus short.

"Sex hits the circus," reported the dissenters, implying that the sight of showgirls in sequins was without precedent. Actually, sex had finally hit the critics.

The list of original costumed events is endless, so are the innovations that abounded in circuses during the vital heyday years. Add to this the many unusual attractions that enlivened the midways and menageries of yesteryear—features like the platter-liped Ubangis and the belligerent Gargantua. Would Mr. Vargas declare these all null and void, along with biblical epics, talking clowns, marvelous riding troupes, singing aerialists, elephant ballets, child xylophonists, living statues, pantomimes, hippodrome races, yodelers, fiddlers, bagpipers, and chorus girls? What are we to revere as the "rich tradition"?

"I believe with all my heart," says Mr. Vargas, "that every generation of Americans is entitled to experience, first hand, the very special thrills, the never duplicated excitement of the real circus, under the big top!"

Good press copy such sentiments make. In truth,

the clever young promoter started with an indoor show and converted to canvas for the same reasons that have driven other producers back to the big top: prohibitive arena rental rates; the loss of concession rights to the arena; and monstrously expensive local musician-union agreements that must be complied with at most auditorium engagements. As a result of these crippling economic factors, Cliff Vargas is now operating under a tent where he has better control over his profit margin. He negotiates reasonable space rates at shopping centers, carries his own band at his own fees and is free to sell all the popcorn and lemonade he can. You may spot the shrewd money man at his novelty stand, diligently cashiering until the last potential purchaser of a pennant or little tin trumpet has gotten away.

The greatest tradition that Mr. Vargas brings to his job is the zeal of an award-winning evangelist. "He's constantly running," says Douglas Lyon, who until he switched to the Beatty-Cole organization in 1977 held the post of National Marketing Director for Circus Vargas. "He has a high energy level. If Cliff Vargas walks on the lot, everyone knows he's there. When the phone rings, I know if it's Cliff Vargas. He has been somewhere in the Midwest and he's called me at four in the morning. 'I got this idea!' And I'll say, 'Cliff—it's four o'clock in the morning.' 'Oh, is it?' 'Yeah, Cliff.' 'Well,' he'll say, 'what do you think about this?'

"He demands the utmost of anybody that he's with. He knows everything that's going on around him. He works 24 hours a day. If I say, 'Cliff, I need to see you,' he'll be on the next airplane or I'll be back to see him. I think his love ultimately is the circus itself. It's the excitement that is generated by a performance, by the crowds, by the tickets, by the business, of the show itself more so than the paper work and the front end of it. He made his money in the phone room operations, which he is now to an extent forsaking with the cold dates (unsponsored engagements) coming along. He is that intense in the cold dates."

Lyon is the man who helped Vargas discover and believe in the power of publicity and advertising. That happened in Los Angeles in 1973 when Vargas (then operating as Miller-Johnson Circus) lost sponsorship for three dates, leaving twelve vacant days to fill. The rising circus man was forced to consider an alternate promotion, and he choose Devinshire Downs for a fill-in date. Performance Director Parley Baer approached Lyon for assistance with

publicity. No circus had played "cold" under canvas in Los Angeles since the Cristiani show in 1959. Southern California was ripe for an old-fashioned ballyhoo. Lyon dispatched an elephant through a car wash ("two years before Ringling did it") and upstaged Henry Kissinger on the ABC evening news.

Mayor Yorty proclaimed it "Circus Day" and celebrities turned out in the droves. It was a "phenomenal success." Vargas watched in awe as thousands of enthused customers lined up at his ticket wagon, laid down hard cold cash, and poured through the marquee to see a circus. Without sponsors. Without a heavy-handed emotional appeal for the local boys club or some distressed birdwatchers fund. No telephone grind had brought the folks in; no, they had been ballyhooed to believe that the circus *itself* was worth patronizing. "All of a sudden, Clifford was getting the recognition he should have been getting for a long time."

The same application was tried out in St. Louis, which "fell flat." Portland, Oregon—their first shopping center engagement later in the year—was uneventful, too. Then came Sacramento, California—another resounding cold date winner. Television stations picked up on a Thanksgiving dinner given for the Vargas personnel under the big top; enthusiastic crowds jammed the tent for the remaining performances.

"From Sacramento on," reports Lyon, "Cliff believed that the way of the circus in the future for him was cold dates." Lyon had proved to Vargas that you don't need the policemen's association or the firefighters' union to pull the people to your doors, not if you have the guts to advertise and promote the circus on its own terms. The two men formed a valuable association, and they moved ahead like pioneers with a great point to prove.

"From November 1973 until we opened again, in January 1974, we went from renting a tent to owning our own tent; from renting trucks to buying twenty semitrucks; to changing our corporate structure from Miller-Johnson to Circus Vargas. In a period of about six weeks, Cliff made moves with leaps and bounds. When the show opened in Dallas, Texas, it snowed the day before we came in there. The show opened on a Thursday night. Cliff wasn't there. He was driving a semi from California and arrived Saturday. He is so intently involved, and at that point the most important thing was getting that truck there, because in it were the ring curbs and the

Circus showgirls endure heavy costume trappings to make fantasies come true. RM.

lights and the sidewall!"

Well over half of all the Vargas dates are now played cold. The show saturates the area with tons of free kids' tickets, blasts the air waves with its name, and treats its customers to a well-run show. "Everything has to work," stresses Lyon. "We play shopping centers. We've found that to be best for our formula, because people naturally go to a shopping center. The children's tickets, the tie-ins, the advertising, having tickets available to the public through ticket outlets are all important. Television is extremely important; it gets people talking about the circus. And once they realize it's under the big top, that's probably the most important single thing. And they come and they see a great show. It's not like being ripped off by some little promoter with a suitcase."

The success of circus Vargas in this crucial area of cold date promotion is nothing less than tremendous considering the stifling dependency in recent times of virtually all American big tops (with the exception of Ringling) on phone room sales. It has positive long term implications. Clyde Beatty-Cole Bros. Circus decided in 1977 to follow suit, with all but two of

their traditional sponsored dates being dropped. Late in the year that organization hired Douglas Lyon, as Vice President and National Marketing Director, to assist with the tricky transition. Showmanship has everything to gain.

Himself a circus fan from childhood, Lyon may be counted among a growing number of buffs who are electing for actual careers in the circus world and whose contributions are proving extremely worthwhile. Notes Lyon, "I think the circus can benefit from people like myself who have an outside knowledge of the entertainment industry (he has worked in rock concerts and recording management) and who just apply it to circuses. It's not a job, because I still enjoy it. I look at it from a historical standpoint, because what we are doing today is creating history."

Cliff Vargas is viewed as the single most important new force under the big top. His accomplishments are formidable and he has advanced rapidly. The question yet to be answered is, can he deliver a great circus performance? His rhetoric, if he ever gets around to taking it seriously, holds promise: "I give our audiences my word that every year, in every way, Circus Vargas will continue to dare, to innovate, to become more exciting!"

In essence, the greatest American "tradition" *is* innovation. Yankee three-ringers at their best fly on the wings of imagination, and they draw endlessly from a rich diversity of forms. Floyd King knew this well, when in 1935 he reflected, "a lot of entertainment for a little money is what the circus gives—a little of almost every form of entertainment blended together—grand opera, vaudeville, musical comedy and burlesque and what not. There is something to please the childish mind as well as the blase amusement critic."

Henry Ringling North affirmed the constant need for new ideas and new modes of presentation when he told a reporter in 1950, "We're trying to outmode that bugaboo of all circuses—that 'What's the use of going again; I saw it last year attitude.' We think we've succeeded to a considerable degree by our constant efforts to get new acts and the large amounts of money we spend to re-dress the show each season. That obviously has helped."

Mr. Vargas has yet to go beyond his own cliche press agentry; beyond such nostalgia-ridden slogans as "The real American circus, under the big top!" and "As it once was in America." He has yet to show us that he really knows what innovation means. The

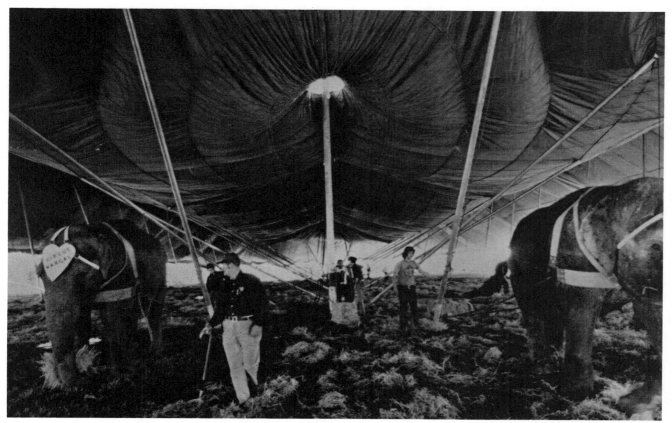

Back to the big top for Cliff Vargas means control of concession sales and freedom from constricting musicians fees in large arenas. CV.

Timeless joy for a world fraught with change. Circus day in the suburbs. CV.

key to turning an average lineup of acts into a spectacle of great and memorable joy is creativity. Tanbark entertainment was never meant to be predictable and ritualistic. Circus Vargas, as presently constituted and stripped of all the "bogus trappings" its press releases so manifestly abhor, is not much more than a European-styled program (with mostly one act at a time) lost in a huge tent that cries out for soaring swirls of acrobats and tumblers and rippling waves of clowns. To be sure, the enterprise is well advertised and promoted, orderly presented, well lighted and orchestrated. The crowds are healthy, and they deserve more.

Let a sense of true experimentation *return* to the big top, yes, "as it once was in America." Let there be novelties new, and unexpected delights; bold staging concepts and stunning new entrances to entrance the eye; let the old and the new parade side by side in startling juxtapositions, yes, "as it once was in America."

Immortality and a Swiss bank account may be within the reach of Cliff Vargas. It's doubtful that will happen until this dynamo of extraordinary promise learns that there is only one great "tradition" worth honoring: SHOWMANSHIP.

Let there be circus!

17
The Feld Bandwagon

"**T**HE most interesting thing about Irvin Feld," commented the company manager of a leading indoor circus, "is that he believes his own publicity."

Who, in case his publicity has failed you, is Irvin Feld? For the equivalent of two presidential terms he has been effectively in charge of our nation's number one circus. When Richard Nixon took up residence in the White House, Mr. Feld joined the illustrious parade of distinguished showmen who have guided the destiny of the "Greatest Show on Earth."

Mr. Feld is an incurable ballyhoo man who would love to carve his initials next to those of P. T. Barnum. Like Cliff Vargas who is returning the circus to the way "it once was in America," wouldn't you guess what Mr. Feld is doing? He's putting "the circus back into the circus." Ringling Bros. and Barnum & Bailey & Feld?

Never has the big top been in cockier hands.

Irvin and Israel Feld and Judge Roy Holfheinze (who lay claim to having introduced to American audiences, in what city and in what year it is not known, bloodless bullfights) bought the circus in late 1967 from the North brothers and their relatives for $8 million. In 1969 they placed it on the New York Stock Exchange, and two years later the "triumphal triumvirate" sold it to Mattel Toy for a price tag of $47 million. (Never mind that the toy company has

Historic Ringling circus sale in Roman Coliseum: John Ringling North, right, *signs over papers to Judge Roy Holfheinz and Irvin Feld.* CW.

since been sued by former Ringling stockholders for grossly overstating the value of its stock, and subsequently ordered to pay them $30 million.)

The Feld who quite naturally assumed the dominant voice was Irvin. Mattel has not challenged his credibility, and although the Judge initially held an option to purchase a controlling interest, beset by ailments and by mounting debts over his costly Astroworld expenditures he settled for a placid Chairman of the Board position. Israel, until his death in 1973, remained passively unobtrusive

189

around an accountant's desk. The three gentlemen, feeling absolutely nothing holy about their new acquisition, proceeded with plans to market the hell out of it. Irvin led the way.

While the good Judge spoke of a day when backwoods families could visit the circus for tickets priced at a dollar a head, his associates adjusted the price of the program magazine alone to twice that amount. They boldly created a second "identical" circus with all the bravura of Noah building a duplicate ark. Now the Greatest Show on Earth would play to twice as many people and make double the money, in two parts—the "Red" and the "Blue" Units—with a one year intermission between. Twin units bearing the same title are not new to the circus world, and what publicists touted "an idea so daring, so sweeping in scope, that no one had ever thought in such cosmic terms" others have dismissed as "only common sense with all the buildings screaming for the show."

The Feld bandwagon has been amazingly successful. The man at the driver's seat, for whatever reasons turn him on, is intently involved. "A genius at what he's doing," estimates Douglas Lyon. Said the late Karl Wallenda, "Feld, I think, as businessman, he's more with his heart and with his

business way. When you be a businessman your heart is with it, too."

"He's selling the circus," emphasizes John Hurdle at the Ringling Museum. "He's going to sell it anyway he can. He's got two units which are making money. He's bringing his circus to the people and it'll keep going. They've done a lot for the show."

Promotion is Feld's first priority. As Harold Ronk sees it, "They promote the circus on a wider scope, partly because of the TV media. They go after the promotion angles. They know how to do this, they're very keen businessmen. This was not so much emphasized in earlier years. This is the big contribution—the angles, they're constantly searching for a new angle to work. This is the vital thing to the circus. If it is not promoted well and the audiences drop off, then I think the interest will drop off. You need that drive that the circus gives, the impact of its arrival, its presence and its departure which brings you back into next season. The audiences are larger now . . . there isn't anything that is a better advertisement than to see a busload of senior citizens or junior citizens or toddlers on their way to the circus, and parking lots filled with buses."

Demonstrating the campaign zeal of a whistle stopper, Feld has taken his case to the American people. Like a politician seeking support for his administration, he solicits and flaunts in trade journal ads the endorsements of national celebrities from sports heroes to Hollywood starlets. Without the rosey platitudes of Joe Namath or Sonny and Cher, would the circus look un-American? Does Feld fear a negative Gallop Poll? A recall at the ballot box? The way he runs, you'd swear the country decided who runs our big tops at general election time. An inner voice seems to cry out:

Irvin Feld. The key is illusion. CW.

New owners put the "Greatest Show on Earth" on the stock market, later sold it to Mattel Toy. CW.

190

Father-and-son producing team: Clown Lou Jacobs, center, *and dignitaries look on as Irvin,* left, *and son Kenneth,* right, *proudly acknowledge Bicentennial honors for their patriotic edition of circus.* HT.

Return the circus to the circus!
Maintain stupendous, tremendous big top leadership!
Vote for the man who has led our clowns and elephants to greater prosperity!
Re-elect Irvin Feld President of the Greatest Show on Earth!

Pom-pom Feld dreamed of being a hard-driving American entrepreneur as a lad of five when he attended his first circus in Hagerstown, Maryland. He felt "a part of it." By the dawning of adolescence he and his brother "Izzy" were following carnivals around the county in an old jalopy, peddling vanilla and lemon extract and rattlesnake oil. (Trust the press kit, kids, from which this information comes.) Shades of future business acumen: the Feld boys bought their goods for a nickel a bottle and foisted them off at county fairs for a buck each.

The bottle merchants advanced eventually to the drug and variety store business, then organized a chain of music centers. From there they ascended to the heights of talent agents, promoting one-nighters for the likes of Belafonte and Andy Williams. They managed Paul Anka from scratch to fame. They took over the operation of the federally owned Carter Amphitheatre in Washington, D. C. They were lauded by a National Press Club award, though presumably not for their active participation in payola—a nasty little practice that Irvin helped to perfect. The practice was long ago declared illegal. Irvin, however, has not lost his touch. He is a master media manipulator.

The key to Feld's success is illusion. With the help of extensive connections in television and the press,

191

Ringling's Bicentennial spec, "Circus Spirit of '76." HT.

Feld has ballyhooed his product well. He has made the circus all things to all people—glittering and antiseptic, safe as candy. His three rings are populated with arm-waving, heart-throbbing hoopla. They are immensely competent upbeat happenings, gorgeously gift-wrapped and slickly attuned to a strut society culture that worships surface over substance. Don Foote's costumes radiate like the shifting hues of an indestructible rainbow. The colors spill out like an enormous ice cream cone so overloaded in flavors it's hard to know what you're tasting—if, indeed, anything. Feld is reaching the tired teenager.

For all of his many allusions to greatness, Feld has not shown himself to be a true innovator. He plays showmanship according to the rules created by his predecessors. He implies continual harsh criticism of the John Ringling North era, yet he is clearly a slave to North's production format. He is overjoyed to quote one of his favorite press agents who notes that he is fully "ten inches taller" than P. T. Barnum;

if the presumptuous statistic were true that would make P. T. a very small man, indeed. Endeavoring to compete with the great Barnum on any grounds is a futile undertaking, especially if you lack originality. How different, really, from Tom Thumb is Michu, "the world's smallest man"? Even if Michu out-littles Mr. Thumb, is that novelty or tradition?

On occasion a few outstanding performers have risen out of the sticky milieu, as was the case with the Bicentennial edition—the one opus Feld has arranged that approaches true brilliance. Therein could be seen Don Martinez, the Carrillo brothers, Petitt, Gunther Gebel Williams, and several refreshing new imported artists. Their contributions were all breathtaking.

Of course, Williams is the crowning coup of the Feld regime; he represents a gold mine of talent and he has been marketed superbly well. The late May Wirth applauded the blond-haired German star. "He is really excellent, he doesn't impinge on the public, doesn't bleed them. He just takes his bows."

192

Some fans are adamant in their conviction that the show depends too heavily on Williams and is therefore inferior as an overall entity. "A handsome man," exclaims one buff, "he is *it* with his charisma and stunning good looks. If one of those tigers decided to eat him, they haven't got a show."

When he first blazed on the American scene in 1969, there was something uniquely contemporary about Williams' casual elegance and natural communion with audiences. In demonstrating never a strain for the spotlight, nor a reach for clamoring applause, he seemed one in spirit with the flower children, the mystics, and the unestablishment

Dazzling are the innovations that Williams has brought to American audiences. HT.

heroes. All he need do was extend his arms outward to the audience in a gesture of blessed communication. Fame and glory were things he seemed already to have confronted, bargained with, and won. He mounted a tiger perched atop an elephant, put his hands together and bowed his head in prayerful meditation, and he personified universal peace. Those were fine, brief, gentle moments in which the center ring realized its own guru.

Williams came along at the exact right moment— at a time when the circus needed a highly personable figure that modern-day audiences could relate to, a figure through whom they could once again discover the timeless magic of center ring. There is no doubt that Gunther Gebel Williams has filled that need— filled it with graceful, no-nonsense animal exhibitions, filled it with his own commanding radiance and with a charisma and charm the circus world may not again see in another of its stars for many years to come.

There is, unfortunately, another side to this equation built on youth and beauty: the day will come—indeed, it is now upon us—when the physical glamour that Gunther and the circus have so heavily relied upon will begin to fade and diminish. Feld and his superstar will end up at a mirror called time; they will be forced to see a pale reflection of past glories. Will Feld then show the same indifference to Williams as he now shows to our great veteran personalities? Catering to the youth syndrome, a cheap and lamentable undertaking that has absorbed much of Feld's attention, may ultimately backfire. In the end, it is not transitory beauty that inspires us. No, it is the spark of true genius to endure. Vitality is the circus world's greatest commodity. Perhaps as Mr. Williams grows older, we will see and enjoy more of his acts. Perhaps he will place further emphasis on greater, more truly amazing animal routines.

In contrast to Williams, and too a few other really

194

"If one of those tigers decided to eat Williams," claimed one fan, "they haven't got a show." HT.

True acrobatic achievement? Many of Ringling's current troupes rely heavily on safety wires and stabilizing poles. HT.

memorable artists, are the performers on loan from various East European countries who work from "mechanics"—safety wires that protect them from fate's fickle finger. They seem out of place on Yankee sawdust, where mechanics are associated with a practice session rather than a finished performance. The feats they attempt are admirable, yet far too many of these performers continually miss their tricks, only to be yanked back to safety by the life lines around their necks. Self-assured professionals they are not. Conceded a production assistant, "They're not sensational enough or electrifying to evoke popular acceptance as a real genuine star."

"They should never be shown," said Karl Wallenda. "When I have a cable on me I can do triple somersaults on that wire and I know if it doesn't go I land on that cable. This is easier than a man makes a somersault on the ground without a mechanic, because he can fall and he can break his neck on the ground. When we practice with the mechanic you can say that's practicing. If they do it without, it would be terrific."

Also of dubious distinction are the apprentice clowns from Feld's Clown College, first year graduates who invariably confuse acrobatic finesse for comedy. The young jesters are beautifully decorative. They are full of boundless energy and determination and they float through the arena like ribbons billowing on a New Year's Eve. Great belly aches they do not inspire. Again, an element of amateurism has infiltrated the circus.

Yet, working with these mediocre materials, Feld the illusionist somehow brings it off. The effect he has achieved is a highly cinematic one. Time was when the circus meant an expansion of our senses at the edge of the unknown, when it had a compelling fascination similar to the lure of science fiction today. At the moment, the Ringling organization is

Michu, the darling of diminutiveness. HT.

197

Circus specs have been greatly charmed by Michu's presence. HT.

giving the public a tantalizing *image* of circus without taxing their nerves much. The preponderance of those questionable safety wires makes possible the enjoyment of basic tanbark skills without the attendant fear of impending danger. As well, the stress on production frills over strong individual acts has given the show a softer edge.

Has the circus lost its guts? Suggested May Wirth, "People, I should imagine, would like to see the performers." The fact is, there are less outstanding performers to see. The Feld formula would appear to be a strategy in compensation—a big splash of color with less heads, more feathers, and a strong solo star around which to build each show: Gunther Gebel Williams on the Red Unit; Elvin Bale on the Blue.

Is razzle dazzle enough? "It's not an organized, one-showman show anymore," as Miles White sees it. "It doesn't hold together as a unit of a show theatrically. It's an industrialist's idea of a show."

Harold Ronk wonders if the other-worldly mystique has been eroded. "I've always said, you can

reach out, almost touch it, but not quite. And this elusiveness is what I think people look for and they hope for. They go to the circus to reach out and touch something, but they're happy when they can't because then it isn't destroyed. And if I were to criticize anything about the circus today, I would say it is a little too accessible. You can get to close to the performer."

Not all the critics have been charmed enough to embrace current artistic goals. The *Christian Science Monitor*, in its 1976 report, noted that none of the acts seemed "as fabulous as the hoopla." A year earlier, the Bicentennial edition (ironically, Feld's best so far) failed to excite the *New York Times*, which called it "The (Not Quite) Greatest Show on Earth." Writers Tony Hiss and David McClelland found the circus more like an ice show without ice: ". . . 45 minutes of showgirls in gorgeous costumes walking through endless production numbers not designed for children of all ages."

Nor was Brendan Gill of the *New Yorker* very impressed, when in reviewing the 1977 opening he

198

reflected, "every year, this lavish and garish mingling of many-colored lights, amplified band music, and busty, bespangled girls strikes me as turning more and more into a fantastically oversized nightclub performance, whose proper habitat is surely the Strip at Vegas."

The matter, clearly, is not whether the production numbers belong in the circus; it is whether they are sufficiently entertaining. Too often of late, these disjointed, laborious, walkarounds have marched us with blinding bravura into a wasteland of meager ideas. "Mardi Gras" (featured in the 108 edition) is a typical case in point. Horribly ill-conceived, it peddled several themes, rambled on far too long, and came off a boring hodgepodge. Hardly could such senseless lavishness compensate for the many second- and third-rate acts that preceded and followed it. Yes, even hoopla can fizzle.

It is within the constitution of a huckster to promise far more than he can deliver, and by far Feld's most exciting productions are his florid predictions of things to come. When he assumed control, it was rumored he would successfully Ringlingize the Western Hemisphere. "By 1973," reported *Variety*, "there will be four Ringling Bros. and Barnum & Bailey units traveling through the world, according to Irvin Feld, President and Chief Executive Officer of the circus . . . he envisions each circus to be virtually equal in quality and up to the highest standards."

Feld saw households canonized in sunburst wagon wheels and gorilla mascots. He and his partners bartered off subsidiary rights for Ringling linen and Ringling health spas, Ringling rock and roll and Ringling hair spray. By 1970, prophesied the president, there would be over 130 products on the market. The possibilities seemed limitless—from Barnum & Bailey mouthwash to Clyde Beatty furniture, Gargantua vitamins and Center Ring prune juice. Funeral parlors wired for calliope music?

Superb Feld import: Pio Nock combined zany humor with drama on the high wire. WT.

199

*Good news for black audiences. Feld booked the King
Charles Troupe from Harlem.* WT.

Life and death for the majority of ordinary citizens does not take place under a tent. I have yet to locate a package of hot dogs bearing the title of one of Feld's properties. When will the third unit of the circus be launched? Where, I wonder, is the movie Richard Irwin supposedly contracted to produce? And that Saturday morning weekly children's special on TV—on what channel will I find it? I have the "Klowns" first and only recorded LP, which I have still to play beyond cut one of side one. Ringling rock and roll doesn't make it to the end, man.

No, circuses have built-in limitations, a fact of life the new owners may be discovering. Who outside a few passionate fans wishes to surround his life with pictures of Jumbo and Michu? Much like the Fourth of July, or Easter, a trip to the big top is a once-a-year pleasure, not the sort of thing you would live with on a daily basis. The circus has institutionalized its fleeting nature beyond domestication. Too much is too much.

When he unveiled the plans for his ambitious

Circus World complex near Orlando, Florida, I sensed Irvin Feld's greatest bid for immortality. I still find the prospectus fascinating. Like the gauche, bigger-than-life program magazines which he crams with pictures and stories of himself, Feld's printed documents are impressive. One of the issues contained a bombastic preview article on Circus World, "The Greatest Place on Earth."

Its construction, in close proximity to Disney World, smacked of a second-rate mind trying to cash in on another man's fortunes. Here, on 750 acres of prime real estate topped with a nineteen-story elephant, Jumbo, would be preserved forever the circus and its associate amusements—cinematic histories of the sawdust trail, carousels and cook houses. Replicas of big tops of the golden age. Sideshows and rides, winter quarters open for public inspection, parades every day, the arrival of the grand old circus train, a theatre of illusions, even a University of Circus Arts for serious aspiring stars.

"What will shortly be the world's most extraordi-

Gifted European stars, such as wire walker Phillip Petit, have been few and far between under the Feld regime. HT.

Shy on showmanship when Feld first booked him in 1969, aerialist Elvin Bale has since developed into a first-rate aerial nut. HT.

nary entertainment center has as its center one man who wanted it so badly he willed it into substance. That Ringling Bros. and Barnum & Bailey will soon be part of our lives is a testament to our dreams."

At the opening of a $6 million preview center detailing the $100 million complex to follow, Feld addressed the crowds: "Anybody who doesn't appreciate what this project is doing for the nation, must be against motherhood, too."

Those in favor of motherhood amounted to a scant three or four hundred patrons each day. The failure

of the park to attract sufficient revenue pushed Mattel's circus-related debts with Wells Fargo bank to the $20 million mark. Circus World was temporarily shut down and a $3 million renovation undertaken as a last-ditch effort to save the costly mistake. The parent company rescinded Feld's authority in the venture and substituted Michael Downs, a former Opryland executive, along with other theme park experts. Circus World has since reopened in augmented format with a live stage show to growing public response. Subsequent Mattel reports to its stockholders have advised them, "There is no assurance that the Company will realize its investments in Circus Park assets and the adjacent land or that, after additional capital investment, if any, the Circus Park will operate successfully."

What became of the vast amusement empire envisioned so eloquently by Irvin Feld? "A complete flop," said the late Floyd King, looking back at what in a different area of the country may have been a smash venture. "The worst location in the world. Thought they'd get an overflow from Disney World. Instead of that Disney got all their business. When a fella went to Disney World, he wasn't thinking about Ringling Bros. Circus winter quarters over there. To hell with that—he wanted to get down to Disney World."

"The park is an albatross," states Douglas Lyon. "A white elephant. Feld is burdened with this thing. I don't think it will ever be built. It's a very idealistic thing."

"No matter how big a fella is," said King, "he can make a mistake sometimes."

Is it possible that Irvin Feld, initially the cold-hearted businessman, hoodwinked *himself* by his own outlandish press agentry?

Figues Lyon, "He went out of his realm, bit off too much. Who is going to be circus-oriented? Kids today are sports-oriented, rock and roll-oriented." Although Circus World has not developed according to Feld's utopian dreams, it is far from a doomed enterprise.

The man behind the ballyhoo has been characterized as a "little dictator." Some say he is haunted by his modest stature, others that he is obsessed with power. The tiniest change in a detail must pass his approval. A little black book in the hands of former performance director Bob Dover recorded the slightest deviation by any of the performers; the new clowns were allowed zero latitude and watched closely. Mr. Dover, to fulfill corporate expectations, toted a clipboard.

201

"They are superior businessmen," says a veteran of clown alley. "But they lack one thing. They have no heart. The heart of the circus is no longer there."

During contract renewal time at the Chicago run in 1972, Feld conducted his own tribunal. Performers were required to make humiliating solicitations for continued employment. "Why should we renew your contract?" was the question posed to each.

The answers varied. An apprentice jester replied curtly, "The fact that I showed up on time."

The Stephenson family, refusing to bow down, pulled its marvelous dogs out of the show.

An irate showgirl told the president where he could shove his so and so circus.

Why such pompous management?

One insider puts it this way: "There was I suppose a pride in the show as a family—of a group. A human type pride that is missing now. It's strictly a business. The Felds are in it to make money. Mr. Feld is not liked generally. Suddenly, he's declared himself the greatest showman on earth and this has rubbed a lot of people the wrong way."

When the Circus Fans Association of America (CFA) convened at Providence, Rhode Island, in 1975 for their annual convention, they were treated to a side of Irvin Feld they had not before seen. Feld honored them as the guest speaker at their final banquet. By the time he reached the podium they had already grown disenchanted. Arrangements had been made in advance to secure a choice block of reserved seats for a performance of the Blue unit. To their dismay, they were shuttled to one end of the arena. They felt snubbed.

Now they had the man in full view as he stood dead center before them on the speaker's rostrum. Eagerly, a few die-hards awaited an exciting scoop or a surprise pronouncement. Feld, par for the course, gifted them with Feld—a rambling dissertation, as one disgruntled member put it, of "we're gonna do this and we're gonna do that crap." The President's historic state of the circus address was highlighted by the tears Mr. Feld shed while speaking of the "standing ovation" accorded to his Bicentennial spec opening night in Venice. (Actually, show promoters were planted through the house to initiate the vigorous reception, a proven technique at political rallies.)

What the fans did get was an eyeful of crass arrogance. Feld, toasting Feld, sent one of his flunkies out for drinks, and when the yes-boy

Sheila Sloan, pushing the feathers forward. WT.

returned there were cocktails for the Ringling VIPs. Circus Fans Association of America officials at the same table sat dry. Then came the moment for Dr. Paul Fitzpatrick, the new CFA president, to address the room. Something reminded Allen Bloom, Feld's right arm, of dental hygiene. Was it the good doctor at the podium? Bloom, in full view of the fans, went to work on his teeth with dental floss.

Unbelievable? Ask the man who runs the circus. He may vehemently deny it. He may even insist it was *Ringling* floss, a sparkling new Center Ring product soon to be available at all participating Barnum & Bailey Drug Stores.

You see, in the great tradition of circus owners, Mr. Irvin Feld is a pathological press agent. The ballyhoo is in the best of hands.

202

18
Move Over, Mother Circus

CLOWNS were up every corridor of Congress, aerialists dangling like ornaments from construction cranes. Toe-tapping dogs stormed television talk shows. Dauntless daredevils were dramatizing the dissident dynasties of Irvin Feld and Abe Pollin, two similarly self-assured impresarios caught up in a monumental tiff. Each man was outlaying over half a million dollars to promote his respective circus. Full pages ads back to back in the *Washington Post* foreshadowed a rugged contest.

"ONLY AT THE ARMORY" warned Ringling Bros. and Barnum & Bailey.

"THE MOST COMFORTABLE BIG TOP IN THE WORLD" boasted Circus America.

"ALONE IN ITS GREATNESS" blasted the Ringling herald.

"TELESCREEN CLOSEUPS AND INSTANT REPLAYS" promised Circus America's.

The imposing figure of Gunther Gebel Williams graced the established circus's posters. Emmett Kelly's sad face dignified the opposing typography.

"The Great Circus Shoot-Out" as the *Washington Star-News* gleefully dubbed it, was underway. ". . . the biggest circus war ever to hit Washington. A complex and bloody battle of pride and politics. The circus world has seen nothing like it since the turn-of-the-century wars."

Earthshaking schisms between equally talented men are the seeds of earthshaking showmanship.

That is the story of how the American circus grew to phenomenal heights during the nineteenth century. The public benefited then, as it was now.

The story begins in April of 1972 when Abe Pollin, a building contractor, elevatored with high hopes to Feld's eleventh floor purple, green, and yellow suite. The Ringling executive fired up a nine-inch Dino label cigar, leaned back, and listened. Pollin leaned humbly forward and declared to Feld, then a good friend, that he needed help in securing a hockey franchise for his new sports arena. It was imperative if the project, about to be constructed, was to be a "viable proposition." Would Mr. Feld exert his "influence" with various arena owners throughout the country, who at that time were preparing to award two new franchises?

Feld released a puff of smoke and said yes—on several conditions. First, he wanted to book his circus into Pollin's lavish showplace on the most favorable terms then existing for any of its U. S. or Canadian engagements. Feld wanted exclusive concession rights and he wanted a chance to buy a big chunk of the hockey team once it came into being.

"No problem, Irv" is what Irv thought Abe told him. "You can put the circus in my arena for nothing, that's the least I can do. Just get me that franchise."

Strange how our recollections differ. Abe recalls telling his friend, "All I'll say now is that you'll get a fair deal out of this. A very fair deal."

Impromptu Barnum: Abe Pollin, left, *opening night at his five-ring Circus America.* CC.

The following summer Pollin got his hockey team. Feld, proudly claiming the credit, relaxed confidently over a bargaining table to consummate his end of the bargain. The agreement he remembered making with Pollin proved about as binding as candy floss in a snow storm. Pollin balked. Feld could bring in the circus if he desired for regular rates. His piece of the action in the hockey team had been whittled down to a mere 3⅓ percent! Concessions? They were negotiable. Quickly the two old "friends" became strained acquaintances.

Feld held out. Pollin continued listing the Ringling name in his advertised calendar of future events. At the same time he surreptitiously got in touch with other personalities. At first he sent his production man, Mark Crowley to Philadelphia, where Circus Vargas was playing. Crowley saw the show and offered Cliff Vargas a crack at the Capital Centre circus dates. Vargas, fearing adverse publicity if he was unable to compete favorably with Ringling, declined the offer.

Pollin then telephoned Karl Wallenda, a man who had been known to produce shows as well as star in them.

"I want to stage a circus as big as Ringling, even better!"

The famous wire walker sighed approvingly. So how can I help you?

Pollin invited Wallenda to meet him in Washington. Wallenda's partner, Jack Leontini strongly advised him against getting involved. The short notice, argued Leontini, made it impossible to deliver a satisfactory product. Wallenda disagreed and deferred to a quasi associate, Paul V. Kaye. He briefed Kaye on Pollin's query and suggested he stand by for possible assistance. Instead, Kaye promptly scheduled his own personal conference with Pollin, desirous of snatching the date himself.

204

When Wallenda showed up at the Capital Centre offices, he was stunned to find Kaye already in attendance. Kaye had cleverly circumvented Wallenda with a cheaper price tag. Diplomatically, Pollin eased the two gentlemen into a coproducing relationship. The friction that resulted over ethics embittered Wallenda, who told me, "Kaye *could* have been my partner; I would have gone with him."

Feld could only bite his lips and hope that a malicious rumor would not materialize. His deepest fears were confirmed on a frosty November morning in 1973 on the construction site of Capital Centre in Landover, Maryland. Abe Pollin hard-hatted up and jumped aboard an elephant to signal the creation of his own Circus America.

From that frame forward, the flak flew furiously.

The shrewd new big top had snuk up alongside the incumbent monarch with outrageous self-confidence, boasting five—count 'em—five rings and four giant sky-high telescreens quadrupling your money's worth. Close-up views were promised at each show of the great Wallendas moving closer to infinity, of Emmett Kelly fussing, still, with an obstinate spotlight, of the Zachinni cannon freaks getting blown out of their minds. Pollin's big top looked like an astral picnic directed by Stanley Kubrick.

For Irvin Feld, it was a five-ring nightmare, a shocking blow to his ego and deplorable evidence of the lack of civility among civilized men. Claimed the Ringling boss, Pollin had reneged on a verbal agreement to book his circus. Feld had only one grim alternative: to play the D.C. Armory—a durable old structure about as glamorous as an International Harvester warehouse.

"Nobody knows what really happened," reported one scribe. "It looked like Abe Pollin was out to get Irvin Feld."

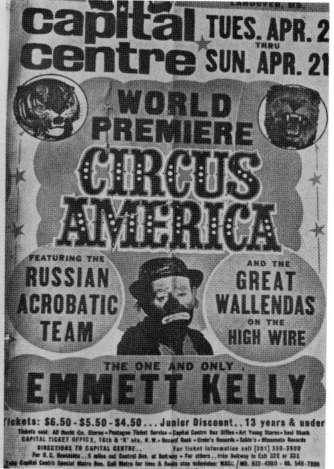

The great "circus shoot-out" pitted Ringling against an alumni of its former stars. WT.

205

Feld told a room full of reporters hurriedly beckoned to his offices that he was "totally amazed." He announced he was slamming a $7.5 million lawsuit alleging fraud, breach of contract, and unfair competition against Pollin and his Capital Centre. He postured feverishly before flashing bulbs and roared like a lion being forced to share the spotlight with a boa constrictor. He lashed out at the tacky tactics of his rivals and took potshots at some of its headliners—former Ringling alumni like Wallenda and Kelly who appeared to be throwing the Mother Circus into competition with its own glorious past.

"I wouldn't dare present a performer who might look aged or winded," scoffed the challenged big-top magnet, claiming to have "retired" Circus America's stars twenty years ago (a remarkable undertaking considering Feld was not then associated with the show). "The average age of my performers is twenty-three—all gorgeous girls and beautiful boys."

A cartoon in the *Star-News* pictured a Circus America clown kicking a Ringling funmaker out of the ring. The accompanying story featured quotes by both rivals. "We are still the Greatest Show on Earth," said Feld. "We're going to put on one hell of a show that all Washington will be proud of," promised the Circus America spokesman.

Writer Louise Lague concluded, "The battle lines are drawn. We need only wait for the fur to fly."

The showmanship that ensued was exceptional. There was skull duggery and counter connivery that Chilly Billy Cole and old Adam Forepaugh would have cheered. For example, when Mr. Feld tried buying a local thirty-second advertising spot on the upcoming national telecast of highlights from his prized circus, he was to his horror informed that the only remaining spots had been taken by Mr. Pollin! Ringling Bros. sponsored by Circus America?

Feld cried fowl play to a U. S. District Court judge.

Pollin's attorney interrupted, "If they can have a circus special, your honor, we want people to know we're having a circus, too!"

The judge, not amused, ordered a disclaimer on all Circus America ads.

Feld took the stand. Snapped the attorney representing his new competitor, "Why didn't *you* put such a disclaimer regarding our show on *your* ads?"

Feld was feldified.

"I don't know what Circus America is! We have tradition, we've been around 104 years!"

The courtroom went up in laughter.

Outside, lines formed at enemy ticket windows. First-string drama critics brushed aside opera assignments to cover opening night of the circus war—Maria Callas, the Living Theatre, and Wings be damned.

The Shriners intercepted Feld's S.O.S. and agreed to be the ostentatious recipients of "a dazzling, sensational evening for the benefit of the Washington Children's Hospital." Naturally, that put hundreds of noblemen on the telephones pushing tickets for the Mother Circus.

Not to be upstaged by allusions to charity (the one thing all circuses are thoroughly professional at doing), Mr. Pollin moved his opening night forward to coincide with Ringling's and willed the proceeds over to three, yes *three* worthy causes: The Columbian Lighthouse for The Blind, Dollars for Orphans, and The Compressed Speech Foundation. Competition in all things, boys.

Running scared, Feld moved frantically backward in time with a bid for nostalgia. He ordered a revival of the old circus sideshow, "INCLUDED IN YOUR TICKET PRICE AT NO EXTRA CHARGE!" Off a dusty shelf came a bearded feminist, Stella, Jolly Dolly the fat lady, and Cairo, the Egyptian Giant.

Pollin moved forward in time with an amazing coup. He engaged a twelve-man Russian acrobatic team, which would mark the first time ever that Soviet Union artists had appeared in an American circus.

Washingtonians surely started counting clowns in their sleep.

Press agents beseeched political big shots for stand-in support. Opening night fever approached

Karl Wallenda, left, points out a rigging problem to Abe and Norris Pollin. CC.

something akin to a championship prize fight. Crowds packed the old Armory and swelled the new Capital Centre clear up to its elite "Sky Suites." Everywhere you looked there were celebrities and senators trying to look natural in greasepaint and struggling for their lives on strange elephants. The late Hubert Humphrey in Ringling red ringmastered in his typical unashamed delight. Spieled the hearty senator while his fellow congressmen rode by on the big bulls, "Aren't those beautiful elephants! I've never seen such good-looking Republicans!"

The new circus, striking a progressive stance, had Art Garfunkel singing about silence and troubled waters. . . .

While all this madness was taking place, I was turning over in my troubled mind available bus service and how I might get there. Being a resident of California, the schedule to either location read approximately seventy-five hours. Never mind the reasons for my transient insanity nor why I chose not to fly Gertrude. Be warned, however, should you contemplate a similar fate—the D. C. bus depot is the end of the civilized world (unless you get your kicks on the run with a firearm), and if you *ever* go Greyhound anywhere, *don't* leave the cooking to them. . . .

"Will passengers continuing through to Washington, D. C. please reboard your bus." Thanks, big mouth, and I still haven't found the ketchup for my cold Post House t-bone.

Anybody who spends three days on a bus to see a couple of circuses should have his head examined, take it from me. Out of my mind? No, I kept telling myself. "You have cotton candy on your brain."

The D. C. terminal at midnight is a midway all in itself, a desolate arcade of passing strangers without the glitter or the jackpots. Then, the man in the White House up the street was hovering behind closed doors in fear, about to be impeached. Tawdry neons cast a flickering glow on the lonely deserted bodies piled up around the shabby concourse as people with money and means skirted past them, arriving and departing. The misbegotten and the losers, they all went nowhere but around in short, repetitive circles. Each one appeared to be searching for something—a dime or a light, or a miracle. . . .

And there was I, hundreds of bus depots from California, in search of my own miracle. I will confess, good reader—to you who have traveled this far with me—that every circus I ever followed after

held out to me the aura of a mystery I might someday fathom, a revelation of man's deepest possibilities through the rich symbolism of raw, poetic nerve . . . into infinity. What *is* the circus? I will tell you what it is: a celebration of man's reach for the miraculous.

The next morning, anxiously I scanned the newspapers. Who was winning the circus war?

"CIRCUS AMERICA ON TOP OF THE HEAP," headlined a Capital Centre ad, quoting from a notice by Roy Meacham of WTTG-TV. "There is something basic, integrity of product as opposed to blatant commercialism. Abe Pollin has assembled a star-studed spectacular . . . Irv Feld has put together a slick package from part of what still may be the Greatest Show on Earth. I can't fault the man for trying to make as much as possible, by splitting his talent between two units, or splitting my nerves with his intrusive souvenir hawks. But given a chance, I'd rather go and send you where the better value is. Maybe next year will be different, but this battle in the great circus war finds Ringling Bros. and Barnum & Bailey the loser, and Circus America on top of the heap."

For a few moments I was numb—excited that another circus could compete so effectively, yet bothered by the thought that the "Greatest Show on Earth" might be considered inferior to a competitor. Art and entertainment being personal matters, Meacham's view was far from the only one to be considered.

"WHO'S ON TOP UNDER THE BIG TOP?" posed a half-page Ringling ad. The answer—a liberal sampling of quotes from the review of the *Washington Post's* prestigious drama critic, Richard L. Coe: "Already a moral can be drawn from Washington's current War of the Circuses. You can't put a circus together overnight . . . Ringling has an authentic assurance and pizzazz no newly formed group could possibly achieve."

"Literally hundreds of turns, pieced together with vitally exact timing and assurance, the sort of thing that takes years of working together. So, if you can see only one of the entries in this hooked-up War of the Circuses, your best bet by far is at the Armory. It looks and was more expensive to create, but you get, a bit cheaper, three hours of dizzying, assured activity."

The more I studied the notices, the more I marveled at what critical attention was being paid this remarkable battle of the big tops. "All things considered," wrote Boris Weintraub in the *Star-*

News, "What may be the most remarkable thing about Circus America is that it is being staged at all . . . if the battle is rejoined next year, Circus America will have one advantage it didn't have this year. It will have established itself as a viable alternative to the Greatest Show on Earth."

Weintraub later issued a delightful quasi-Nader "Consumer's Guide to The Circus War." It was a neat feat of straddling the fence while pretending to give an edge to the Mother Circus.

Both shows did brisk business. Patrons whipped back and forth between the Armory and Capital Centre, intrigued with the differences. The options given them heightened their interest. The public became truly circus-conscious, a rare occurrence for this day and age. Whose juggler was best? What clowns had better routines? Were the aerialists at the Armory as daring as those at Capital Centre? Who turned the most somersaults?

Two children were comparing notes. "Circus America has better acts!" said the one. Argued the other, "The Ringling Bros. is more fun!"

In the sparks of a big-top showdown loyalties are tested and solidified. Performers work harder to please, and audiences harder to show their appreciation. There was much to enjoy at both arenas. Mr. Feld's wares have been amply discussed in preceeding pages. Let me turn to Mr. Pollin's.

Exhilarating new ideas marked the bold, arresting showmanship of Circus America. In luxurious, vendor-free comfort patronizers of Abe Pollin's production were treated to a breathtaking glimpse of the circus moving into a futuristic age. Five magnificent sawdust rings tinted in rich colors of red, green, and yellow. Superb illumination, even some psychedelic lighting effects and cosmic space sounds for a couple of aerial displays. The opening parade moved at a swift, refreshing gait. To a captivating new song—"It's Circus America Time!"—thousands of new fans sighed with a special sense of something different ahead. My pulse quickened: up on the giant telescreen was a huge projection of the krinkled, forlorn face of Emmett Kelly, making his heralded entrance at the parade's end!

The procession of superstars, both old and young, staggered my senses: Tarzan Zerbini, sticking his head into the jaws of a "blod-thirsty" lion and laughing all the way. Young Cookie Arturo, "The Great," hanging from a trapeze while in full motion, only by his toes! The Nerveless Nocks and the Fearless Bauers dangling upwards with dizzy abandon at the tips of seven swaying poles, then sliding rapidly down the spars head first!

There were delightful close-ups on the telescreens, if you chose, of Victor Julian's pretentious and exacting dancing cannines . . . of Norbu, the "Almost Human Gorilla" rampaging the audience. . . .

. . . and the spellbinding Gene Mendez flashing across the high wire like a bolt of lightning . . . and the impeccable twelve-man Russian Acrobatic Team offering nothing less than perfection . . . and the very inventive young Flying Americans—two troupes of trapeze artists working side by side on double riggings to whamo space patterns . . . and Johnny Luxem racing madly over the "Wheel of Destiny" . . . and Wayne Zacchini soaring out of the tip of that human cannon projectile . . . AND. . . .

Karl Wallenda, highest man on the "human pyramid," never more thrilling, never in greater control. His unrelenting presence alone was a marvel to behold. The audience stilled to an icy hush while slowly he began his ascent to the top of a chair

Realizing the arena's ultimate lure: Circus America presented performers like Tarzan Zerbini in the flesh and on giant telescreen close-up images overhead. CC.

"Circus Journey into Outer Space" filled arena with
compelling space-age effects. CC.

Circus America's incredible Russian Acrobatic Team. CC.

Norbu, the "almost human gorilla" rampaged Capital Centre audiences. CC.

balanced hazardously on a bar that joined the shoulders of two men on bicycles one behind the other. All this, dead center on the wire and without a net below or safety wires from above. Carefully, he rose to a standing position, perfectly erect at last, throwing his arms out like a God taunting the laws of gravity and laughing at human weakness and fear. One year from his seventies, Wallenda was still a sensation up there—open, alive, forever free. And upon his safe return to the other side, the house collapsed into a limp, resounding ovation. Aristotle would have judged it a true catharsis.

Circus America, asserted its harshest critics, lacked the pacing and animation of the established circus against which it was competing. The dissenters were valid, to a point. Only time could smoothen out the stilted transitions between certain acts and the lulls in a few displays. "Nothing is so bad in the circus as a pause," Fred Bradna once reflected. Circus America would have had fewer hesitating moments had there not been so many chiefs stirring the soup in different directions: there

Triumphal, unrelenting Karl Wallenda (above Ricki) at the summit of control. CC.

The Leighs on their giant revolving "Space Wheel." CC.

was Wallenda, Kaye and Leontini, not counting Michael Crowley, Pollin's man in charge of overall supervision who spent most of his time mediating between the bickering producers. Also conspicuously missing was a crackerjack ringmaster; Phil McDonald's laborious, velvet smooth announcements lacked punch. Rather than push the pace forward, McDonald called attention to himself.

Still, one could not argue with the show's basic brilliance: great acts in a great setting. "A solid core of superior circus turns," wrote Richard L. Coe. The music was exceptionally fine and the production concepts were artful and imaginative. An aerial ballet staged by Paul Kaye must rank as one of the finest ever. It began on a deceptively simple note, with thirty-two girls working webs amidst a shower of bubbles to the song, "Raindrops Keep Falling on My Head." Then, suddenly, the mood changed. . . .

. . . into the "serene" setting cycled the mod Cookie Arturo on silver chrome, easy-rider style, touches of hip humor. After his "cool" entry, he

Searching his shadow for meaning, America's favorite tramp, Emmett Kelly, at Circus America. CC.

proved in the air to be the finest single trapeze artist to come along in years, moving with that certain ease that only a few have ever attained. An electric base guitar incorporated into the score by musical director Jack Cervone added a chilling nuance to Arturo's stunning toe-suspension climax. The best of the past, the best of the future.

Not since the advent of John Ringling North had an American circus spoken to its own time with such daring imagination. For Abe Pollin, Circus America was a tremendous personal victory. Coming from literally out of nowhere and putting together, virtually overnight, a five-ring zinger, he had achieved what few men ever dream of doing. Pollin's success is proof positive of the power of the competitive spirit—the yeast that is missing in today's circus world. What has brought us to a point of apathy?

I recall a cluster of loyal Ringling fans outside the Armory after the show, standing at a bus stop in a state of limbo, each one clutching their souvenir program magazine as a child clasps a security blanket when a stranger draws too close. How dare another circus try to equal theirs! It had become to them a sacred emblem of life's perpetual dreams, of its cycles of hope and beauty—like Miss Liberty and Christmas Eve and a Fourth of July picnic. The public's sentimental attachment to the Mother Circus has given it an edge that would take another show many years to achieve.

Historian Fred D. Pfening, Jr., commented at the end of the dismal 1956 season, when Ringling folded its tents for good and people thus concluded that circuses were a thing of the past, "It is my feeling that too much emphasis is placed on the Ringling Bros. show as representing the 'circus' in the United States . . . unfortunately, many folks, particularly the general public, do not realize that there are a number of other shows operating very successfully."

What has happened? Harold Ronk remembers as a boy being captivated by a number of big name shows. "In all due respect to Ringling Bros. Circus, it never was the only circus in my mind as a boy. As a matter of fact, when I first saw Dorothy Herbert she was with Hagenbeck-Wallace. I remember that Clyde Beatty was with Russell Bros. So there were always great attractions on all the shows. They all had big name show stoppers, big performers. And Ringling certainly was one of the greats, but as a boy I didn't classify it as the only one and others as secondary. They were *all* great to me."

How times have changed. Ronk respects the need for diversity and believes that circus goers should have viable choices. "There's a public waiting for all circuses, no matter what their size or where they're playing." Yet Ronk, too, is mystified by Ringling's uncanny monopoly over public sentiment. "I swear, right now, tonight, if no one else showed up (more than a scattering of people), if there were two elephants in the back, they'd open the curtains and two elephants would come out and there'd be *something*, because it is a *way*. It's *indestructible*." It's the Mother Circus, a rarely challenged institution, Mr. Ronk.

It's a pity the spirit of rivalry has virtually vanished from the big tops. "Circus America was healthy for the whole amusement industry," remarked Douglas Lyon, pointing out that the shows today "are not in a growing pattern, but very content with their little territories."

There was bullish talk in the Pollin camp of a national tour. Strategists questioned whether Pollin could generate on the road the winning set of circumstances he had fostered at home: playing the underdog, engaging an all-star cast and using technical innovations to sell it. Capital Centre itself drew customers on the basis of its being a new arena, and the illustrious feud between Pollin and Feld garnered much free publicity. Moreover, the problem of booking enough buildings for a continuous tour was complicated by constricting contracts that Feld has imposed on many of the auditoriums he plays in, making it near impossible for a rival show to organize a cohesive route.

The building contractor began doubting his own genius. Conjectures Lyon, "Pollin had to ask himself, 'Am I in the circus business or in the business of running this building?' " The answer evidently was not in favor of epochal sawdust entertainment. The impromptu showman had proved his point to Irvin Feld, and wasn't that what the tiff was all about? The things that give birth to great circuses often have nothing to do with great art at all.

After one heroic bout, it appeared that the battle of the big tops had fizzled. Starting in 1975, Ringling Bros. and Barnum & Bailey played both Capital Centre and the D. C. Armory each season. Insiders guessed that Feld compromised some to placate his autonomous former friend Abe Pollin and thus prevent further embarassing complications.

But *hold your horses!* All is not over, *yet.* In 1978 Pollin suddenly announced to the press that Ringling's spring engagement at Capital Centre had become increasingly incompatible with a heavy schedule of regularly slated and playoff games for the Centre's basketball and hockey teams. In an effort to resolve the conflict, Pollin approached Feld about moving the circus dates forward to the holiday season. Feld was unable to comply, and the two gentlemen again parted ways. Pollin quickly revived the Circus America title and assembled a twenty-performance 1978-79 edition, which premiered on Christmas day.

This time around, ironically the new Circus America was a one-ring outing. Richard L. Coe, reviewing it in the *Washington Post,* was mesmerized: "From Moscow to San Diego, from Lillian Leitzel to Elvin Bale, I've never seen so dazzling a sequence of star turns as the second half of the new Circus America . . . . this one-ring sizzler will be a hard-to-top circus."

The production was deemed a success, with repeat engagements virtually assured. With that, naturally the prospects for a national tour of Circus America had brightened.

Playing Barnum to the hilt, Irvin Feld may discover that down the sawdust trail are other big tops, and that you can never tell in which one may lurk an Abe Pollin, or another Irvin Feld, playing Barnum, too.

Long live the benefits of the great "Circus Shoot-Out"!

19
Cry, Clown, Cry

Oh, listen to the band! Disciples of discords, merry murderers of melody, mad masters of off-keys in reed and brass, grotesque soloists in lost chords, ludicrous symphonists seeking the musical heights and attaining only laughs—the clown band.
—from Hagenbeck-Wallace program magazine, 1935

WE have reached the chill winds of autumn. In the air are rumors the circus will not survive many more. Are we to believe them?

It is 3 A.M. on a humid March morning in Florida where for Ken Dodd, Clyde Beatty-Cole Bros. Circus producing clown, another precarious spring is unfolding. Oblivious to the static buzz of a pictureless television screen, Dodd fiddles with an opening in the top of a wooden head. Never mind a stack of mismatched fabrics lying on a sofa or a hundred other materials yet to be cut and joined. One thing at a time. Finally, out of the wooden head pops a cuckoo bird. The inventor is tickled. Next item: find some red thread.

First, Dodd clicks off the TV and pours another cup of coffee. A few sips of forced relaxation and he returns, blurry-eyed, to the maze of half-constructed paraphernalia: angelic halos, duck feathers, gigantic bow ties, enormous hot dogs and french fries. No luck finding the thread, so he applies glitter to a Chinese gong and calls it a night.

Believe, for a moment, that the creator will locate a full complement of merry andrews to bring his zany ideas to life. Or maybe he won't. Dedicated jesters are a vanishing breed.

Hours later, Dodd is back on his feet, retesting the cuckoo bird, searching for red thread, realizing suddenly that today rehearsals begin. He calls winter quarters about long steel pins for a new gag spoofing acupuncture. "I need the pins today! We've

Producing clown Ken Dodd (astride elephant) with his Beatty-Cole funmakers. Ensemble clown alleys are on the decline. KD.

215

got to start working with them!" The master of madness reports to the mirror for an abrasive bout with his razor (clowns are undomesticated), hurries through a bowl of cereal he forgot to eat yesterday and darts out the door loaded down with medical uniforms and operation room gadgetry, clownville style. He is scheduled to meet with his screwball associates for a first runthrough of the clinical takeoff. Ailments will be assigned to some, acupuncture licenses granted to others. Heads will jam for fresh ideas. The effect desired is for Clyde Beatty-Cole Bros. audiences to be hilariously diverted by clown alley's version of the trendy pain-killing practice—wherein once the patient's needles have been pulled sprays of colored water gush from the skin penetrations. Through the eyes of a practicing buffoon, life is full of holes.

Regarded generally as the nation's finest producing clown since the late Paul Jung, Kenneth Dodd is satirically in step with the times. Ever-open to new twists on time-proven guffaws, Dodd refuses to join the bandwagon of tired routines and easy employment that might be called ritual circus (sponsored by the Elks and the local policemen's association and other such organizations). Like Jung, who for years on the Ringling show was given a free reign and all the clowns he needed, Dodd has enjoyed a similiar mandate, on a smaller scale, from his boss Frank McClosky. A good clown alley does not come into being overnight, and Dodd's merry backsliders— some of them longtime associates and all of them responding to a strong artistic head—have developed a true ensemble spirit. There's a whimsical tilt to their thrust, an aura of elegant nonsense about them. They come at you sideways, off axis— victorious dropouts and overgrown babies, mad hatters without their hats and safecrackers in high heels. Their cockeyed unity is devastating: you can feel your heart unwinding backwards and all your well-founded scruples fluttering away, discheveled. Correct Yankee buffoonery elevates us to a state of happy confusion.

"It's a challenge," says Dodd with enthusiasm. "You get an idea, sketch it out, you start to build it. It's a very rewarding thing to see it finished and go into the ring and hear the people laugh. That's my little show out there. It makes it worth sitting up all night sewing or hammering props together. The whole thing in general excites me. I'm just as excited now after twenty years as when I first saw it."

Dodd has occupied an enviable position with

Louis Nagy, third from top *entertained Ken Dodd when he was a youngster. Nagy now works for Dodd,* above him. KD.

Beatty-Cole, although in 1977 he was forced to leave the show for an indefinite period owing to illness in his family. In his place, his capable cohort Jimmy James has taken over, and with the addition of several younger clowns he is keeping the comedy ranks alive.

Assuming that Ken Dodd returns, will his past good fortunes continue? Although he was allowed a budget for ten men, finding dependable wise guys to fill the slots has become more difficult. In 1976 Dodd carried only seven joeys. By 1986 how many might he have? The show is currently undergoing drastic organizational changes. The wonderful clown alley that Dodd created may now be a thing of the past.

When he is available to resume his career, Dodd may find the options discouraging. If he transferred to Circus Vargas he might have problems convincing the boss to hire more than the three clowns he normally employs. Should he contract his services to a producer of sponsored indoor dates, Dodd would experience the frustration of trying to keep intact a group of joeys over a series of sporadic engagements here and there. In any event, the ensemble spirit he has fostered would be highly difficult to achieve elsewhere.

216

Jimmy James with showgirls on the Beatty-Cole lot. KD.

Or Dodd could retire to the Showfolks Club in Sarasota and join the nightly circle of disheartened laughmakers bemoaning their plight. The man behind the bar there is Alfredo Landon, a gifted European tramp clown who has served for Dobritch and Kaye. Landon counts himself one of the casualties of the era of diminishing full-season tent shows and scattered Shrine circus dates.

To be a serious-minded jester in this country, just ask Landon. Who, he might ask, wants you? Not the Shriners, who with a combined total of over 400 annual shows in various North American cities and towns probably keep more acrobats and monkeys out of the unemployment lines than any other single producing force. Why don't the good Shriners care if they see a professional clown working on the payroll? Because many of them enjoy hiding out two or three days a year behind big red noses and polka dot frills. In their opinion they are as funny as some of the so-called pros they have seen. Since the Shriners sell the tickets to their affairs, they are not at the mercy of critics or advertising for box office oompha. They can afford to do as they please and their friends—the ticket holders—usually go along with it.

Independent producers bidding for these guaranteed bread-and-butter Shrine dates are, of course, accommodating. If they can get by without bringing in a set of funmakers, that's less expense for them. It's a sad fact of life that has driven the jollies out of jolly men like Landon. Cries one, "the producer ask twenty thousand, thirty thousand for the date. So many clowns, five thousand. No got to bring clowns, save five thousand. The Shriners are happy. For the people it. . ."—he waves his hand angrily, making the point. "Not one of those guys who work, three or

217

four or five day a year can be a clown. This guy do it in one day. He see what the other clowns do. The guy see, he copy. That's the truth!"

"We're on the endangered species list," adds Danny Chapman, another gifted cutup contributing to the argument. Nothing reflects more the fragmented, chaotic state of the circus in America today than the plight of these men.

P. T. Barnum in a different day is reported to have said, "Clowns are the pegs upon which to hang a circus." Is he being proven wrong? In his era, Barnum could not escape the colorful brigades of loony pranksters and suave misfits that cluttered hippodrome tracks with infectious merriment. They crashed off collapsing table tops, rode proudly in wagons pulled by pigs and in jalopies that reared up and snorted on their hind wheels. Made a dandy racket and made their irreverent presence felt everywhere. They were an integral part of the action. The venerable P. T., rightly so, testified to their howling importance.

Dan Rice was then a superstar. The celebrated goof-off endeared himself to Yankee patrons with a trained pig Lord Byron and to first-class employers for as high as one thousand dollars a week. In our time, Emmett Kelly is the only funny man with true name-drawing power, and he has gone where there is money for a marquee-worthy comic—to the night club scene.

Barnum did not forsee the future of "sponsored" shows, nor could he have envisioned the diversified entertainment outlets that would claim our best comedians. Would P. T. still call them "pegs" if he could see some of today's token jesters at work? Relegated, as often they are, to quick inconspicuous walkarounds, have they been ignored into obscurity? Whereas in the 1930s a small truck show like Barnett Bros. would carry twelve clowns, fifty years later you will not see that many on most of our *biggest* shows. Scarcely will you count more than five "funny" faces.

Don't be shocked if there's not a single harlequin on the bill. In 1972, Dory Miller's resplendent five-ring enterprise, Carson & Barnes Circus, toured successfully without the "pegs" for seven straight months. No ominous jinxes or crippling spells befell the show. No irate customers wanted their money back—and there wasn't one merry-maker on the payroll! Royal Hanneford that same season failed to utilize the services of a professional fool. Owner Tommy Hanneford, the funniest man

on a horse, gave his audiences all the stomachaching fun they needed.

How necessary, anyway, are the masters of mirth when they can't tickle the house beyond a few half-hearted giggles? Not very much in the opinion of the show directors who place minimum value on their contributions. Why present an unfunny pretty face? Lackluster lunacy is never missed. In a subsequent season Carson & Barnes featured a delightful foursome of Mexican comics whom audiences greeted with marked pleasure whenever they entered the tent. The star of the group was a mini-jester, Eleazor Hernandez, charmingly cast as the victim of numerous mishaps. His reaction to a falling egg hitting his noggin and splashing down his forlorn face was priceless. Children waited for him to return. So did their parents.

Many producers have given up on the "endangered species" and don't expect much from the boys who come knocking at their doors with worn out routines. Perhaps, also, because the wages

Nineteenth-century buffoon Dan Rice was the highest paid circus clown. He originated the Uncle Sam character and, with his eyes on the presidency, ran unsuccessfully for Congress in Pennsylvania. CW.

218

Today, our most famous living clown, Emmett Kelly, finds night-club engagements more profitable. CW.

they offer a clown are demoralizing, they are reluctant to make demands on his creativity. One promoter who has a string of weekend Shrine shows subcontracts with a husband and wife team for a five-man clown alley. They receive $450 a day to distribute as they wish. Naturally, they keep at least $300 for themselves and give two hired clowns about $35 each. The fifth member is usually a Shriner picked up at each local stand. Struggling to make ends meet on a couple of days work a week, the two assistant joeys can hardly afford a private bath at the YMCA, while the two producing clowns lodge upwards of one grand every Friday. Cry, clown, cry.

There's not much to laugh about. The entertainment values that emerge from such shoddy payscales are an affront to the business. A guy can earn more money selling popcorn and lemonade than he

Medium-size shows of yesteryear engaged twenty or more laughmakers. RM.

Today's clowning chores on Circus Vargas—America's largest tent show—are handled by three wise guys, two of whom are pictured here. CV.

can by spilling out his heart in baggy trousers. Or he might combine the two callings, as a great many clowns are doing out of necessity, and help the manager unload tons of pink ice and cracker jack. Then he might land a private bath at the YMCA. It's a pity that our funmakers are reduced to the ranks of coloring book merchants and novelty peddlers. Where on continental soil would a jester be allowed to abominate his craft in a like manner? And people ask, why is the circus "dying" and why is it not taken seriously anymore? The state of clowning in this country is a symptom of the apathy of our circuses in matters of art. Expresses Harold Ronk with concern, "I think that small shows that don't give circus audiences something better than just mediocrity are in danger. Because I think that in spite of an instinctive feeling that a youngster and his parents have for circus just basically, I think you can't possibly disappoint them with mediocrity and sustain circus this way."

Enter Irvin Feld and his highly touted Clown College. You might acclaim Mr. Feld's kooky academy of lower learning. You might see right through it. According to the press agents, it is striving madly to fill the void. Whatever, it is a shrewd exploitation of the problem not without substantial benefits to circuses in general.

Established in 1968, its long-term effects are yet to be felt convincingly. Feld opened the doors of opportunity to a host of bright young faces, while at the same time escorting to an early retirement some top Ringling funsters. You can't replace an inspired wacky army overnight, and Feld's boys have a long way to go. Their big production gags fizzle as often as

Once attended by a score of happy faces, the clown wedding, in 1976, was given this abbreviated version by Kaye Continental joeys. MO.

they crackle and there have been moments when the relief they provided was far from comic. "Now let them be clowns for a couple of years," says Struppi Hanneford, "and they'll probably develop their own styles and maybe a few will find their way to the top." Indeed, that is happening in some cases, but there are problems. . . .

The way to the top may be a path marked "out of order." Were Feld truly concerned with the quality of comedy on his two units, he would be endeavoring to build up strong ensemble companies based on promising apprentices rather than letting go at the end of each season most of the new faces to make way for other new faces. Clown College may have created a void as big as the one it was intended to fill for its potential is continually being sacrificed for promotional purposes.

"An unbelievable publicity gimmick," says Ken Dodd. "It has been nothing but a winner. There *has* to be a turnover. Now, where do these new clowns go? This is the pattern I have watched. If you have

twenty clowns this year and you have twenty more clowns coming in and you can only have twenty clowns, there are twenty that have to go somewhere."

Out the door, boys. Make way for the feminists from North Dakota who want to be clowns. Step aside for the Jesuit priests who want to be clowns. "Let's say they go out and get a group of Navajo indians," poses Dodd theoretically. "And they make them clowns. It's a *fantastic* thing. They say, 'DIRECT FROM THE RESERVATION—ALL NAVAJO INDIANS!' This is a gimmick and it just never fails to be a winner."

What has Clown College accomplished? It has flooded a vanishing market with warm bodies, and some of them will no doubt distinguish themselves. For that credit is due Irvin Feld. Clown College has provided a tremendous introduction to the big top for scores of talented newcomers; it has given many of tomorrow's potential comic stars a start. The school stresses visual and acrobatic qualities, its

221

Constant turnover among Ringling's apprentice jesters precludes strong ensemble development. HT.

graduates are distinctly colorful and energetic. "They try very hard," comments one producing clown, "like the bell just rang and school is out." They are the fleeting gems on Feld's ever-changing carousal of shallow comedic figures. Some will achieve brillance.

All that glitters is not gold. Seasoned merrymaking is a gift of birth and of eccentricity, nurtured through years of posturing before all kinds of crowds. Paul Jung once said, "To be a good clown you *have* to take it seriously . . . There is no worthwhile school for clowns except the long hard school of theatrical experience."

"The Ringling clowns *try* to be funny," says Tommy Hanneford. "When you try to be funny that's when you're not funny."

"So many of them think," observed a disappointed fan, "all they have to do is run around and make a lot of noise and fall down and they are funny. And they are *not.*"

Believe it or not, a good clown is a real character, and characters we can relate to have personality quirks far deeper than what the pretty lines on a youthful face can suggest. The bizarre and the grotesque are true attributes of the lovable fool. Beyond his makeup he is very real, indeed, which is why born comics become more, not less amusing with age. Which is also why Ken Dodd as a producing clown is no respecter of youth for youth's sake. "A *19*-year-old *tramp?*" he asks. "The makeup has to read—character comes through."

What makes people laugh? Says Dodd, speaking of his idol, the late Harry Dann, "he could make anything funny. Just walking across the ring. Every movement was what you expected to see of a clown."

While Dodd is constantly experimenting with new ideas, he takes exception to the critics of traditional elements of slapstick. "If you're doing a comedy cannon act and if you don't have an explosion it's kind of ridiculous, don't you think? I just came out of the tent and we dropped our pants and everybody stood up and screamed. Now, who is right—the five thousand people who just saw me do that or this one guy that's sitting here and saying,

222

Turning the simple to the ridiculous: Horace Laird, with Cole Bros. Circus, 1946. CW.

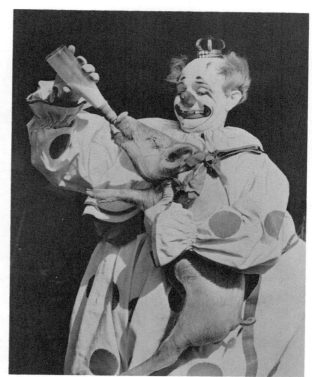

Felix Adler. RM.

Joe Lewis. RM.

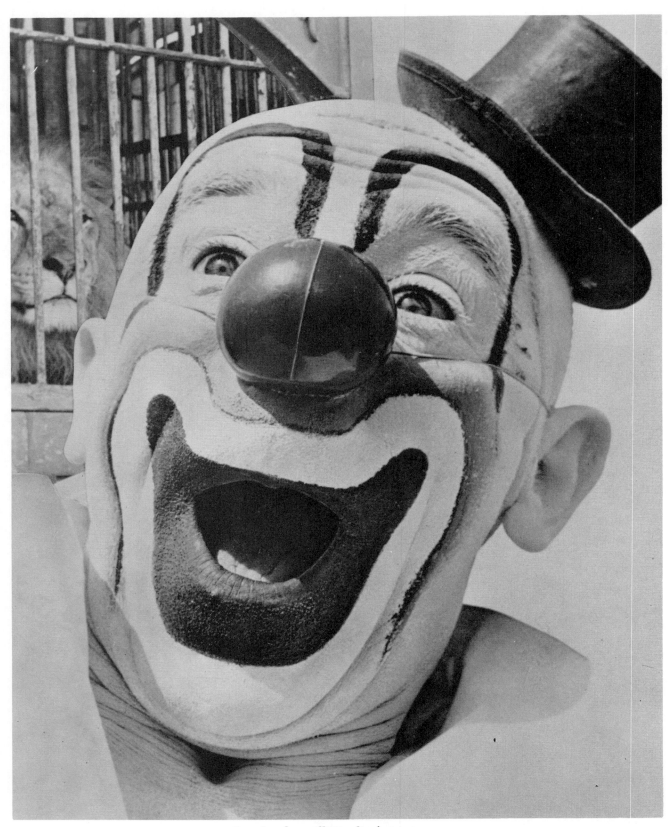

Lou Jacobs, still Ringling's top joey. RM.

"That's my little show out there," says Ken Dodd. "It makes it worth sitting up all night sewing or hammering props together." KD.

'Well, the clowns . . . all they did was shoot fireworks and drop their pants.' "

The age of an applicant seeking work in Dodd's alley does not influence significantly his chance one way or the other. Fifty-year-young Bill Smith, after eleven years with the Army and twelve with the Navy, decided to recycle his youth. By chance he put on a face for an Optimists' Club outing in New Mexico. Smith loved it. His new found hobby turned into a professional commitment to help children "enjoy their childhood." Not finding much joy, however, in some of the makeshift shows he'd been touring with, Smith finally drew up a resumé and forwarded it to the Beatty-Cole show. Soon he was being interviewed by Ken Dodd. The master jester was impressed, and Smith got a job in Dodd's crazy factory.

When Dodd was a wee lad paying his first visit to

the Big Show, he was entranced by Louis Nagy's portrayal of a fat lady. Nagy still performs his charming imitation, now under the canvas of Beatty-Cole, and Dodd was happy to report with a glow in his eye, "He works for me now."

Should Nagy reapply for work on the Ringling show, he might be met with the same indifference other veterans have experienced—a familiar question, "Have you filled out an application for Clown College?"

One old-timer took the question seriously, applied for admission and was accepted. They advised him if he could pass the final exams with flying colors, well maybe . . .

Attentively, the duffer took a seat on the ringcurb with his fellow classmates—emancipated housewives and Navajo indians—while the "experts" lectured in the arts of "Facial Expression," "Fundamental Gymnastics," and "Comedic Body Movement." He learned about Big Top Nutrition, even heard about Godot. He participated dutifully in exercises in "Cutting and Draping," tried learning how to spell "Acrobatableaux," rode an elephant feigning the excitement of a child. He took copious notes on "Transportation and Logistics," sighed impressively over a speech on "Arena Choreography." The old codger took a crack at Yoga and damn near fell asleep. He posed for numerous publicity shots with a Montana car salesman and an ex-junkie from Harlem, both converted buffoons.

The master of mirth waited out nervously the results of his final audition for a contract with Ringling Bros. and Barnum & Bailey. When the list was at long last posted, his name was on it!

The graduate with a degree in merriment prepared victoriously for opening night at Venice, Florida. He would never clown the same way again. He was now an educated fool versed in modern methodology. He strolled onto the arena floor feeling a great sense of joy in being back. He was confident as never before, he had passed all the tests, sigma cum laude. Our renovated merry andrew decided to execute a pratfall, Clown College style. Engineering the move with precision, he placed it over the "antic axis point," timed it perfectly and descended to his fanny with flawless technique.

Nobody laughed.

20
Ten More Bars!

WHEN judgment day arrives, I'll lay odds it's Merle Evans who brings it in with a rousing fanfare. In his youth, he once stood erect on a hillside in a white robe, raised to his lips a coronet and blew away for the benefit of a gathering of Holy Rollers convened in a riverside tent meeting. A spotlight illuminated his lean frame. The unusual appearance had been prearranged by facetious minds. The zealous Christians mistook the Kansas windjammer for Gabriel and fled in all directions, convinced the world had come to an end.

It seems fitting to conclude my narrative on the exceptional men and women of the circus with a tribute to Merle Evans, considered "The maestro of the circus world." May Wirth projected enthusiasm and stamina, Leitzel poetry and fire, the Wallendas courage. Merle Evans has all these qualities. His life, his blood, his music *is* circus. I do not think there is a man living who understands better what the big top is all about.

In 1919 he became musical director of the Ringling show, a position he filled with few interruptions for fifty years. At one point along the way, Evans was featured in *Ripley's "Believe It Or Not"* as the bandmaster who played 7,790 performances in succession "without missing a show in twenty-two years."

Once he did leave the bandstand, in Washington, D.C., during an outbreak of ptomaine poisoning that was claiming most of the troupe. Staggering

around in the backyard, Evans quickly decided the bug did not displease him, though, as much as the sound of his musicians faltering a cue. He hurried

A burst of shimmering brass power, led by Maestro Merle Evans, at the forefront of the "Greatest Show on Earth" for fifty seasons. RM.

227

back to rejoin them before anyone in the audience realized he had left.

Evans never sacrificed his homespun ways. He enjoyed telling people, "I haven't met a person or a bag of popcorn I didn't like."

Born the son of a coalmine foreman in a small town outside Columbus, Kansas, young Merle blew to life at ten or thereabouts, when with a brand new $16.95 John Slater coronet he took up residence in a woodshed for six hours a day, much to the consternation of surrounding residents. "The strongest sound in the state" they soon called him. Merle played his horn while he sold newspapers and dispensed with other of his boyhood chores. His first public performance was in a Methodist church, where he played "Onward Christian Soldiers" while leading a group of children around the churchyard. He advanced without a formal degree to a musician of burning energy and ambition.

When he was fifteen years old, the S. W. Brundage Carnival came to his town. Merle applied to Cleve Pullen for a job in his band. Pullen asked for a demonstration from Merle, and the applicant whipped out his coronet and proceeded to blow Pullen nearly off his feet. Merle was awarded a ten-dollar-a-week assignment that required erecting and dismantling the merry-go-round and taking part in a motley of noisemakers organized to arouse public attention. Merle formed a valuable friendship with his boss, Pullen, who was a fine E-flat clarinetist.

From there, Merle free-lanced with other traveling concerns, alternately taking up more practical jobs such as tooting for his supper at a Salvation Army or raking balls in a Salina, Kansas, poolroom. Invariably, with each stationary job he grew quickly impatient, always drifting back to the open road. He sold phonographs and instruments, tried putting together a medicine show with Pullen. The partners employed their horns to attract prospective customers for their skunk oil remedies. Evans did not find the enterprise to his liking and soon gave it up.

Pullen took over directorship of the Cotton Blossom Showboat band and talked Merle into joining him. Up and down the Mississippi they toured. Merle enjoyed fishing along the big river when he was not playing music or dreaming about the future.

Evans wrote to the Miller Brothers 101 Ranch Wild West Show, inquiring if they had an opening for an "experienced" band leader. To his surprise, he was hired to form an eighteen-piece group. The company's star was Buffalo Bill, and Merle played for the famous rider on his last transcontinental tour.

Slowly, Evans was moving closer to the challenging world of big-top action. While working with the Walter Savage Stock Company, his path crossed that of Ringling Brothers Circus in Sioux City, Iowa. He took in a performance there. His eyes were opened to a whole new future in music. After the show, Merle struck up a lively conversation with Lew Graham, the sideshow manager. Hopeful of impressing the Ringling official, Merle went on about musical tastes and previous credits and composers and musicians he knew and. . . .

"Hold on, young man," interrupted Graham. "Now, why don't you try for the bandleader's position?"

Overjoyed with the hint of a job offer, Merle sent off a query, "crudely written," to the circus headquarters. And later, while jamming with Gus Hill's Minstrels, he was observed in action by a very impressed Ringling agent, Charles Wilson. "What was great for me, if I do say so, I was a pretty good coronet player. I got my style from Horris Murphy, who played boat shows, and who died at age ninety-three in 1974. I could blow 'em off the sidewalk in those days."

Shortly thereafter, Merle received a telegram from Charles Ringling: HAVE POSITION FOR YOU AS LEADER OF RINGLING CIRCUS BAND. REPORT AT YOUR EARLIEST CONVENIENCE.

That nearly blew Merle off the sidewalk. Excited by the sudden offer, he traveled to New York in March 1919, in the finest fashions he could obtain in his hometown of Columbus—high top laced shoes, a checkered cap and long sleeves, and a gladstone bag with more of the same. Laughing over it in retrospect, he confesses, "I was really a hick, and had never went to New York before."

During his first run-through with the band at Madison Square Garden, Evans drew a raised eyebrow from the worldly John Ringling, whom he had not yet met. Ringling spotted the country boy going through the motions of a maestro and asked his brother, Charles, "Who's that hayseed on the bandstand?"

"Why," answered Charles, "that's our new bandleader, John. The guy's name is Merle Evans."

"Charles, take the guy out and buy him some clothes!"

The Kansas coronetist was diplomatically mea-

When Evans joined the combined Ringling-Barnum Circus, in 1919, its mammoth big top contained three rings and four stages, and could seat fifteen thousand souls. CW.

sured and fitted for a brand new wardrobe befitting the current fashions east of the Mississippi. They never tried tampering with the "hayseed's" music, though. From the heart it came. Merle Evans leaped overnight to circusdom's most honored podium, with virtually no big-top experience to his name save for his one tour with Buffalo Bill. The newly combined Ringling Bros. *and* Barnum & Bailey Circus was a great success, and much of the credit went to the first-of-may who played a coronet in his right hand and led the band with his left.

John Ringling's earlier reservations were quelled. "Young man," said the top man of the Big Show, "you damn near blew me out of my box!"

Charles Ringling embraced Evans, delighted he had hired him.

"You're the greatest we ever had."

At the end of his first season, Evans was approached by Charles about his feelings on a pay raise. Evans asked for ten dollars a week more than he had been getting; he got fifteen dollars. Each season a similar raise followed. After a few years, Charles told him, "You can stay with this show as long as you want."

His music became synonymous with circus. Evans championed a rich, wide open style of diverse tonal and rhythmic qualities. F. Beverly Kelley, an ardent admirer of the sound, called him "the Toscaninni of the big top" in a *Saturday Evening Post* story. Earlier, in 1930 as a first-of-may radio publicist for the Ringling show, Kelley had sold RCA Victor on the idea of making the first commercial

record of a circus band. Later, he spent two years talking to the producers of the Fitch Bandwagon radio program, who in 1941 agreed that the circus band belonged on their weekly airing of big American bands. For seven years thereafter, Evans and his windjammers enjoyed a once-a-year special before a

Maestro Evans and his windjammers in rehearsal, at Sarasota during the 1950s, for another season. RM.

229

live audience at NBC. When they first hit the airwaves in 1941, the mail response was the heaviest the long-time radio show had ever experienced, and six consecutive follow-up appearances were immediately scheduled. Kelley narrated, and for one he wrote a special number saluting Merle and using his nickname "Abba Dabba" (a term the Maestro applied to his favorite fancy deserts). Merle scored the number and Kelley sang it with the band.

When they cut an album for Columbia records in 1940, Kelley recalls being the only "unpaid musician, standing on a chair atop a table near a separate hanging mike to blow the equestrian director's whistle at proper points for the band's segues from one kind of number to another, matching the action of the part of the show the band was scored for: from a clown walkaround one-step to a flying act waltz . . . and at the end into the gallops at break-neck tempo."

Because Merle Evans is the only circus bandleader who has successfully recorded, his music has been accepted and embraced by the American people as the authentic sound of the big top. The Maestro's prolific releases all bear his unmistakable imprint. In 1967, London Phase 4 issued an album of the sounds and the music of the circus. Arranged and conducted by Merle Evans, then approaching his fiftieth year with the "Greatest Show on Earth," it is possibly the most exciting record of its kind ever produced. It sold extremely well.

The Ringling bandleader traveled to England a few winters to conduct the Bertram Mills Circus band. In the mid-1960s, he accompanied a troupe of American performers through the Soviet Union. While he was there he shared with Russian musicians his popular scoring techniques. Over the years he has served on various workshops at universities across the nation. To this day, though he retired from the circus in 1969, Evans travels thousands of miles each summer making guest appearances with college and civic bands. Wherever the maestro goes, he wears the familiar Ringling red embroidered with gold leaf. Crowds rise to their feet.

Back in 1926, when the Ringling family hosted a farewell gathering at the old Madison Square Garden, scheduled for demolition, the famed circus bandmaster was in attendance. Reported *Variety*, "Without Merle Evans, it would not be a Ringling affair."

The maestro's gallops and marches and his explosive fanfares were born out of an era of hurricane-paced performances. Then, the entire show includ-

The bandleader backstage before the show. "Without Merle Evans," Variety *once wrote, "it would not be a Ringling affair."* RM.

ing the hippodrome races was delivered in two hours and fifteen minutes flat. John Ringling checked his watch closely and would not tolerate the slightest let-up. With Evans on the bandstand, he had little need to worry.

". . . I enjoyed it. I'd stand up there day in and day out, in front of that band, blasting away. I took an interest. I liked to see the show do business and do well. I did everything to help put it over . . . Music can mean *so much* to the performance." Indeed, in the truest sense of the word *performance*, Evans' music was an integral part of every moment of action.

Traversing half a century at the circus podium, Evans' style changed with the times. His records are formal concert pieces, meticulously rehearsed and performed. His music in-performance was the most colorful of all. To rephrase Jane Johnson's wonderful remark about John Ringling North, I am inclined to say of Merle Evans, you simply cannot judge his music by ordinary standards because it is not

Riders in an early 1920s Ringling spec "Garland Entry"
wait for a familiar Merle Evans march to cue them in. CW.

ordinary music. It moves at quick, hurly-burly angles, like a speeding roller coaster whipping over steep crests and around treacherous curves. Under the big top, Evans might be faulted for technical deficiencies, for lapses into the predictable and for occasional inadequate personnel. In the canvas days it was more difficult with the wages and working conditions offered to attract and sustain a first-rate force of windjammers day in and day out. The acoustics were severely limiting. Such were the variables Evans had little control over; his sound, accordingly, fluctuated.

Whatever its merits, you will thrill to the varied textures of his charts, to the rich, resonant inner voices, and if you close your eyes the wondrous mosaic of circus action does not diminish in the least degree. And what color! All the poetry and the pomp is there—the twisting and whirling of daredevils in defiance of the laws of nature, the breathtaking dives of the flyers and the roar of lions and tigers. There, too, are the mud-stained sequins, the uneven movements of the elephants and the flawed ballet

Alfredo Codona. "You just had to like him," said Evans.
"He did it so easy." CW.

231

girls, the sudden lashes of wind and rain against frayed canvas. Under the big top, Evans never escaped the transient human drama that surrounded him. Too sensitive was he to this incredible world.

"Thank you," sighed a group of blind children to the maestro following a matinee performance of the "Greatest Show on Earth." "With your music, Mr. Evans, we *saw* everything."

No doubt, they saw a world of imperfect dreams. The music they heard was the fitting metaphor for this world. The swift tempo changes, the strange shadings, the surprise transitions from one melodic idea to its opposite—this all accomplished with lightning speed characterizes not only the circus but the music of Merle Evans. My blood has tingled to the tapes of those scores as performed under the big top. Few if any circus bandleaders have approached

the complexity of the Maestro's expansive charts. They incorporated Dixieland and grand opera, Souza and Strauss. They traversed the spectrum from Bach to Broadway, from Stephen Foster to tin pan alley to Rimsky-Korsakoff.

"I'm a great guy to grasp at everything," Mr. Evans explained to me. "I like a lot of action when I get in there."

Evans is an outstanding composer of many stirring marches and fanfares. His brilliant "Symphonia March" paints a vivid picture of unstopable three-ring fever. Gradually it builds in melodic urgency to a roaring affirmation of catapulting acrobats and flyers. One sees a big top overflowing with action.

". . . Leitzel was kind of odd to get to. You'd play her in—she'd come in and she'd take off her cape and

Maestro Evans leads the band through Stravinski's score for "Ballet of the Elephants," Madison Square Garden, 1942. "The hardest music I ever played." RM.

232

Ringling's bandmaster, costumed for the 1954 finale, "U.N." RM.

Merle Evans had traversed a long, winding journey from the big tops of yesteryear to the modern arenas of the late 1960s. "As his years have gone by," said Harold Ronk, "he still had that vitality." ME.

she'd kick off her shoes. And she'd move and touch the rope and throw the rope out and catch everything. Then we'd change the music, she'd go up and she'd roll up her back on her arm and we'd catch the drums, and catch her up there and we'd play the best waltz for her, 'Crimson Petal.' "

Evans' unwavering passion to keep the show moving drove him, some seasons on four occasions, to a complete resetting of the score. Out came trunks full of arrangements from his vast collection. Each act got fresh music. "I liked to lay out the music. We played cold the next day. It pepped up the show."

After the circus began playing indoor engagements, local musicians at each stand were used in lieu of a full touring contingent. This, along with the superior acoustics available in modern auditoriums and arenas, resulted in a smoother sound. Still, the flavor that was distinctly Evans always rang through.

"He was a joy to work with," says Harold Ronk. "The minute he blew into the coronet you were always aware that he had taken over. It was a very driving, authoritative sound. There was never any hesitancy about it. It was always firm. Even in his last year with the show, I felt this about him. As his years had gone by, he still had that vitality. There was always a force."

Whether indoors or under canvas, I will never forget the Ringling bandleader playing for Gena Lipkowska as she danced in a ring of liberty horses, "Stranger in Paradise"; for high-wire comic Pio Nock, "Oh, My Papa"; for a troupe of aerialists descending at the completion of their hazardous routines aloft, "Hallelujah." Still alive in my mind is a huanting Russian march Evans played for Ingor Rhodin, the superb Swedish dressage rider. I asked him about that march, and he told me he acquired it while traveling through Russia with the American troupe. He explained further that rarely did he use the music imported acts brought with them; rather, he played it for *other* acts, *other* years!

His sensitivity to unforeseen occurrences is remarkable. When a cage full of tigers who had erupted in a bloody fight were finally subdued, the band celebrated the trainer's return by swinging into a victorious rendition of "Happy Days Are Here Again."

On another occasion, when a sudden tornado ruined the snare drum, Evans kicked a water bucket in the drummer's direction and cried, "Turn up the bottom and carry on!"

. . . *Evans led the band heroically on while the big top turned to flaming cinders in Hartford, Connecticut, 1944.* RM.

Once when the Wallendas lost control of their balance and tumbled from their pyramid, miraculously they all grabbed onto the wire or each other and clung desperately while a makeshift net was prepared below. The band, responding to its uncanny leader, played a moving version of "My Hero." Old guard observers maintain the audience was so touched by the music that it mistook the dramatic, near-fatal accident as part of the act!

. . . there is an ominous odor in the air now. The year is 1944; the place, Hartford, Connecticut. The band is blowing full steam ahead. Alfred Court's wild animal acts are coming to an end, and the great Wallendas are preparing aloft to begin their fantastic wire walk.

Smoke appears. Flames are on the move somewhere in a huge circus tent.

"FIRE!" somebody screams.

The big top is threatened. Yellow and red flashes swirl along the upper reaches of the canvas, lunging forward like a deranged killer bent on destroying everything in his path. The tigers are hurriedly directed to safety through the chutes adjoining their cages to the wagons outside. Confused and terrified crowds of people begin dominoing onto each other in a wave of hysteria.

"STARS AND STRIPES FOREVER!" shouts Merle Evans at the bandstand. His thirty men, riveted by the heroic commands of their leader, play on. The circus must never be without music. Evans knows this, has spent his whole life proving it . . .

The band booms out loud and clear the familiar Souza piece. Patrons are leaping from the bleachers onto the ground and darting in chaotic directions, struggling in a mass of screeching humanity for a way out of the nightmare.

The entire tent is ablaze. The "ageless delight" has gone up in flames, and the dreams of the nineteenth century are beginning to die. Children of all ages are scrambling over ring curbs and stakes, running into poles and props, racing frantically to beat the mounting odds against them.

The fire surges towards the bandstand.

"REPEAT!" hollers Evans, the captain of a ship he will be the last to desert. One hundred sixty-eight souls are trapped in the burning holocaust, doomed to spend their final moments on earth in the cinders of a failed dream. In silence? No, not in silence. Strange as it seems, as tragic as it was, they will depart from mortality with the music of life's eternal fantasy ringing in their ears.

Charred canvas topples onto the musicians. White hot cables fall perilously close to the brass section.

"*TEN MORE BARS!*" shouts the bandmaster from Columbus, Kansas, the hayseed with a heart of Gabriel who refuses to abandon the ageless delight until it is no more. He struck up the first fanfare, and he will strike the last.

The kettle drumheads catch fire.

"JUMP!" commands the maestro, releasing his faithful men only seconds before one of the king poles crashes to the bandstand.

. . . echoes of yesteryear, painful, reoccurring echoes of a lifetime packed with the joys and sorrows of a shifting, restless world on the move. Like a change in the music, the opposing themes of sunshine and shadow drift away then return . . . time leaps backwards and forwards, the images rush violently through his blood like old lovers refusing to be silent or forgotten. . . .

. . . outside in the sun, over a carpet of well-manicured green grass a gentle breeze dances. A robin bobs aimlessly down the street from one mailbox to another. Inside, the maestro sits in a soft sofa—reminiscent yet never fully reclined. The road is permanently in his blood. . . .

. . . the lines on his face shaped by the winds of adversity, they are the tarnishes of years of railroad sidings at dawn, of battered, bumpy rides atop bandwagons down the Main Streets of America, and of torrid afternoons under oppressive canvas. . . .

. . . "She's going to swallow first this curved sword and you will notice that she has to twist her body in order that the sword can go down her curved neck."

. . . "Silence please, ladies and gentlemen, while

Honored by Sarasota, Merle Evans, the "Toscaninni of the big tops," rides aboard a circus bandwagon from a bygone era. RM.

the daring young aerialist attempts a triple somersault through the air!"

. . .ruuummmmmmmmmm, poppp, katoppp . . . rummmmmmmmzzzzzzzztttttttttsssssszzzzzz. The flyer soars to the top of the big top, lets go, hurls himself around three times and is caught perfectly in the hands of the catcher.

passshhhhhh, BOOM BANG, a drumroll and a blast of trumpets take off. A burst of applause, and crashing brass and coronet power signals the entrance of equestrians and rope spinners. . . .

How many fanfares ago is Lillian Leitzel twirling over and over way up there? . . . is May Wirth jumping through hoops on her favorite horse, Joe? . . . are the Great Wallendas crossing the wire through icy stillness?

. . . How many fanfares ago is Howard Barry

cursing out Blacaman on a hot, frustrating Fourth of July in Des Moines, Iowa, screaming at him to get inside the tent and hypnotize his crocodiles?

. . . is Balanchine conferring with Igor Stravinski over a ballet for "young" elephants?

. . . can you hear Cecil B. DeMille asking the boss in disbelief, "We show on the side of that *hill*, Art?"

. . . are the sounds of the midway magic in the ears of young and old alike?

"PROGRAM MAGAZINES! CIRCUS PROGRAM MAGAZINES! STORIES AND PICTURES OF ALL THE BIG STARS TO BE SEEN INSIDE THE BIG TOP!"

"RESERVED SEATS HERE! CHOICE, CENTRALLY LOCATED GRANDSTAND RESERVED SEATS!"

". . . first, this curved sword, and you will notice

235

. . . the last parade? Memories race backwards in time as the bandwagon moves forward, from which the Maestro waves his salutations to a world almost too young to remember. . . . RM.

that she has to twist her . . .
body. . . ."
RUMMMMMMMZZZZZZSSSSSSSSSMMMMM
PPPPPPPPPP BANGGGGGGGG!!!!
"CHILDREN OF ALL AGES! JOHN RINGLING NORTH WELCOMES YOU TO THE GREATEST SHOW ON EARTH!"
Stop.
No, you are merely a guest of the Maestro's, sipping a coke while he talks, quietly searching his face, his eyes and his hands for a clue to the passion behind the big top. Questioning, probing, hoping. . . .

Someday, today will be the good old times.
If you will ride each rainbow as it climbs
And cheer what's here, then someday you will say
God bless this yesterday!
. . . "TEN MORE BARS!"

Dreams? No, the lingering refrains of yesterday's magic. The ghosts of Dan Rice and Doc Spaulding, of Jumbo and P. T. and Adam Forepaugh and Charles Siegrist and the Clarkonians, of Poddles Hanneford and John Ringling and Jerry Muggivan and Zack Terrill and Clyde Beatty and Bird Millman, of Codona and Leitzel and Colleano and Gargantua and Barbette and McClain and Modoc and Hartford and Butler and Dobritch and . . . and
STOP.

. . . The show is o'er—the races run
"All out and over" rings the cry.
The lights are lowered one by one;
The crowds depart—"Good night—
        Goodbye!"

Where has the parade gone?
. . . to a peaceful meeting on a quiet afternoon.

236

You are gazing in the eyes of the man who at eighty-three possesses the same indelible spark of boyish enthusiasm and raw courage that he felt when he first saw Ringling Bros. Circus in Sioux City, Iowa. And in his presence you can feel the wanderlust and hoopla that have drawn down the sawdust trails of time the wizards of sight and sound. Drawn them on red wagons, in gaudy pullman cars, in trucks and on foot. Drawn them from all parts of life to be water boys and wire walkers, candy butchers and press agents, riggers and ringmasters and big-top tycoons. Drawn them to bring the ageless delight to children of all ages through the ages. . . .

And you sense he will never let go, not Merle Evans—not any of them who were truly "with it."

. . . He talked of "the glamour and all the baloney that goes with it. The horray and the excitement, and the people. And a town *everyday*. That was the main thing. If I had to do it all over again, I'd be glad to do it again. Oh, I love the circus."

I asked him, were there things about circus life that ever got you down?

"No," he answered, "I don't think I was ever downhearted with the circus."

Then, with a glow in his eyes, he summed it all up in words no poet could equal. The great Maestro of the circus world told me something I will never forget:

"Everyday was a big day for me. Every day was circus day."

Index

Adkins, Jess, 90
Alferetta Sisters, 34
Al G. Barnes Circus, 25, 71, 81, 94, 110, 183, 184
Alzana, Harold, 119
American Circus Corporation, 22, 60–62, 71, 101–4
American Federation of Actors, 108–10
Anderson, John Murray, 115, 117, 123, 184
Anka, Paul, 191
Apollo Trio, the, 183
"Arabia," 183
Arbuckle, Fatty, 71
Ardelty, Elly, 119
Arno, Peter, 115, 116
Around the World, 35
Arturo, Cookie, 167, 168, 208, 212, 213
Astley, Philip, 22, 179
Astroworld, 189

Baer, Parley, 185
Bailey, James A., 97, 138, 139, 147, 163
Baker and Lockwood, 113
Balanchine, George, 114, 115, 119, 120, 124, 125
Bale, Elvin, 67, 68, 198
Bale, Trevor, 22, 23, 68
Ballantine, Bill, 145
Ballard, Edward, 61, 101, 102, 104
"Ballet of the Elephants," 114–26
Barbette, 30–38, 115–17, 120
Barnum, P. T., 66, 127, 138, 139, 163, 218
Barnum & Bailey Circus, 73, 94, 183
Barry, Howard, 106–13
Barstow, Richard, 173
Bauers, the, 208
Bauman, Charlie, 26, 119
Beatty, Clyde, 25, 90, 143, 183
Bece, Norman, 63
Belafonte, Harry, 191
Berosini, Josephine, 119
Bertram Mills Circus, 130, 230
Bigson, Arthur, 60
Billboard, the, 110, 112, 121, 123, 172, 183

Biller Bros. Circus, 31
"Birth of A Rainbow," 67
Blacaman, 106–13
Blood of A Poet, 35
Bloom, Allen, 202
"Blue Eagle Jail," 180
Bowers, Bert, 61, 101, 102, 104
Bowman, Ted, 72
Braden, Frank, 26
Bradna, Fred, 52, 99, 139, 212
"Bride and the Beasts," 22
Bronett, Francois, 176
Brunn, Francis, 119
Buck, Frank, 106
Buffalo Bill, 228, 229
Burke, Major John, 86
Burke, Michael, 160–63
Butler, Roland, 22, 119, 129, 145

Ca d'Zan, 99
Caesar, Irving, 117
Cairo, the Egyptian Giant, 206
Canestrellis, the, 169
"Carnaby Street," 174
Capital Centre, 203–14
"Carnival in Spangleland," 34
Carrillo Brothers, the, 192
Carson & Barnes Circus, 72, 218
Castle, Hubert, 72, 73, 119
Cervone, Izzy, 162
Cervone, Jack, 169, 213
Chapman, Danny, 218
Cherokee Ed's Historical Wild West Show, 93
Christian Science Monitor, the, 198
Christiansen's Horses, 81
Christy Bros. Circus, 60, 77
Circus America, 28, 203–14
Circus Circus (Las Vegas), 76
Circus Fans Association of America (CFA), 202
Circus Kings, 73
Circus Maximus (ancient), 19–20

239

Circus Maximus (produced by Paul Kaye), 176
"Circus Polka," 117, 126
Circus Vargas, 179, 180, 182, 184–88, 204, 216
Circus World (Florida), 200–201
Cirque Medrano, 38
Clarkonians, the, 81
Clown College (Venice, Florida), 197, 220–22, 225, 226
Clyde Beatty Circus, 31, 33
Clyde Beatty-Cole Bros. Circus, 90, 186, 216
Codona, Alfredo, 48, 81, 139
Coe, Richard L., 207, 212, 214
Cole, "Chilly Billy," 93
Cole Bros. Circus, 90, 91, 105
Colleano, Con, 70, 81
Concello, Antoinette, 139, 150, 173
Concello, Arthur, 61, 63, 138–64, 173
Concellos, the, 139
Cotton Blossom Showboat, 228
Court, Alfred, 25, 26, 119, 234
Coxey, Douglas, 86
"Crimson Petal," 233
Cristiani, Cosetta, 45
Cristiani, Lucio, 40
Cristiani, "Papa," 39
Cristiani, Pete, 40, 43
Cristianis, the, 40, 119
Cronin, S., 184
Crowley, Mark, 204, 212
Crowson, Bill, 112
Cucciola, 119
Cunningham, George, 184

Dailey Bros. Circus, 62
Dann, Harry, 222
Dan Rice's Great Floating Paris Pavilion Circus, 105
Davenport, Ben, 62
Del Oro, Pinito, 118, 119
DeMille, Cecil B., 147, 149, 150
Disney on Parade, 37
Disney World, 200, 201
Dobritch, Al, 171, 176
Dobritch International Circus, 165, 168–72, 176
Dobritch & Swedish National Circus, 176
Dobritch, Lola, 119
Dod Fisk Circus, 101
Dodd, Kenneth, 28, 44, 215–17, 221–25
Dover, Robert, 201
Downie, Andrew, 82
Downie Bros. Circus, 110
Downs, Michael, 201

Esclante, Phil, 112
Elford's Whirling Sensations, 34
Evans, Merle, 57, 81, 119, 120, 125, 150, 162, 174, 180, 227–37
Evans, Nena, 146, 149, 151, 161

Faludis, the, 174
Faughnan, Richard, 55, 57
Feld, Irvin, 189–208, 214, 220–22
Feld, Israel, 189–91
Fellows, Dexter, 86
Fewless, Tom, 172
Fields, William, 134

"Fitch Bandwagon" (radio program), 229
Fitzpatrick, Paul, 202
Flying Americans, the, 208
Foote, Don, 192
Forepaugh, Adam, 59, 86
Forepaugh-Sells Bros. Circus, 97
"Forty-niners" (Ringling stockholders), 163

Gaona, Tito, 119, 167, 174
Gaonas, the, 174
Garfunkel, Art, 207
Gargantua, 115, 124, 127–37, 140
Gargantua, Mr. and Mrs., 116, 130–37
Garrido, Ugo, 173
Geddes, Norman Bel, 114, 115, 123, 158, 184
Genders, Tuffy, 150, 161
George Matthew's Great London Circus, 173
Gentry Bros. Circus, 91, 113
Gibsons, the, 172
Gill, Brendan, 198
Goebel Lion Farm, 113
Gollmar Bros. Circus, 101
Gould, Morton, 34
Gould, Rose, 119
Graham, Lew, 228
Graham, Rubye, 117
Great Amburg Shows, 101
"Greatest Show on Earth." See Ringling Bros. and Barnum & Bailey Circus
Greatest Show on Earth (film), 147–51
Greer, Edward, 73, 74
Gumpertz, Samuel, 104, 105, 108
Gus Hill's Minstrels, 228

Haag, Emily, 105
Hackett, Ella, 74
Hackett, Sarah, 74
Hagenbeck-Wallace Circus, 25, 62, 71, 74, 91, 94, 95, 106–13, 183
Half Moon Hotel (Coney Island), 104
Hamilton, General Alexander, 178
Hamilton, Tody, 85, 86
Hanneford, Poodles, 71, 107, 110
Hannefords, the, 81, 169
Hanneford, Struppi, 33, 44, 168, 169, 171, 172, 221
Hanneford, Tommy, 71, 81, 218, 222
Hargrove, James, 63, 64
Hargrove Productions, 64
Hartford fire, 143, 145, 151, 234
Helliott, John, 25
Hemingway, Ernest, 39, 117, 119
Herbert, Dorothy, 213
Hergotti Troupe, the, 173
Hernandez, Eleazor, 218
Hiss, Tony, 198
Holfheinze, Judge Roy, 189
"Holidays," 118
Holtzmair, Wolfgang, 22
Hoover, Dave, 25
Houcs, the, 172
Howe's Great London Circus, 101
Humphrey, Senator Hubert, 207
Hunter, Martha, 134
Hurdle, John, 20, 75, 190

"Indian Summer," 169
International Telephone Solicitors Association, 64
Irwin, Richard, 200

Jacobs, Lou, 119
James Bros. Circus, 63, 172, 173
James, Jimmy, 216
John Ringling Hotel, 117
John Robinson Circus, 60, 101, 183
Johnson, Jane, 124–26, 139, 143, 230
John Strong 1869 Circus, 64, 179
Jolly Dolly, 206
Jomar, the, 117
Jumbo, 127
Jumbo (film), 35
Jung, Paul, 216, 222

Kaye, Paul, 169, 171, 172, 176, 204, 205, 212
Kelley, F. Beverly, 81, 229, 230
Kelley, John, 62
Kellner, George, 176
Kellner, Matthew, 176
Kellner, Sid, 172, 173, 176
Kelly, Emmett, 57, 119, 169, 203, 205, 208, 218
Kernan, Walter, 161
King Bros. Circus, 90–93
King, Floyd, 61, 69, 86–95, 103, 166, 186, 201
King, Howard, 91
King, Karl, 180
Klowns, the, 200
Knights of Columbus, the, 62
Knoblaugh, Edward, 159
Ku Klux Klan, the, 63

Lague, Louise, 206
Lamont, William, 74
Landon, Alfredo, 217
La Norma, 119, 168
La Tosca, 35
La Tour, Octavie, 48
Lavrenovi Duo, the, 173
Lawson, Willis, 161
Leitzel, Lillian, 48, 81, 83, 227, 232, 233
Leontini, Jack, 204, 212
Lewis, Ronnie, 33
Light of Asia, the, 86
Lintz, Gertrude, 127
Lipkowska, Gena, 119
Long, Hillory, 81
Luxem, Johnny, 208
Lyon, Douglas, 64, 65, 185, 186, 190, 201, 213, 214

McClain, Walter, 119, 125
McClelland, David, 198
McClosky, Frank, 150, 161, 216
McDonald, Phil, 212
MacMans, John T., 124
Madam Cherie, 83
Madison Square Garden (New York), 52, 79, 82, 100, 101, 121, 139, 1
   162, 228, 230
"Mama's In The Park," 117, 118
"Mardis Gras," 199
Martinez, Don, 167, 192

Mattel Toy, 189, 201
May, Earl Chapin, 96, 166
Meacham, Roy, 207
Mendez, Gene, 55, 208
Michu, 192
Miller Bros. 101 Ranch Wild West Show, 228
Miller, Dory, 72, 218
Miller-Johnson Circus, 64, 185
Mills Bros. Circus, 44
Milman, Bird, 81
Mister Mistin, 119, 151, 178
Mix, Tom, 104
Mlle Toto, 127, 130–37
Mlle Toto Room, 117
Modoc, 114, 123, 126
Moore, Chester, 86
Moore, Sonny, 172
Morales, Antonio, 172
Morales Family, the, 72
Muggivan, Jerry, 61, 96, 101–4
Murphy, Horris, 228

Nachman, Gerald, 181
Nagy, Louis, 225
New York Hippodrome, 71
New Yorker, the, 198
New York Stock Exchange, 189
Nobles, Ralph, 72
Nock, Pio, 233
Nocks, the, 119, 169, 208
Noel, Pablo, 28, 67
Norbu, 208
North, Henry Ringling, 22, 71, 73, 105, 114, 116, 121, 124, 125, 127,
   140, 186
North, John Ringling, 22, 26, 39, 81, 114–26, 127–34, 139–64, 173, 176,
   178, 184, 192

O'Brien, Pogey, 58, 59
Olympia Theatre (London), 84
"On Honolulu Bay," 118
"Oriental Romance," 183
Orpheum circuit, 34

Palace Theatre, 34
Palacios, the, 169
Paramount Pictures, 147, 149
Parkinson, Tom, 172, 173
"Pavan," 34
Payola, 191
Petit, Phillipe, 48, 67, 192
Pfening, Jr., Fred D., 213
Phelps, William, 22
Phillips, Captain Arthur, 127
Picasso, 67
Pickle Family Circus, 180
Pickman, Milton, 158
Pinkerton detectives, 62
Pissoni, Larry, 180
Polack Bros. Circus, 30–38, 73, 178
Pollin, Abe, 203–8, 212–14
Pompey, 20
Prince, Andre, 173
Pullen, Cleve, 228

"Rainbow Around The World," 119
Rajah, 25
Reed, Della, 22
Rhodin, Ingor, 119, 233
Ricard, Tex, 100
Rice, Dan, 22, 86, 180, 218
Ricketts, John Bill, 22, 177–79, 182
Ringling, Albert, 68, 69, 98, 183
Ringling, Alf. T., 98, 104
Ringling, Audrey, 104
Ringling Brothers, the, 59, 60, 62, 68, 71
Ringling Bros. and Barnum & Bailey Circus (also the "Greatest Show
    on Earth"), 52, 62, 67, 83, 90, 97, 110, 113, 121, 143, 147, 167, 173,
    174, 176, 189–202, 203–8, 212–14, 229
Ringling Bros. Circus, 77, 82, 95, 181, 228
Ringling Bros. Grand Carnival of Fun, 96
Ringling Bros. United Monster Railroad Shows, Great Triple Circus,
    Museum, Menagerie, Roman Hippodrome, and Universal World's
    Exposition, 96
Ringling, Charles, 22, 23, 25, 62, 99, 100, 102, 104, 228, 229
Ringling, (Mrs.) Charles, 142
Ringling, Edith, 104
Ringling, John, 69, 70, 82, 94, 96–105, 228–30
Ringling, Mabel, 99, 105
Ringling Museum of the Circus, 61, 75
Ringling, Otto, 59, 68, 69, 98
Ringling, Robert, 142, 143
Ripley's "Believe It Or Not," 227
Robbins Bros. Circus, 72, 112
Robinson, Blossom, 183
Rodriguez Brothers, the, 169
Rogers & Harris Circus, 62, 63
Ronk, Harold, 173, 174, 181, 190, 198, 213, 220, 223
"Root Hog or Die," 180
Rose, Billy, 35
Royal Hanneford Circus, 218
Ruarke, Robert, 151, 153
Russell Bros. Circus, 143, 213
Russian Acrobatic Team, 206, 208

Sands & Astley Circus, 101
Santa Rosa Fairgrounds Pavilion, 30, 52
Saturday Evening Post, the, 229
Scallera, 35
Schepp, Dieter, 54, 55, 57
Schepp, Jana, 54, 55
Schmidt, Hugo, 174
Sells & Gray Circus, 90
Sells Brothers, the, 93
Sells-Floto Circus, 22, 66, 71, 81, 82, 101, 112
Sells-Sterling Circus, 110, 113
Selznick, David O., 147
Seven Lively Arts, 35
Sherwood, Bob, 66
Shieve, Hurbert, 62
Showfolks Club of Sarasota, 48, 217
Shriners and Shrine Circuses, 33, 52, 167, 176, 206, 217, 219
Siegrist, Charles, 67
Silverman, Sime, 79
Sinott, Earl, 72
Six Flags (Texas), 52
Smith, William, 225
Soules, Gerard, 119
Sovet Union (Ringling tour), 230
"Spangleland Powwow," 33

Sparks, Charles, 81, 110
Sparks Circus, 81, 94, 104
Spaulding, "Doc", 86
Stark, Mabel, 25, 81
Stebbins, the, 169
Steinbeck, John, 19
Stella, The Bearded Lady, 206
Stephensons (Dogs), the, 119, 173, 202
Stern, Louis, 73
Stravinski, Igor, 114, 115, 117, 119, 120, 125, 126
Strong, John A., 178, 179
Strong, John, Jr., 178, 179
Strong, Linda, 178
Strong, Sandra, 178
Sully, William, 182
S. W. Brundage Carnival, 228
"Symphonia March," 232

Tasso, Dieter, 119
Terrell, Zack, 90
Thomas, Jose, 129
Till The Clouds Roll By, 35
Tim McCoy Circus, 110
Tom Mix Circus, 112
Tonito, 119
Toung Taloung, 86
Truzzi, 119
Turner, Aaron, 178

Unus, 119

Vargas, Clifford, 177–80, 182, 184–89, 204
Variety, 60, 66, 79, 82, 90, 94, 104, 123, 125, 130, 183, 199, 230
Vasconcellos, Roberto de, 119
Vertez, 162
Victor Julian's Dogs, 119, 208

Wallace Bros. Circus, 39–47
Wallace, Harvey, 94, 166
Wallenda, Carla, 52
Wallenda, Gunther, 55
Wallenda, Herman, 52, 55, 56
Wallenda, Karl, 20, 48–57, 69, 70, 81, 190, 197, 204, 205, 208, 212
Wallenda, Mario, 55
Wallenda, Ricki, 48, 51, 72
Wallenda, Rietta, 57
Wallendas, the, 69, 205, 227, 234
Walter L. Main Circus, 82, 94
Walter Savage Stock Company, 228
Ward-Bell Flyers, the, 34
Ward, Mamie, 139
Washington, George, 177, 182
Washington Post, the, 203, 214
Washington Star-News, the, 203, 206, 207
Webber, Herbie, 172
Weintraub, Boris, 207, 208
Welles, Orson, 35
Wells Fargo Bank, 201
Westinghouse, 158
White, Miles, 115, 117, 119, 120, 125, 151, 198
White Tops, the, 173
Whitehead, Robert, 108–10, 112

Wilde, Cornel, 147
Wilkins, Willie, 94
Williams, Andy, 191
Williams, Gunther Gebel, 26, 67, 68, 192–95, 198, 203
Williams, Robert, 143
Wilson, Charles, 228
Winchell, Walter, 143
Wirth Circus, 82
Wirth, Frank, 82, 83
Wirth, George, 84
Wirth, May, 75, 81–84, 100, 192, 198, 227
"Wizard, Prince of Arabia," 73, 183

Woodcock's Elephants, 172

Yankee Robinson Circus, 101
Yorty, Mayor Sam, 185

Zacchinis, the, 205
Zacchini, Wayne, 208
Zdravkos, the, 173
Zerbini, Tarzan, 28, 29, 108
Zoeppes, the, 119
Zorina, 123

791.3   81-4598
Ham   Hammarstrom, David
        Behind the big top.

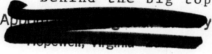

1. Books may be kept two weeks and may
be renewed once for the same period, except
7 day books and magazines.

2. A fine is charged for each day a book is
not returned according to the above rule. No
book will be issued to any person incurring
such a fine until it has been paid.

3. All injuries to books beyond reasonable
wear and all losses shall be made good to the
satisfaction of the Librarian.

4. Each borrower is held responsible for all
books charged on his card and for all fines ac-
cruing on the same.